OFFICIAL
ECLIPSE 3.0 FAQS

eclipse

the eclipse series

SERIES EDITORS   Erich Gamma ▪ Lee Nackman ▪ John Wiegand

Eclipse is a universal tool platform, an open extensible integrated development environment (IDE) for anything and nothing in particular. Eclipse represents one of the most exciting initiatives hatched from the world of application development in a long time, and it has the considerable support of the leading companies and organizations in the technology sector. Eclipse is gaining widespread acceptance in both the commercial and academic arenas.

The Eclipse Series from Addison-Wesley is the definitive series of books dedicated to the Eclipse platform. Books in the series promise to bring you the key technical information you need to analyze Eclipse, high-quality insight into this powerful technology, and the practical advice you need to build tools to support this evolutionary Open Source platform. Leading experts Erich Gamma, Lee Nackman, and John Wiegand are the series editors.

Titles in the Eclipse Series

John Arthorne and Chris Laffra, *Official Eclipse 3.0 FAQs*, 0-321-26838-5

Kent Beck and Erich Gamma, *Contributing to Eclipse: Principles, Patterns, and Plug-Ins*, 0-321-20575-8

Frank Budinsky, David Steinberg, Ed Merks, Ray Ellersick, and Timothy J. Grose, *Eclipse Modeling Framework*, 0-131-42542-0

Eric Clayberg and Dan Rubel, *Eclipse: Building Commercial-Quality Plug-Ins*, 0-321-22847-2

Steve Northover and Mike Wilson, *SWT: The Standard Widget Toolkit, Volume 1*, 0-321-25663-8

OFFICIAL
ECLIPSE 3.0 FAQS

John Arthorne
Chris Laffra

✦Addison-Wesley

Boston • San Francisco • New York
London • Munich • Paris • Madrid
Capetown • Sydney • Tokyo • Singapore • Mexico City

The publisher offers discounts on this book when ordered in quantity for bulk purchases and special sales. For more information, please contact:

U.S. Corporate and Government Sales
(800) 382-3419
corpsales@pearsontechgroup.com

For sales outside of the U.S., please contact:

International Sales
(317) 581-3793
international@pearsontechgroup.com

Visit Addison-Wesley on the Web: www.awprofessional.com

Library of Congress Cataloging-in-Publication Data
Arthorne, John.
    Official Eclipse 3.0 FAQs / John Arthorne, Chris Laffra.
        p. cm.
    Includes bibliographical references and index.
    ISBN 0-321-26838-5 (pbk. : alk. paper)
    1. Computer software—Development. I. Laffra, Chris. II. Title.

    QA76.76.D47A776 2004
    005—dc22

                            2004011197

ISBN 0-321-26838-5
Text printed on recycled paper
1 2 3 4 5 6 7 8 9 10—CRS—0807060504
First printing, June 2004

To Catherine
—JA

To Carla
—CL

Contents

Foreword

As Chris and John describe later in this book, the Eclipse Project began in 1999 at IBM's Object Technology International (OTI) subsidiary. At the time I was CEO and president of OTI and so was very involved in the decision to proceed with Eclipse, which was initially conceived as a successor product to the VisualAge family of software development tools. VisualAge, especially VisualAge for Java, was a commercially successful IDE. But it was also a closed environment built on proprietary APIs and did not integrate well with other vendors' tools. Only the IBM/OTI team could enhance or extend the product. Beyond these issues, though, it was becoming apparent from customer feedback that more was required than a simple rewrite of VisualAge. There was growing demand for a *tool integration platform*—a programming environment that would not only provide kernel IDE functionality but also allow developers, third-party vendors, and users to seamlessly add their own extensions, personalizations, and enhancements.

The vision of the Eclipse Project team was to extract the essential infrastructure underlying VisualAge—or any other IDE for that matter—and to package and deliver it as a platform. In effect, the team wanted to strip out all the IDE functionality that was specific to a particular programming language, development task, or programming model. The hope was that there would be substantial residual function left behind that could then be restructured to form a content-neutral and programming language-neutral foundation on which IDEs and similar products could be built from components. It was a bold venture, as there was no guarantee that anything practically useful would result, and there was certainly a lot of soul-searching and hand-wringing in the early days of the project.

The result was Eclipse: a tool-integration platform together with a set of components—"plug-ins" in the Eclipse vernacular—that could be seamlessly assembled into a wide variety of software development products. The Java development tools (JDT)—the Eclipse Java IDE—became our proof-point. It was built in parallel by a separate team, led by Erich Gamma of Design Patterns fame, that operated independently from the Eclipse Platform team. The JDT team had no special privileges; it had to use the same API as any other third-party product and was allowed no "backdoor" access to the Eclipse Platform. The intent was that, despite these constraints, the finished JDT should be indistinguishable from a purpose-built, vertically integrated IDE product like VisualAge. Of course, this goal was in fact realized, the Eclipse Project was a success, and the Eclipse community was born.

In the two years since the Eclipse code base was released into open source by IBM, its growth has been quite stunning, especially for those of us involved at the beginning of the venture. It has without question exceeded our wildest imaginings. Tens of thousands download the Eclipse SDK every week from more than 50 mirror sites around the globe. Thousands of Eclipse plug-ins are now available from open source and commercial suppliers. Software vendors are now shipping several hundred commercial products based on Eclipse. As of June 2004, approximately 50 companies are members of the Eclipse Foundation, which hosts Eclipse open source development. The first Eclipse Developer Conference—EclipseCON 2004—was held in Anaheim in February 2004, with more than 220 companies and organizations and nearly 25 countries represented.

Although I had a very amicable separation from OTI and IBM a couple of years ago, I continue to be actively involved with Eclipse. My main role today is leading the Eclipse Foundation Technology Project, whose mission is to engage the research and academic communities. And, of course, if you want to know more about this, Chris and John have provided a very nice section in the *Official Eclipse 3.0 FAQs* on this subject. It has been particularly interesting for me to see the uptake of Eclipse within the research community. In retrospect, one could perhaps have anticipated this. Software researchers necessarily build on the work of those who have gone before, and, of course, as time progresses our technology pyramids keep getting higher. Complexity is our nemesis—the low-hanging fruit was picked long ago, and most interesting problems are not simple anymore. Consequently, experimentation usually requires complex infrastructure, "plumbing" as we often call it. Most researchers spend far too much time building, rebuilding, and fixing this plumbing and far too little time developing new ideas. Given the nature of research, there are seldom any applicable standards for such infrastructure; these come only much later, when the research has matured into products. Consequently, researchers up to now have had to live and work in their own vertical towers, sharing their ideas but only infrequently sharing code. Eclipse has fundamentally changed this context, however, by providing a means to create and share that necessary common infrastructure, particularly for investigators in such areas as programming languages, tools, and environments. Researchers can focus more of their time on their real mission—innovation—and much less on the hated plumbing tasks.

So when Chris and John approached me to write this foreword to their new book, I was flattered and pleased to be asked but also, I confess, a bit perplexed. I had known and worked with both for many years at OTI and held both in high regard. I recruited Chris to help us start a new development lab in Amsterdam in the mid-1990s. The venture was a great success, and Chris developed into a very fine lab director, despite the usual hurdles and bumps along the way, which probably had a lot to do with the good friendship that developed between us as we worked our way through these. John joined OTI as a coop student and rose through the ranks, as it were, invariably choosing to get down and dirty working in middle- and low-level system code—making compilers work and that sort of thing. So even without seeing their book, I was sure that it would be a worthwhile addition to the Eclipse portfolio. But not having worked closely with either for several years, I was not exactly sure what they were up to or what the book was trying to accomplish.

It was a genuinely pleasant surprise when I looked at it. In my role as the "Eclipse outreach person" for research and academia, I get "How do I do this with Eclipse" questions continually, and I am a long way from being an Eclipse expert. In fact, as Eclipse has grown and become both deeper and broader as a platform, it is probably true that no one is an "Eclipse expert" any more. *Official Eclipse 3.0 FAQs* immediately struck me as a great idea. For one thing, I can, and do, use it myself. But more important, I hope that it will give the thousands of users and developers who venture into Eclipse for the first time the courage to just dive in and get started, knowing that they have a life jacket to keep them afloat and a compass that will guide them through the experience. For the more experienced hands, I suspect that this book will become a (virtually) well-thumbed desktop reference, there to remind you of all those things you know you know but can't quite recall. For many, it will likely be the plug-in version that they will reference and use most often, although I suspect that a few Luddites are out there, who, like me, on occasion still enjoy the reassurance and tangibility of the printed page.

I also happen to think that the emphasis on the Rich Client Platform will prove to have been prescient. After a few years of experimentation with browser-based applications, there has lately been a resurgence of interest in old fashioned desktop apps—the "fat client" seems to be back but this time in the guise of a tonier, slicker, and more sophisticated "rich client." The rich client has learned some ease-of-use and desktop-management lessons from the Web browser and aims to offer a much better out-of-the-box experience. It remains to be seen how this is all going to play out in the marketplace, but Eclipse seems very well positioned to provide a development platform for this new generation of rich client applications. As we have seen with the research and the academic communities, nothing succeeds quite so well as being in the right place, at the right time, with the right function. So the emphasis that Chris and John have placed on this topic is timely, to say the least.

Finally, I have to say that I think the decision to write the book entirely as a plug-in was very bold and very cool. It has a certain self-referential flavor to it which is very appealing to old Smalltalk programmers, such as Chris and John and yours truly. And it provides a very nicely integrated addition to the online documentation already available for Eclipse programmers and users. Whether you are an experienced developer, a newbie, an end user, or simply a curious bystander wondering what this Eclipse excitement is all about, I recommend this book to you. I guarantee that it will be both a good read and a great investment.

Brian Barry
Eclipse Foundation Technology Project Lead
Ottawa
April 2004

Preface

Most of the numerous Eclipse books published over the course of 2003 and 2004 cater directly to novel users and/or starting contributors to the platform. Other books have a particular focus on a specific vertical domain, such as modeling, or on a special niche, such as the underlying design principles of the platform.

This book has been carefully sculpted to fit a particular niche market of its own: Eclipse enhancers with at least some experience in writing Eclipse plug-ins. Our goal was to make this book the definitive guide to the wealth of other relevant Eclipse books, online articles, newsgroups with thousands of messages, mailing lists, and other random sources of Eclipse information, such as wikis and online FAQ lists.

A Brief Exploration of FAQs

An FAQ is a Frequently Asked Question. We pronounce the acronym FAQ as it is spelled: F-A-Q. On the Web, FAQ lists are ubiquitous. A Google search on "FAQ" results in 60 million pages, with FAQs topic ranging from early music to Esperanto to fly fishing to Perl to the X Files to XML programming. With an average FAQ size of 27K, this thriving online ecosystem of FAQs represents a whopping 1.6 petabytes of valuable, distilled domain knowledge.

In the more modest context of this book, an FAQ is a question that is frequently asked by *Eclipse developers*; hence the title of this book. Of course, we mean developers who extend the Eclipse Platform by writing new plug-ins. Developers who write random Java programs and happen to use Eclipse as an integrated development environment will find less guidance.

Naturally, even when considering that "wisdom lies in the question," a long list simply of *questions* would be rather depressing; most readers will not instantly know the answers to the majority of the questions. Therefore, this book also includes *answers* and guides you to even more sources of more detailed information.

The Target Audience for This Book

Official Eclipse 3.0 FAQs is targeted primarily at software developers interested in writing their own plug-ins to the Eclipse Platform, either for personal use or as part of a professional product. This audience consists of all the categories including and below Configurers (Figure P.1) in the Eclipse contribution pyramid described by Gamma and Beck (2004).

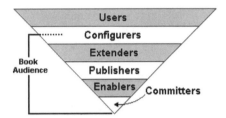

Figure P.1   The Eclipse contribution pyramid

Everyone below the level of Users in this pyramid is somehow involved in creating and using plug-ins to customize their Eclipse environment, or publishing plug-ins for use by the greater community. This book targets all these groups of Eclipse plug-in writers. Rather than focusing on end-user questions, we discuss how Eclipse has been implemented, what techniques are being used, what extension points are published, and what application programming interfaces (API) are available. The goal is to provide an authoritative reference for all plug-in writers: from those writing simple extensions to their environment to those writing complete Eclipse-based applications of their own.

If you are interested only in using Eclipse-based applications as an end-user, an introductory Eclipse book might be more appropriate. No effort is made here to provide an exhaustive reference for Eclipse end-users. We intentionally keep answers brief and as concise as possible. Where appropriate, the included references are intended to provide more explanation when our quick answer is too terse or cryptic. Many projects are supported by the Eclipse Foundation, but this book focuses almost exclusively on the core Eclipse Platform. If you are interested in some of the other projects under the Eclipse umbrella, we highly recommend perusing the other titles in the Addison-Wesley Eclipse Series.

If you have been using Eclipse for a while and have written your first plug-in(s), you might be ready to better integrate them into the platform and iron out the wrinkles and erase the rough edges. In that case, this book will prove an indispensable guide. The questions answered here have been harvested from people who have been asking the very same questions you are facing now. Some of the questions are tough to answer, as we have discovered over the past year of writing.

This book refers to many online Eclipse articles and books and the overwhelmingly large platform documentation. By reading this FAQ book first, we believe that you will save yourself a lot of time in finding the information you are looking for.

The Eclipse Versions These FAQs Cover

Eclipse is a fast-moving target. Every six weeks, a stable build is released with significant new functionality, making it extremely difficult to write a book with the potential to remain relevant for a long time. In this FAQ list, we have chosen version 3.0 of the Eclipse Platform as our primary target. However, our focus is on core concepts and principles that are relevant to most, if not all, versions of the platform. In some cases, a redesign of architecture or API warrants specific answers for different versions of the platform. Major discrepancies between 2.1 and 3.0 are pointed out, and we sometimes give different answers for 2.1 versus 3.0. We generally do not delve into topics that are relevant only to versions of the platform prior to Eclipse 2.1.

However, all the example snippets were tested primarily on the latest 3.0 builds, and you may need to reverse engineer those examples for older versions of the platform. Of course, for some functionality that is new in Eclipse 3.0, no pre-3.0 answer can be given.

A final caveat: This book went into production just after the 3.0M9 milestone build. This build represents a nearly feature-complete preview of what the final Eclipse 3.0 will be. We have covered only material that we are confident will remain correct when the final release goes out the door. With that said, there could be minor discrepancies between the information in this book and the final 3.0 release. We will try to maintain corrections and clarifications on the book's Web site (http://eclipsefaq.org).

How to Read This Book

This book consists of 20 chapters in three parts. Each chapter contains a number of FAQs, consisting of

- A question in the form an Eclipse developer would pose it

- A concise, to-the-point answer

- References to other FAQs, articles, and books

One way to read this FAQ book is to glance over the table of contents, look at a few random FAQs, and use the book primarily as a desk reference. In that case, the included index at the end of the book or an online search engine will be invaluable.

Another way is to read this book from front to back. The chapters have been carefully written so that the next question is closely related to the current one or directly elaborates on a common theme. If you take this route, keep in mind that we have made the somewhat arbitrary distinction between "user questions" (Part I) and "developer questions" (Parts II and III). Of course, every developer is also a user, so we often had difficultly deciding exactly where a question should lie. Does it make sense to explain how a user builds a plug-in before describing exactly what a plug-in is? Novice users may find it necessary to flip back and forth between Part I and the remainder of this book as they grow into the simultaneous roles of "user" and "developer" of the platform.

Online Updates to This FAQ

This FAQ list is found online at this book's Web site (http://eclipsefaq.org). At that site, you can search and browse FAQs and propose new categories and questions for which the editors of the FAQ list may post answers.

Furthermore, from that Web site, FAQs can be downloaded as an Eclipse plug-in, in the form of Hypertext Markup Language (HTML) files. The plug-in allows for searching with the common Eclipse Help search (through **Help > Help Contents...**) to efficiently find your way through this FAQ list. Any reference made in an FAQ to other FAQs, documentation, or articles is done through HTML hyperlinks.

How This Book Was Written

"Eat your own dog food" is one of the most important guiding principles the Eclipse development team follows. As soon as possible, Eclipse was used to develop Eclipse itself. It is the most secure way to iron out bugs in the system. If you force yourself to use your own product, you are bound to make sure that it works well. Naturally, we adopted the same style while writing this book.

To write this book in the true Eclipse spirit, we developed a plug-in that extends the following extension point:

```
<extension point="org.eclipse.help.toc">
   <toc file="toc.xml" primary="true"/>
</extension>
```

The `toc.xml` file provides a topical ordering over the large collection of FAQ files. We realized early that we would go through quite a few editing steps before finalizing our ordering. We envisioned changing question titles, ordering in a given section, creating new FAQs, and discarding some others. Moreover, we also wanted to have a lot of FAQ cross-references. Finally, we wanted to offer readers both a soft-copy version of the FAQ and a hard-copy printed version. Being good computer scientists, we decided that we had to build some of our own tooling to ease our work. Of course, we downloaded available open source technology when and where appropriate.

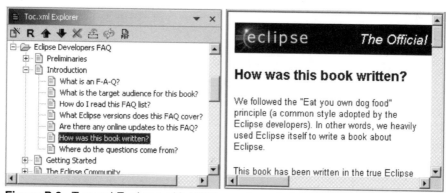

Figure P.2 Toc.xml Explorer with HTML preview window

In writing the documentation for Eclipse 2.1, the Eclipse team devoted a lot of energy to managing the integrity of the documentation. Changing a section topic could result in changing a name in various unrelated locations. We decided to write an explorer for the `toc.xml` file to automate file editing, ordering, renaming, and cross-linking. Figure P.2 shows a screen dump of our Toc.xml Explorer with HTML preview window in action.

A second problem we faced was our wish for one master source for both the plug-in and book incarnations of the FAQ list. We decided to edit and maintain only the plug-in version and to generate the book from the plug-in with an automated script. For this conversion, we used HTMLDOC, a great tool for generating a Portable Document Format (PDF) version of a book from a set of input HTML files. This results in the best control over the printed end result. We also developed some rudimentary Eclipse support for HTMLDOC to allow automatic generation of camera-ready manuscripts from any plug-in containing a toc.xml file.

While we were at it, we also wrote an Eclipse HTML editor with basic code assist and syntax highlighting. Finally, we wrote a number of sample Eclipse plug-ins that are available from the book's Web site and on the book's CD-ROM.

Spider Diagrams

To generate diagrams of relevant Eclipse object structures, we used enhanced Spider diagrams. Spider diagrams were introduced by Erich Gamma and Kent Beck to illustrate complex object relationships. The Spider plug-in is a graphical object explorer. It shows objects as nodes in a graph. References between objects appear as arcs. The Spider plug-in is licensed under the Common Public License (CPL) and can be downloaded from the Spider Web site (http://www.javaspider.org).

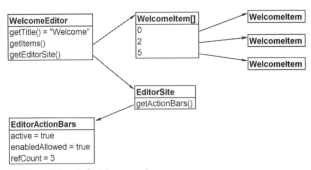

Figure P.3 A Spider graph

For this book, we downloaded Spider and enhanced it only slightly to improve its visual appearance for printed matter and added support for exporting a graph to a bitmap image on the file system.

Figure P.3 shows a sample Spider graph containing an instance of class `WelcomeEditor`. When the method called `getTitle()` is invoked on it, the string `"Welcome"` is returned. The `getItems()` method returns an array with six `WelcomeItem`s. Of the six, items 0, 2, and 5 are shown in Figure P.3. When `getEditorSite` is called on the `WelcomeEditor` object, an instance of `EditorSite` is returned. One of its methods, `getActionBars()`, returns an instance of `EditorActionBars`. Two of its fields—`active` and `enabledAllowed`—have a value equal to `true` and the `refCount` field has a value of 3.

Unlike Unified Modeling Language (UML) diagrams, Spider diagrams show a reference graph of live objects and their values. Spider diagrams are derived from the actual object model of a live, running Eclipse instance. Java reflection is used to inspect objects and obtain symbolic information.

Conventions Used in This Book

Throughout this book, we use *italics* for emphasis, FAQ titles, special terms, and book titles. We use `code font` for code fragments, file names, class names, method and field names, strings, and objects. We use **bold font** for menu paths, key names, and perspective and view names.

Optionally, an FAQ is followed by a list of related FAQs, book references, or URLs for related Web sites. Such a section is highlighted by having the following image in the text margin:

The table of contents mentions both FAQ numbers and the page on which the FAQ can be found. For brevity, the index at the end of the book only refers to the FAQ number.

The Origin of the Questions

We collected good questions from various sources and then wrote our own answers:

- Eclipse newsgroups (http://eclipse.org/newsgroups)

- The eclipse.org articles (http://eclipse.org/articles)

- Eclipse developer mailing lists (http://eclipse.org/mail)

- Interesting discussions in the descriptions of many Eclipse bugs

- Feedback from Eclipse code camps and developer conferences such as EclipseCon

- Personal discussions with Eclipse committers

- Varying other sources of Eclipse information (http://eclipse.org/community/main.html)

- Our own personal experience with development of Eclipse

Structure of This Book

Part I (Chapter 1–4) discusses the organizational structure of the Eclipse Project and lays the fundaments for plug-in development. It explains where to download Eclipse, how to extend the platform by writing a plug-in, and how to use the Eclipse development environment to edit Java code. After reading Part I, you should become comfortably familiar with the strengths and abilities of the Eclipse Platform.

Part II (Chapters 5–14) describes Eclipse as a generic application platform, the so-called Rich Client Platform (RCP), with which stand-alone applications other than development tools can be built. The Eclipse plug-in architecture allows software developers to grow an application by picking and choosing the plug-ins they need to meet their goals. This has proven a godsend for the development tooling domain, which was previously dominated by monolithic products that were nearly impossible to customize and that rarely interoperated with each other.

Along the way, the Eclipse community took an unexpected left turn. While the Eclipse Foundation is still dedicated primarily to tool development, many members of the open source community around Eclipse started to see things differently and began to use the Eclipse Platform to build things other than development tools. They built games, chat clients, and news readers, and consulting companies started building all sorts of custom applications on top of the Eclipse Platform. They realized that a component-based platform with a vast store of open source components already available was ideal for rapidly creating all kinds of applications. Part II will still be interesting for development tool writers, since a great deal of the Eclipse Platform's functionality has been pushed down into this generic layer.

Part III (Chapter 15–20) discusses the Eclipse IDE Platform and will be of interest to those who want to enhance the Eclipse IDE with new behavior. These chapters cover FAQs relating to the broad assortment of plug-ins that round out the Eclipse SDK and include a chapter on extending the Java development tool (JDT) plug-ins, as well as a large chapter that guides you along the various steps of writing an IDE for your own programming language. Many of the plug-ins that make up the Eclipse IDE Platform, such as those providing text-editing functionality, search and compare support, and even repository support, may be interesting for RCP applications.

Erich Gamma and Kent Beck, *Contributing to Eclipse* (Addison-Wesley, 2004)
The Eclipse FAQ Web site (http://eclipsefaq.org)
HTMLDOC (http://www.easysw.com/htmldoc)
The Spider Web site (http://www.javaspider.org)

Acknowledgments

It takes a village to write a book on Eclipse.

First of all, books have a nasty habit of stealing away cycles from regular work activities. In our case, our management at IBM Ottawa Labs has been supportive of the effort to produce this book from the very day we proposed it. In particular, we thank John Duimovich and Mike Wilson. Furthermore, our thanks extend to Paul Buck, former OTI lab director. Chris will miss the trips to Starbucks. Finally, by actively going out and inviting developers to write about software, we would like to thank both Lee Nackman and Danny Sabbah for creating the right creative environment at the IBM Software Group for writing books.

Book publishing is a funny business. Publishers have to deal with cut-throat competition and acquisitions editors run the risk of being reduced to bean counters who can talk only in terms of profit/loss analysis. On the other hand, authors most often simply seek an outlet for their creativity. If they want to strike it rich, they had better try to write the next *Harry Potter*. The Addison-Wesley acquisitions editor for the Eclipse Series, John Neidhart, is a unique person who deeply understands the technical book publishing market and can also mold a sometimes confused author with never-ending positive suggestions and recommendations. Editors have to be patient, highly responsive to e-mail, and work at insane hours, following bizarre schedules. Thanks, John, for being our own Jerry McGuire.

Thanks also to Tyrrell Albaugh, John Fuller, Lisa Iarkowski, Raquel Kaplan, and Evelyn Pyle, the Addison-Wesley production team that guided us through the various phases of the book-writing process. With characteristic patience and determination, Marcellus Mindel, Judy Keen, and Adrian Cho at IBM Ottawa helped us navigate the book-publishing waters on the IBM side. Much of the shape, form, layout, and even writing style of our book are heavily inspired by the seminal *C++ FAQs: Frequently Asked Questions* by Marshall Cline and Greg Lomow. The Eclipse Series team, formed by John Neidhart, Erich Gamma, Lee Nackman, and John Wiegand, shared our vision and took the risk with us to develop a version for Eclipse. Thanks!

Finally, without the collective energy and creative output of the entire Eclipse team and the support teams at IBM and other locations, this book would have been meaningless. We apologize to all Eclipse developers for publishing a book with our names on it. In fact, the names of all Eclipse developers should be on the cover as this work directly reflects their creative achievement.

Special Acknowledgments from John

I owe thanks most of all to my wife Catherine, without whom this book may never have been written. Her exuberance and work ethic continually provide me with a model that, on my better days, I strive to emulate. For the countless evenings and weekends that she has been supplanted by this book, I cannot begin to repay. An apology is also due to my family and friends, who have seen more of my laptop than my face over the last year. I hope you all know you are far more important to me than my work will ever be.

Special Acknowledgments from Chris

I sincerely thank my dearest Carla for her never-ending support and positive approach during this endeavor. Furthermore, this book is dedicated to Bob for allowing Daddy to "work on his computer" and not play with his Bionycles, Power Rangers, and Rekonstructors. Finally, I wrote this paragraph while looking over my younger son, Koen, who has been given new chances in life, thanks to the incredible staff at the Children's Hospital of Eastern Ontario, Ottawa (http://www.cheo.on.ca).

Reviewers of This Book

Several members of the Eclipse community have spent considerable time reviewing this book, proposing FAQs, providing guidance, recommending alternative solutions, or pointing out blatant errors in the manuscript. Any errors or omissions that remain are the sole responsibility of the authors, who are in great debt to Erich Gamma, Chris Grindstaff, D.J. Houghton, Kai-Uwe Maetzel, Lee Nackman, Nashib Qadri, Pascal Rapicault, Estelle Ringenbach, Darin Swanson, Dave Thomson, John Wiegand, and Brian Wilkerson.

☞ Marshall Cline and Gregory Lomow, *C++ FAQ, Second Edition* (Addison-Wesley, 1999)

Part I. The Eclipse Ecosystem

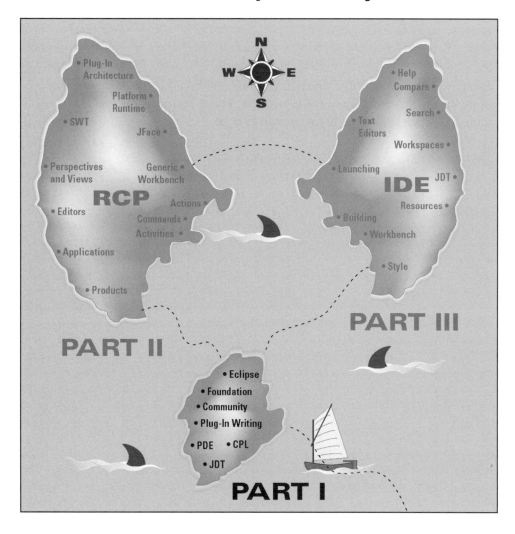

Chapter 1. The Eclipse Community

Eclipse has taken the computing industry by storm. The download data for the Eclipse Software Development Kit (SDK) is astounding and a true ecosystem is forming around this new phenomenon. In this chapter we discuss what Eclipse is and who is involved in it and give you a glimpse of how large a community has put its weight behind this innovative technology.

An open source project would be nothing without a supporting community. The Eclipse ecosystem is a thriving one, with many research projects based on Eclipse, commercial products that ship on top of Eclipse, lively discussions in newsgroups and mailing lists, and a long list of articles and books that address the platform. The following pages will give you a roadmap of the community, so that you will feel more at home as you come to wander its winding streets.

What is Eclipse?

FAQ
1

Eclipse means a lot of different things to different people. To some Eclipse is a free, state-of-the-art Java development environment. To others, Eclipse is a flexible environment to experiment with new computer languages or extensions to existing languages. To yet others, Eclipse is a comprehensive framework that deploys many advanced and modern software design and implementation techniques.

> Zawinski's Law: Every program attempts to expand until it can read mail. Those programs that cannot so expand are replaced by ones that can.
>
> —Jamie Zawinski

The official party line is, *Eclipse is an open (IDE) platform for anything, and for nothing in particular*. Eclipse is *open* because its design allows for easy extension by third parties. It is an *Integrated Development Environment (IDE)* because it provides tooling to manage workspaces; to build, launch and debug applications; to share artifacts with a team and to version code; and to easily customize the programming experience. Eclipse is a *platform* because it is not a finished application per se but is designed to be extended indefinitely with more and more sophisticated tooling. Eclipse is suitable for *anything* because it has been used successfully to build environments for wide-ranging topics, such as Java development, Web Services, embedded device programming, and game-programming contests. Eclipse has no *particular* focus on any vertical domain. The dominance of Java development tooling in Eclipse is merely historical. The platform has no explicit or implicit support whatsoever for Java development as provided by the Java development tools (JDT). The JDT has to play according to the same rules as all the other plug-ins that use the platform.

When this book was being written, Eclipse itself could not read mail yet, but, of course, products based on Eclipse *do* exist that can read mail. That sums it all up.

Speaking more technically, Eclipse is built on a mechanism for discovering, integrating, and running modules called *plug-ins*. A contributor to Eclipse delivers as one or more plug-ins an offering that manifests itself with a product-specific user interface (UI) in the workbench. Multiple, usually unrelated, products can be installed in one Eclipse instance and happily live and cooperate to perform a certain task. The class of end products includes IDEs, but also so-called rich clients, applications that benefit from the Eclipse Platform design and its components but do not look like an IDE. Examples of the latter category include the latest generation of applications based on IBM Workplace Client Technology, the first of which will be Lotus Workplace Messaging 2.0 and Lotus Workplace Documents 2.0.

FAQ 2

What is the Eclipse Platform?

Those who download the generic Eclipse Platform—usually by mistake—are somewhat confounded by what they see. The platform was conceived as the generic foundation for an IDE. That is, the platform is an IDE without any particular programming language in mind. You can create generic projects, edit files in a generic text editor, and share the projects and files with a Concurrent Versions System (CVS) server. The platform is essentially a glorified version of a file-system browser.

As an end user, what you don't see when you download and run the platform is that the architecture is designed from the ground up for extensibility. In fact, everything you see is a plug-in, and everything you see can be tweaked, replaced, or augmented using various hooks. To draw a computing analogy, it's like the Internet Protocol (IP): exceedingly generic, not terribly interesting by itself, but a solid foundation on which very interesting applications can be built.

A carefully designed subset of the Eclipse Platform has been produced in Eclipse 3.0: the Rich Client Platform (RCP). Despite the name, this is not the version of the platform sold for fat profits to rich clients. This is the portion of the platform that is interesting for non-development-environment applications. We thought this part so interesting that we dedicated almost half the book to RCP alone.

Where did Eclipse come from?

Eclipse started out as proprietary technology, led by IBM's subsidiary, Object Technology International (OTI). IBM wanted to reduce the large number of incompatible development environments being offered to its customers and to increase the reuse of the common components in those environments. By using the same common framework, development teams could leverage one another's components, integrate to a high degree, and allow developers to roam among projects.

Eclipse did not emerge from thin air but evolved from a long product line of development environments, of which the earlier ones are IBM VisualAge for Smalltalk and IBM VisualAge for Java. Both of these products were written in Smalltalk. The IBM VisualAge Micro Edition product was the first serious—and actually quite successful—experiment with writing the entire IDE in Java. Many concepts found in Eclipse have been tried out in that product already. However, for third parties, it proved difficult to extend the product with new components, mainly for two reasons: (1) it was not designed with a component model in mind, and (2) it essentially was a monolithic, closed-source product.

A small team of experts set out to take the experiences of the previous years of designing and implementing development environments. The result was Eclipse, a platform designed from the ground up as an integration platform for development tools. It enabled partners to easily extend products built on it, using the plug-in mechanisms provided by the platform. The subsequent path to open source and enabling of a much wider audience and ecosystem was a natural progression.

The Eclipse open source project was announced in November 2001 by a group of companies that formed the initial Eclipse Consortium. From there, the small initial project burgeoned into a collection of related projects that formed the basis of dozens of commercial applications.

What is the Eclipse Foundation?

From a small IBM-led project, Eclipse has grown into a framework deployed by a wide assortment of commercial backers. The Eclipse Foundation is a true open source project, with a board of directors governing the direction of the core platform and an ever-growing number of technologies and projects built on it. As a completely independent organization since February 2004, the foundation has a suitably complex organizational structure and plenty of exciting legal documents that you can read at eclipse.org. Each of the more than 40 foundation members has either direct or indirect representation on the board of directors, along with two representatives from the community of Eclipse committers. Most importantly, all the member companies are following the Eclipse charter by making a commitment to release Eclipse-compatible offerings and to provide continued support for the community of users, researchers, and developers. It is remarkable how quickly Eclipse has grown from a small internal project into the enabling platform for all kinds of areas, such as application development, modeling, programming language research, and so on.

 FAQ 1 *What is Eclipse?*

How can my users tell where Eclipse ends and a product starts?

You cannot see where Eclipse ends and a product starts, and this is intentional. The platform itself is written entirely as a set of plug-ins, and the product plug-ins simply join the "soup of swimming plug-ins." To bring some order to the chaos, the platform does maintain a history of configurations. When a new plug-in is installed, a new configuration is created. To obtain insights into the current configuration of the platform and its update history, consult either **Help > About... > Configuration Details** or the Update Manager. There you can discover the installed plug-ins that are part of the Eclipse Platform and those that were installed afterward.

Having said that, an Eclipse-based product can exert a certain amount of branding on the appearance of the final application. In particular, a product will usually replace the workbench window icon and splash screen. The product can also configure a set of preferences that will ship as the defaults for users of that product. See Chapter 14 for more details on productizing an Eclipse offering.

 FAQ 250 *What is an Eclipse product?*

What are Eclipse projects and technologies?

FAQ
6

The Eclipse Foundation oversees a lot of activity, with contributors numbering in the hundreds. To organize these activities, Eclipse is divided into projects and subprojects. The four main Eclipse projects in June 2004 were:

1. *The Eclipse Project.* The three outputs of this project are the Eclipse Platform, Java development tools (JDT) and Plug-in Development Environment (PDE) tools. These three components comprise the Eclipse SDK, a full-featured Java IDE with all the necessary features for building Eclipse plug-ins. The Eclipse SDK is what much of the wider software development community equates with the term *Eclipse*. This book focuses entirely on the components produced by the Eclipse Project.

2. *The Eclipse Tools Project.* Examples of development tools based on Eclipse are tools for visual editing, C/C++ development, UML development, quality assurance (QA), graphical editing, modeling, profiling, and even COBOL.

3. *The Eclipse Technologies Project.* Projects in this category are oriented toward research and experimentation into future directions for the platform. These projects are not always intended to become part of products today but instead to explore cutting-edge ideas for future Eclipse-based products. Some of these projects, such as the Equinox project to develop a new Eclipse runtime infrastructure, may migrate into the base platform or other core projects. Topics include aspect-oriented programming, collaborative development environments, Eclipse education, and the Open Services Gateway initiative (OSGi).

4. *The Eclipse Web Tools Platform.* This project to develop tools for J2EE is still in its infancy, but has generated a great deal of excitement about its potential to lay the groundwork for high-quality, interoperable development tools for building Web applications.

FAQ 7

How do I propose my own project?

First check whether your activities can be performed under an existing project. The list of projects is continuously growing, covering a wide range of research topics and product ranges. The Eclipse subprojects are overseen by a project management committee (PMC). If you have compelling reasons to start a new tool or technology, contact the PMC of either the Eclipse Tools Project or the Eclipse Technologies Project.

Having a proof of concept definitely supports your arguments, of course. Furthermore, before you contact the PMC as an individual, it does not hurt to first find other people and Eclipse Foundation members who would like to collaborate with you on the project. If interested in your project, the PMC will guide you through the steps required to establish it as an official Eclipse project.

 FAQ 6 *What are Eclipse projects and technologies?*

FAQ 8

Who is building commercial products based on Eclipse?

Each member of the Eclipse Foundation has committed to delivering one or more products based on Eclipse. For example, IBM has moved almost all of its IDE products to the Eclipse Platform. At EclipseCon 2004, many companies showed exciting demos of upcoming products based on Eclipse, including several products based on the new Eclipse RCP.

In April 2004, the following companies had commercial Eclipse-based offerings: Advanced Systems Concepts, Borland Software, CanyonBlue, Catalyst Systems, Codefarm, Embarcadero Technologies, Ensemble Systems, Ericsson, ETRI (Electronics & Telecommunications Research Institute), Flashline, Fujitsu Software, Genuitec, Hewlett-Packard, Hitachi, IBM, INNOOPRACT Informationssysteme, Instantiations, Intel, Logic Library, M7, MERANT, Metanology, Micro Focus, MKS, MontaVista Software, Oracle, Parasoft, QA Systems, QNX Software Systems, Red Hat, SAP, SAS, Scapa Technologies, Serena Software, SilverMark, SlickEdit, SuSE, Sybase, Teamstudio, Telelogic, Tensilica, TimeSys, and Wasabi Systems.

What open source projects are based on Eclipse?

Thousands of projects of various sizes are based on Eclipse. A small number are directly supported by the Eclipse Foundation as official Eclipse projects but a far greater number can be found elsewhere on the Web. Many are hosted at such sites as Source Forge or can be found in the various Eclipse plug-in listings floating around the Web. The following are the best-known portals for finding Eclipse-based plug-ins:

- *http://eclipse.org/community.* Acknowledging the losing battle of trying to track the growing list of Eclipse plug-ins, this page lists other Eclipse information sites that have lists of plug-ins.

- *http://www.eclipse-plugins.info.* This site is probably the longest running Eclipse information portal, best known for its exhaustive catalog of known open source Eclipse plug-ins. If you have a plug-in that you want the world to know about, get it listed here!

- *http://www.eclipseplugincentral.com.* A newcomer to the world of Eclipse portals, this site has an excellent Eclipse news feed and a growing catalog of open source Eclipse-based projects.

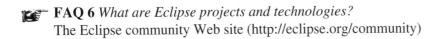 **FAQ 6** *What are Eclipse projects and technologies?*
The Eclipse community Web site (http://eclipse.org/community)

What academic research projects are based on Eclipse?

Much of the academic research on Eclipse is propelled by the Eclipse Innovation Grants, a financial stimulation project funded by IBM in 2003 and renewed for 2004. The award winners are prominently profiled at the Eclipse community Web site (http://eclipse.org/community).

The Eclipse-oriented research projects have topics that vary widely, such as educational software, modeling tools, program analysis, reverse engineering, aspect-oriented programming, alternative language support, Design Patterns, automated testing, software lifecycle support, groupware techniques, debugging, optimization, and software requirement analysis and specification.

Essentially, all these projects benefit from the strengths of Eclipse: an open source platform that is easily extensible, and very well documented. Using Eclipse gives these research projects a running start and allows them to focus on pushing the envelope in the specific vertical domains they are targeting.

 The Ecesis Project (http://eclipse.org/ecesis)

Who uses Eclipse in the classroom?

A growing number of universities worldwide are deploying Eclipse as a vehicle for computer science classes. The platform itself can be used very well as an example of state-of-the-art software. Analysis of the Design Patterns adopted in Eclipse could alone easily fill a curriculum for a year. In addition, Eclipse can be used by students to write their own plug-ins. With minimal effort, interesting topics can be explored and impressive results obtained.

Various sources of classroom materials are circulating. International universities that are known to teach courses about Eclipse include, but are not limited to, Carleton University in Ottawa, Ontario, Ecole des Mines de Nantes in France, University of Tuebingen in Germany, Royal Military College of Canada in Kingston, and University of British Columbia in Vancouver.

Owing to the success of using Eclipse in the classroom, the Eclipse Ececis Project was formed in late 2003. Its goals are collaboration and participation in the development and use of open *free* courseware for Eclipse and related technologies.

 The Ecesis Project (http://eclipse.org/ecesis)

What is an Eclipse Innovation Grant?

FAQ
12

This is a monetary grant by IBM to perform innovative research based on the Eclipse Platform. The grant varies from $10,000 to $30,000 based on the scale of the project. For a comprehensive and up-to-date list of award recipients, see the innovation grant Web site.

 Eclipse Innovation Grants
(http://www.ibm.com/software/info/university/products/eclipse/eig.html)

What Eclipse newsgroups are available?

FAQ
13

As with most technologies, Eclipse started out with a single newsgroup. Now, all major, and some smaller, Eclipse projects have their own newsgroups. Some are more active than others. Some have a very specific scope, and others are more broad in their coverage of discussion topics. The Eclipse newsgroup (http://eclipse.org/newsgroups) page has a complete index of the current Eclipse newsgroups and a description of their focus areas.

The most active newsgroup is news://news.eclipse.org/eclipse.platform, with around 1,500 postings per month. Before you post a question to any newsgroup, it makes a lot of sense to search the platform newsgroup for an answer. Chances are that the question has been asked before, and the answer can be found there quickly.

The newsgroups are archived at the Eclipse Web site, and the search engine at the Eclipse Web site (http://eclipse.org/search/search.cgi) can search them quite efficiently.

**FAQ
14**

How do I get access to Eclipse newsgroups?

The Eclipse newsgroups are password-protected to protect them from spam and trolls. Visit http://eclipse.org/newsgroups/index.html and request a free password to access the newsgroups. The same password can be used to browse the Eclipse mailing list archives.

**FAQ
15**

What Eclipse mailing lists are available?

Although Eclipse newsgroups are intended for users and extenders of the platform, the mailing lists are specifically targeted at those who are actively contributing to the development of Eclipse itself. Messages focus mainly on new areas of development, administrative messages about release dates and build information, and general discussions of the subtopic controlled by the mailing list.

> **Warning:** Unless you are actively contributing to an Eclipse project, have a vested interest in the topic, or have special expertise to contribute, you should simply *read* the archive for the mailing list and *ask questions* on the corresponding newsgroups.

 The Eclipse mailing list page (http://eclipse.org/mail)

**FAQ
16**

What articles on Eclipse have been written?

The online archive of Eclipse articles contains more than 50 articles written by the Eclipse experts, often the committers of the Eclipse projects described in the articles. When printed in sequence, the online articles contain more than 500 pages of deep knowledge of the Eclipse Platform.

The audience for the online articles is extenders of the platform, so it makes a lot of sense to consult the articles before trying to write your own Standard Widget Toolkit (SWT) widget, implement a preference page, react to workspace resource change events, launch an application from Eclipse, support drag-and-drop, use

Draw2D, internationalize your plug-in, turn your plug-in collection into a product, write an editor for your favorite programming language and integrate it into Eclipse, use a tree viewer, use decorators and markers, or create CVS branches in your team project.

In addition to the online Eclipse articles, a wealth of Eclipse experience is reported on the IBM developerWorks® Web site, with many articles and code samples.

☞ The Eclipse articles page (http://eclipse.org/articles)

What books have been written on Eclipse?

FAQ 17

In June 2004, books on Eclipse, other than this one, included the following:

- Frank Budinsky et al., *Eclipse Modeling Framework*, Addison-Wesley, 2004 (http://www.aw.com)
- Berthold Daum, *Eclipse 2 for Java Developers*, Wiley, 2003 (http://www.wileyeurope.com)
- Berthold Daum, *Java-Entwicklung mit Eclipse 2* (German), DPunkt, 2003 (http://www.dpunkt.de)
- Berthold Daum, Stefan Franke, and Marcel Tilly, *Web-Entwicklung mit Eclipse 3* (German), DPunkt, 2004 (http://www.dpunkt.de)
- Eric Clayberg and Dan Rubel, *Eclipse: Building Commercial-Quality Plug-Ins*, Addison-Wesley, 2004 (http://www.qualityeclipse.com)
- Bill Dudney, *Eclipse Live*, SourceBeat, 2003 (http://www.sourcebeat.com)
- David Gallardo, Ed Burnette, and Robert McGovern, *Eclipse in Action: A Guide for the Java Developer*, Manning, 2003 (http://www.manning.com)
- Erich Gamma and Kent Beck, *Contributing to Eclipse*, Addison-Wesley, 2003 (http://www.aw.com)
- Wonjin Heo and Jiwon Jun, *Total Eclipse (Korean)*, Youngjin Publishing, 2003 (http://www.youngjin.com)
- Steven Holzner, *Eclipse: A Java Developer's Guide*, O'Reilly, 2004 (http://www.oreilly.com)
- Junya Ishikawa et al., *The Complete Eclipse Guidebook: From Installation to Plug-In Development* (Japanese), ASCII, 2003 (http://www.ascii.co.jp)

- Shinji Miyamoto, Shinichi IIda, and Yu Aoki, *Java Developers Guide to Adopting Eclipse* (Japanese), SoftBank Publishing, 2003 (http://www.sbpnet.jp)
- William Moore et al., *Eclipse Development Using the Graphical Editing Framework and the Eclipse Modeling Framework*, IBM RedBooks, 2003 (http://www.redbooks.ibm.com)
- Stanford Ng, Stephen Holder, and Matt Scarpino, *JFace/SWT in Action*, Manning, 2003 (http://www.manning.com)
- Steve Northover and Mike Wilson, *SWT: The Standard Widget Toolkit*, Addison-Wesley, 2004 (http://www.aw.com)
- Joe Pluta, *Eclipse: Step by Step*, MC Press, 2003 (http://www.mc-store.com)
- Sherry Shavor et al., *The Java Developer's Guide to Eclipse*, Addison-Wesley, 2003 (http://www.aw.com)
- Carlos Valcarcel, *Eclipse Kick Start*, Sams Publishing, 2004 (http://www.samspublishing.com)
- Rob Warner and Robert Harris, *The Definitive Guide to SWT and JFace*, Apress, 2004 (http://www.apress.com)
- Seongjun Yun, Sang-Min Cho, and Jeong Il Song, *Eclipse: Reinforcing the Java World* (Korean), Hybird, 2003 (http://hybird.net)

FAQ 18

How do I report a bug in Eclipse?

To manage and track Eclipse bugs and feature requests, the Eclipse Project uses Bugzilla. The main entry point to the Eclipse Bugzilla can be found at https://bugs.eclipse.org.

Do not be shy; post a bug if you see something wrong, even if you are in doubt whether it really is a bug. The committers of the relevant component will quickly decide what to do with your bug report. Also do not think, *Someone else will report the bug or at least the Eclipse developers themselves will see something so obvious.* Even the obvious things need to be documented and reported to be fixed. Your help is crucial in continuously improving the quality and robustness of the Eclipse Platform.

Before posting a bug, be sure to check whether it has already been posted. You can use the Eclipse Bugzilla search engine. Search instructions can be found at the Bugzilla page under the heading **Help With Bug Reporting**.

In short, Bugzilla is split up into "products," representing the major areas of interest in Eclipse: C Development Tools (CDT), Eclipse Modeling Framework (EMF), JDT, and so on. To post a bug on the generic Eclipse infrastructure, choose **Platform**. Choose the component, such as UI, that you want to provide feedback on, and be sure to follow the bug-writing guidelines mentioned on the bug report Web site. You will need a password to access Bugzilla. This is mainly for your own protection; the intent is to keep the spammers out.

Writing good bug reports or feature requests is an acquired skill. A great place to learn the basic etiquette is, "How to Ask Questions the Smart Way," by Eric Raymond and Rick Moen. Note that Eric and Rick are not affiliated with Eclipse, and you should not contact them with your Eclipse questions. Their article is linked from eclipse.org and can be found easily on the Web using your favorite search engine.

Keep in mind that the Eclipse committers are few, and the community is large. Bugzilla tracks thousands of defects and requests, and the committers have limited time to investigate vague, poorly described, or inaccurate reports. Always include the Eclipse build number in your bug report, which can be found in the **Help > About** dialog.

FAQ 19 *How can I search the existing list of bugs in Eclipse?*
FAQ 20 *What do I do if my feature request is ignored?*
Eric S. Raymond and Rick Moen, "How to Ask Questions the Smart Way" (http://www.catb.org/~esr/faqs)

FAQ
19

How can I search the existing list of bugs in Eclipse?

Visit the Eclipse bugs Web site to search for an existing bug report. The Eclipse Project uses Bugzilla for bug reporting and uses it to not only store bug reports but also feature requests, plan items, and architectural discussions. Before posting a bug, see whether it has been posted already. If you find yourself overwhelmed by the Bugzilla query page, you're not alone. Look for the link at the bottom of the query page, **Give me a clue about how to use this form**.

Eclipse Bugzilla (http://bugs.eclipse.org)

What do I do if my feature request is ignored?

Don't be put off by little or no initial response to a feature request logged in Bugzilla. Sometimes, the committers are focusing on feature deadlines or other priorities, but rest assured that everything logged to Bugzilla is at least read by one or more committers within a week. If your request gets no response, you can do some things to help speed up the process.

First, make sure that your request is well described and motivated. Eclipse Bugzilla gets many feature requests, so you need to "sell" your request to the committers and convince them why your request is important. If you are requesting a feature, demonstrate why it is useful to not only you, but also others. If you are requesting new API, you need to describe your main use cases and describe why they cannot be implemented using existing API. Keep in mind that as stewards of their individual plug-ins, committers have an obligation to prevent feature bloat. API is typically added to a plug-in only if it can be demonstrated to be broadly useful to a large number of downstream consumers of that plug-in. If every little requested feature were added without rigorous scrutiny, every plug-in in the platform today would be at least twice as big and probably much slower in execution.

Once you have convinced the committers that your request is valid, keep in mind that there is no guarantee it will be implemented for you. They still have only limited time and are focused primarily on major features in the development plan. However, at this point, you are welcome to implement the feature yourself and attach a patch of your implementation to the bug report. Committers will then review your patch and either apply it or reject it. If they reject it, they will describe their technical or other reasons and will often work with you to get it into suitable shape for releasing. Don't forget: In open source, as in much of the world, there is no such thing as a free lunch. The Eclipse committers will implement your feature only if they believe that it is truly useful to the users of their component. If they suspect that you are simply asking them to do your work for you, you'll be out of luck.

☞ **FAQ 18** *How do I report a bug in Eclipse?*

Can I get my documentation in PDF form, please?

Documentation for Eclipse SDK releases is available in PDF form from eclipse.org. Obtaining PDF documentation for other Eclipse software, or for non-release builds is a bit more involved.

When you download Eclipse code, documentation is provided in the form of HTML files, made accessible through a table of contents contained in a file called `toc.xml`. The contents of the HTML files can be browsed and searched easily with the Eclipse help system (see **Help > Help Contents**). The same information can be found online at the Eclipse documentation Web site.

Converting HTML to PDF form is somewhat labor-intensive. Although tools are available, such as HTMLDOC, to automatically convert HTML to PDF, the exact selection of files to include in the PDF and in what order requires some extra work. The best approach is to start with the `toc.xml` file and either write a conversion script or develop an Eclipse plug-in, as is done in the `tocviewer` plug-in used to write this book.

Since June 2004, Eclipse downloads come with PDF versions of the documentation. Check this book's CD–ROM or the Eclipse download site.

HTMLDOC by Easy Software Products (http://www.easysw.com/htmldoc)
eclipse.org documentation page (http://eclipse.org/documentation/main.html)
eclipse.org downloads page (http://eclipse.org/downloads)

Where do I find documentation for a given extension point?

At least three simple ways exist to find documentation for extension points:

1. Use platform help. See **Help > Help Contents > Platform Plug-in Developer Guide > Reference > Extension Point Reference**

2. Go online to the Eclipse Project documentation site

3. While contributing an extension point using the PDE Manifest Editor, select the **Extensions** tab and choose **Add > Add... > Generic Wizards > Schema-based Extensions > Details**

Note that **Search > Plug-in Search** lets you search for all uses of a given extension point.

 Online Eclipse documentation (http://eclipse.org/documentation/main.html)

How is Eclipse licensed?

The answer to this question depends on what aspect of Eclipse you are talking about. Everything you see on eclipse.org is governed by the Eclipse Web site terms of use (eclipse.org/legal). This document describes what licenses apply to the content, along with other legal information such as export control information. Everything you contribute through the Web site, including the Eclipse mailing lists, newsgroups, and CVS repositories, is governed by these terms of use.

Any software you download from eclipse.org is governed by a similar user agreement. This document, contained in a file called `notice.html` in the `eclipse` install directory, describes the licenses and other legal information that applies to the software. Each Eclipse plug-in typically has additional legal information in a file called `about.html`.

Unless otherwise noted in the Web site terms of use and software user agreement, most Eclipse content is licensed under the Common Public License (CPL). The CPL is approved by the Open Source Initiative (OSI). The OSI is a non profit corporation dedicated to managing and promoting the Open Source Definition for the good of the community, specifically through the OSI Certified Open Source Software certification mark and program. Approval by the OSI bestows confidence on a license that it really is "open source." The OSI also makes copies of approved open source licenses available on their Web site. The Eclipse Public License (EPL) is a new license, very similar to the CPL, that was introduced when the Eclipse Foundation was created. The EPL is currently undergoing OSI certification, and will eventually replace the CPL for any new content contributed to the Eclipse Foundation.

You should always speak with a lawyer for complete interpretation of any license, but it is safe to say that in essence the CPL provides free, unrestricted access to the source code and other creative matter it covers. CPL-licensed code can be redistributed or sold without making royalty payments to the copyright holders. The fact that dozens of companies are shipping commercial Eclipse-based products is a strong indication that the CPL is widely regarded as a safe, liberal open source license.

CPL FAQ (http://ibm.com/developerworks/library/os–cplfaq.html)
CPL version 1.0 (http://www.opensource.org/licenses/cpl.php)
eclipse.org Legal FAQs (http://eclipse.org/legal)

Chapter 2. Getting Started

Eclipse can be seen as a very advanced Java program. Running Eclipse may sound simple—simply run the included `eclipse.exe` or `eclipse` executable—yet in practice, you may want to tweak the inner workings of the platform. First, Eclipse does not come with a Java virtual machine (JVM), so you have to get one yourself. Note that Eclipse 3.0 needs a 1.4-compatible Java runtime environment (JRE).

To use Eclipse effectively, you will need to learn how to make Eclipse use a specific JRE. In addition, you may want to influence how much heap Eclipse may allocate, where it loads and saves its workspace from, and how you can add more plug-ins to your Eclipse installation.

This chapter should get you going. We also included some FAQs for plug-in developers who have already written plug-ins and want to get started with plug-in development for Eclipse 3.0.

Where do I get and install Eclipse?

FAQ
24

The way you download Eclipse depends on how close you want to be to the "live stream." Following are the release types that can be downloaded from the Eclipse download site (http://eclipse.org/downloads), in increasing level of closeness to the CVS HEAD stream:

- *The latest release*, used by most products in the market. These releases have little risk of surprises, yet those builds can be up to 6 months behind what is being worked on now. Example version numbers for these releases are 2.1.2 and 3.0.

- *Stable builds* (so-called milestone builds), which are typically 6 weeks apart and deliver a major collection of stable features. These builds are moderately tested, making them reliable enough for the needs of most developers. An example is Eclipse 3.0M4, which refers to the milestone 4 build of Eclipse 3.0.

- *Integration builds*, done every week and sometimes more in case of failure or when closer to a release date. These builds integrate contributions from various Eclipse subteams to test the collaborations of various plug-ins. Build names start with the letter "I."

- *Nightly builds*, which provide a view of the contents of the CVS server's HEAD stream at midnight (Eastern Standard Time) each night. You can compare this build to the result of musical chairs. The music stops at midnight, and the build captures what was released at that instant. Mileage accordingly varies. Build names start with the letter "N."

Each release or build has a corresponding set of build notes and test results. Be sure to consult these notes before selecting a given build. Automated test suites are run against the nightly and integration builds. Having a build pass the tests can increase the confidence level people have in them. In all cases, the builds are shipped as a compressed archive, and installation is a simple matter of unzipping them anywhere on your local machine.

Alternatively, you may have already installed Eclipse without knowing it. Many commercial products are based on Eclipse, and so while installing these products, you often install a given version of Eclipse. These products usually are not shy about being based on Eclipse, so you can easily discover the location of the eclipse installation by investigating the installation directory of the product. Usually, the directory will contain a subdirectory called eclipse that contains the embedded Eclipse instance. While running your product, you can activate the menu option **Help > About ...** and then click on the Eclipse icon to see what version of the platform is being used.

 The Eclipse download site (http://eclipse.org/downloads)

How do I run Eclipse?

When you unzip the Eclipse SDK, it creates a base install directory called eclipse. The directory layout looks something like this:

```
eclipse/
    features/          the directory containing Eclipse features
    plugins/           the directory containing Eclipse plugins
    eclipse.exe        platform executable
    cpl-v10.html       the CPL license
    install.ini
    jre/               the JRE to run Eclipse with
```

```
notice.html
readme
startup.jar          classes needed to start the platform
```

You can start Eclipse by running `eclipse.exe` on Windows or `eclipse` on other platforms. This small launcher runs a JVM with the following arguments:

```
java -cp eclipse/startup.jar org.eclipse.core.launcher.Main
```

If available under the `eclipse/jre` directory, the Eclipse JRE will be used; otherwise the launcher will consult the `JAVA_HOME` system path variable. A better option is to explicitly specify a JVM of your choice, using the `-vm` command-line argument:

```
eclipse -vm c:/jre/bin/javaw.exe
```

You should always use `-vm` so you can be sure of what VM you are using. Installers for other applications sometimes modify the `JAVA_HOME` variable, thus changing the VM used to launch Eclipse without your knowing about it.

The first time the `eclipse` command is executed, the platform creates a workspace directory, such as `eclipse/workspace`. The workspace will contain all your projects, along with private metadata computed by various plug-ins.

In Eclipse 3.0, you are prompted to choose a workspace location on start-up. Previously, the platform stored the workspace in the Eclipse install directory by default. In all versions of Eclipse, you can manually specify the workspace location on the command line, using the `-data <workspace-path>` command-line argument. The easiest way to quickly start Eclipse on different workspaces for versions before Eclipse 3.0 is to create shortcuts or shell scripts for each launch. The use of `-data` is advised because using the default workspace location will make it much more difficult for you to upgrade to new versions of Eclipse.

FAQ 26 *How do I increase the heap size available to Eclipse?*
FAQ 260 *Who shows the Eclipse splash screen?*

**FAQ
26**

How do I increase the heap size available to Eclipse?

Some JVMs put restrictions on the total amount of memory available on the heap. If you are getting **OutOfMemoryError**s while running Eclipse, the VM can be told to let the heap grow to a larger amount by passing the -vmargs command to the Eclipse launcher. For example, the following command would run Eclipse with a heap size of 256MB:

```
eclipse [normal arguments] -vmargs -Xmx256M [more VM args]
```

The arguments after -vmargs are directly passed to the VM. Run java -X for the list of options your VM accepts. Options starting with -x are implementation-specific and may not be applicable to all VMs.

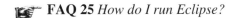 **FAQ 25** *How do I run Eclipse?*

**FAQ
27**

Where can I find that elusive .log file?

Whenever it encounters a problem that does not warrant launching a dialog, Eclipse saves a report in the workspace log file. The log file can be looked at in four alternative ways.

1. **Window > Show View > PDE Runtime > Error Log**. This gives you a view with the contents of the .log file.

2. **Help > About Eclipse Platform > Configuration Details**. This prints out a great number of details about the environment and also concatenates the .log file. Great for including in a bug report.

3. Locate the file yourself, see workspace/.metadata/.log.

4. Start Eclipse using -consoleLog. This will print the messages that normally go to the .log file in the enclosing shell/command window.

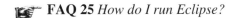 **FAQ 121** *How do I use the platform logging facility?*

Does Eclipse run on any Linux distribution?

Eclipse should work fine on any Linux distribution that has GTK+ 2.2.1 and higher—SWT is based on GTK2—and a 1.4 JRE. Motif versions require Open Motif 2.1, which is included in the Eclipse distribution. Although the Motif distribution has performance comparable to Windows, its clunky appearance makes GTK the widely preferred choice on Linux.

However, the Eclipse development teams are able to perform thorough testing only on a limited set of platforms. Consult the release notes included with each Eclipse build for a detailed list of officially supported platforms. As of June 2004, this list included the platforms in Table 2.1.

Portability of Eclipse is defined mainly by the underlying Java runtime—Eclipse 3.0 needs a Java 1.4 runtime—and by what platform SWT runs on; namely, all graphical UI in Eclipse are based on SWT. Table 2.1 lists various standard Java runtimes. However, earlier versions of Eclipse have also been compiled with `gcj` (http://www.klomp.org/mark/classpath/eclipse-gnome-gij.png) and even made to run on .Net, using IKVM on the CLR or Mono through the amazing work of Jeroen Frijters (http://www.frijters.net).

For any given Eclipse build, the supported platforms are listed in the readme file included with the download (`readme_eclipse.html` in the `readme` directory).

☞ The Eclipse download site (http://eclipse.org/downloads)
   IKVM (http://www.ikvm.net)

Operating System	Processor	Desktop	Java 2 Platform
Microsoft Windows XP	Intel x86	Win32	Sun Java 2 SDK, Standard Edition, version 1.4.2_03
Microsoft Windows XP	Intel x86	Win32	IBM 32-bit SDK for Windows, Java 2 Technology Edition, version 1.4.1
Red Hat Enterprise Linux WS 3	Intel x86	GTK	Sun Java 2 SDK, Standard Edition, 1.4.2_03 for Linux x86
Red Hat Enterprise Linux WS 3	Intel x86	GTK	IBM 32-bit SDK for Linux on Intel architecture, Java 2 Technology Edition, version 1.4.1
SuSE Linux 8.2	Intel x86	GTK	Sun Java 2 SDK, Standard Edition, 1.4.2_03 for Linux x86
SuSE Linux 8.2	Intel x86	GTK	IBM 32-bit SDK for Linux on Intel architecture, Java 2 Technology Edition, version 1.4.1
Sun Solaris 8	SPARC	Motif	Sun Java 2 SDK, Standard Edition, 1.4.2_03
HP HP-UX 11i	hp9000 PA-RISC	Motif	HP-UX SDK for the Java 2 platform, version 1.4.2.00
IBM AIX 5L version 5.2	PowerPC	Motif	IBM 32-bit SDK for AIX, Java 2 Technology Edition, version 1.4.1
Apple Mac OS X 10.3	PowerPC	Carbon	Java 2 Standard Edition 1.4.1 for Mac OS X
QNX Neutrino RTOS	Intel x86	Photon	IBM J9 VM for QNX

Table 2.1 The Eclipse Reference Platforms

I unzipped Eclipse, but it won't start. Why?

Invariably, with several hundred thousand downloads of Eclipse every month, Eclipse does not start at all for a few users . These failures typically stem from software configuration problems on the host machine or an unusual hardware configuration. If you are already a power Eclipse user, you might be tempted to skip this question. However, even the most advanced Eclipse user will occasionally have problems starting an Eclipse build. So, with a nod to David Letterman, here is a "top ten" list of the most common start-up problems, along with suggestions for solutions.

1. *Cannot find a VM.* Eclipse requires a JVM to run and does not include one in the download. You need to grab a VM yourself; the Eclipse downloads page has pointers to where you can get one. You may have a VM, but Eclipse cannot find it. To avoid possible conflicts, always specify the VM you are using with the -vm command-line argument.

2. *Bad VM.* All versions of the Eclipse Platform require at least a JDK 1.3 VM. Eclipse 3.0 requires a 1.4 VM. The Sun 1.4.0 VM is known to be flaky, so you are best off with a recent 1.4.2 VM. Also, you may not get much sympathy from Eclipse if you are using a home-grown or experimental JVM. Use a reputable VM. If you run into trouble, always try a VM from a major distributor and see whether the problem goes away.

3. *Unsupported platform.* Make sure that the architecture and the operating system of your machine match one of the supported systems described in the file readme_eclipse.html. Eclipse will not run on Windows 95 or Commodore 64, for example. If your machine does not match one of the configurations described in the readme, it may still run, but you are on your own!

4. *Lack of appropriate native widget toolkit.* If you download, for example, the GTK version of Eclipse, then you need to make sure that you have GTK (GTK+ 2.1.1 or higher) on your computer and that it is correctly installed.

5. *Incorrectly unzipped.* Believe it or not, about once a month, a user reports start-up failure: The user has unzipped Eclipse without selecting the use folder names option. Make sure that the result of unzipping is an

install tree with an `eclipse` directory at its root. The Ark unzip utility in KDE is known to mangle Eclipse zips, so use a different unzip program to install there.

6. *New Eclipse unzipped on top of older Eclipse.* Do not do this. Either install Eclipse in a brand new directory or use the Eclipse Update Manager to upgrade an older Eclipse. You can still keep your old workspace. Look in the Eclipse `readme` file for more details.

7. *Buggy build.* It is not always user error. Some integration builds, and even the odd stable build, will have start-up problems under certain configurations that were not well tested. For example, build 3.0M6 would fail to start up if you restarted with an old workspace after unzipping new plug-ins into the `plugins` directory. If you are a new user, always start with the most recent official Eclipse release to be sure you are using the "least buggy" version possible. For more advanced users willing to accept less stable builds, consult Bugzilla to see if your particular start-up problem has already been reported.

8. *Xerces problem.* Prior to Eclipse 3.0, Eclipse used a version of Xerces for parsing XML files, but certain distributions of 1.4 JVMs included a different version of Xerces with the same package names. This should not be a problem with Eclipse 3.0 or higher. See FAQ 108 for more details.

9. *Disk full or out of memory.* Eclipse, especially 2.1 and earlier, does not always gracefully report disk-full errors or out-of-memory errors. Make sure that you have adequate disk space and that you are giving the Java VM enough heap space. See FAQ 26 for details.

10. *None of the preceding.* When all else fails, try asking on the eclipse.platform newsgroup. Be extremely specific about what operating system, VM, Eclipse build, hardware, and so on, you are running. Attach any error details that you have found in the Eclipse error log. You will find, especially on Linux and Mac, where configuration can be a lot more complicated, that the community is fairly helpful in getting new users going and will generally make an effort in proportion to the effort they perceive that you have made. You are almost guaranteed to get no response if you simply say, "Eclipse will not start." If a well-described newsgroup post does not get any response, enter a bug report.

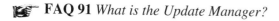 **FAQ 26** *How do I increase the heap size available to Eclipse?*
FAQ 108 *Why doesn't Eclipse play well with Xerces?*

How do I upgrade Eclipse?

FAQ
30

Run the Update Manager, using **Help > Software Updates > Find and Install...
> Search for updates of the currently installed features**. The Update Manager
will visit the Eclipse Web site and offer updates for the features you have
installed and allow for easy update from Eclipse 2.1 to 3.0, for instance. You can
use the Update Manager to upgrade only between official Eclipse releases.

If you want to upgrade to stable stream releases or even nightly builds, you have
to live on the edge. Download a new build from the Eclipse download Web site
(http://eclipse.org/downloads) and unzip it in a new directory. We strongly
recommend against unzipping over your existing Eclipse version as unexpected
side effects may occur. Complete upgrade instructions are always included in the
Eclipse `readme_eclipse.html` file included with every build in the `readme`
directory.

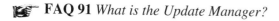 **FAQ 91** *What is the Update Manager?*

How do I install new plug-ins?

FAQ
31

Your best approach is to use the Eclipse Update Manager.

More experienced plug-in developers—and sometimes lazy plug-in
publishers—have learned to find the `eclipse/plugins` directory and install their
plug-ins there manually. This obviously is a more dangerous approach, as no
certification takes place about the suitability of the plug-in; it may rely on other
plug-ins not available in your installation. In the case of compatibility conflicts,
you won't find out until you use the plug-in that it might break.

You may compare installing plug-ins to installing applications on Windows. You
can, of course, install your dynamic link libraries (DLLs) in the `System32`
directory or play with the `PATH` environment variable. But, how are you going to
remove the application later when you no longer need it? On Windows,
specialized installation programs have been devised, and uninstallation is easy

through the **Start** menu. The Eclipse Update Manager can be seen as the Eclipse equivalent of InstallShield and the Windows Registry combined.

For day-to-day development and prototyping of small plug-ins, you might still be tempted to use the manual installation process. You could, but we strongly advise against it. Creating a feature and a corresponding update site is child's play using the PDE wizards and will greatly improve the quality of your work. Eventually, you will want to share your fruits with others, and having an update site ready from the start will make it much easier to boast of your Eclipse knowledge to your friends and colleagues.

FAQ 69 *How do I create a plug-in?*
FAQ 89 *How do I create a feature?*
FAQ 91 *What is the Update Manager?*
FAQ 237 *What is the purpose of activities?*

Can I install plug-ins outside the main install directory?

Users who like to "live on the edge" will be frequently installing new builds of Eclipse. When a new build is installed, a manual step is generally required to copy over any extra plug-ins from the old build to the new one. We all know how much programmers hate manual steps, so it would be nice if there were an easy way to link a set of external plug-ins into Eclipse builds. A mechanism to do that is called a *product extension*.

A product extension must be laid out on disk in a certain way so the Eclipse configuration tools can recognize it. Following is the disk layout for a product extension that contains a single plug-in called `org.eclipse.faq.examples`.

```
eclipse/
    .eclipseextension
    plugins/
        org.eclipse.faq.examples/
            plugin.xml
            examples.jar
        ... optionally more plug-in directories ...
    features/
        ... features would go here ...
```

The file `.eclipseextension` is empty, acting as a special marker that tells install tools that this is an Eclipse extension. Other than that special file, the layout is the same as that for an Eclipse product. Plug-ins go in a directory called `plugins`, and if the extension contains features, they go in a sibling directory called `features`.

Once you've got this directory structure set up, you have to link the product extension into your plug-in configuration. In Eclipse 3.0, you simply go to **Help > Software Updates > Manage Configuration**, choose the option called **Link an Extension Location**, and select the extension directory when prompted. That's all there is to it! As long as you keep the same workspace when you upgrade to a new build, the product extensions will automatically be available in the new configuration.

 FAQ 30 *How do I upgrade Eclipse?*
FAQ 33 *How do I remove a plug-in?*

How do I remove a plug-in?

You should not remove plug-ins from Eclipse. Plug-ins should be installed as *features* using the Update Manager. The same Update Manager can be used to disable plug-ins by disabling the feature they belong to. Run **Help > Software Updates > Manage Configuration...**, select the feature of interest, and disable it with the task shown in the right window.

When a feature is disabled, all its plug-ins will be disabled also. They are still available on disk, and they can be enabled at any time in the future. To physically remove the feature and its plug-ins, you will have to manually remove the feature from the `eclipse/features` directory and its plug-ins from the `eclipse/plugins` directory. We advise extreme caution here. Remove the wrong ones, and you may have quite some trouble restoring your Eclipse to a stable state. Unless you care a lot about hard disk use, we recommend leaving the plug-ins where they are.

How do I find out what plug-ins have been installed?

One way of finding out is to select **Help > About Eclipse Platform >**. From this dialog, click **Plug-in Details** to get a list of all installed plug-ins, along with vendor and version information. If you instead click **Configuration Details**, you will be rewarded with a full credit report of your current Eclipse installation. The main sections contain information about your system properties, what features and plug-ins have been installed, preferences specified by you, the Update Manager log, and a dump of the error log, which lists problems that have been reported by various plug-ins.

 FAQ 111 *What is a configuration?*

Where do I get help?

Eclipse offers extensive help through the menu option **Help > Help Contents...**. This will launch a Tomcat server to run from inside your Eclipse, and a browser is opened to show the contents. The help browser has a useful search engine to search the entire Eclipse documentation. Sometimes, this help text is confusingly referred to as the online help, perhaps because the help is replicated online at the Eclipse Web site (http://eclipse.org/documentation/main.html). However, your local help will also work when you are disconnected from the network.

Alternatively, more focused, context-sensitive help can be invoked at any time by pressing F1. The currently selected widget is offered a chance to honor the help request. Its containment tree is walked upward until a suitable localized help can be furbished. A pop-up will appear near the mouse, and links to the documentation are provided. If the help does not seem helpful, remember how the search path for F1 help works and feel free to enter a bug report to ensure that help is provided at the proper level.

Select **Help > Cheat Sheets...** for step-by-step instructions on common tasks. The steps have convenient links to topic-related help.

If you don't find the answer you need in the help system, there are plenty more sources of information on Eclipse. On eclipse.org you will find a plethora of resources, including articles by Eclipse experts, newsgroups, mailing lists, and lists of books and tutorials. Perhaps best of all, the Eclipse source code is the most reliable place to look for information. The source never lies and is always up to date!

☞ **FAQ 274** *How do I add help content to my plug-in?*
FAQ 275 *How do I provide F1 help?*

How do I accommodate project layouts that don't fit the Eclipse model?

FAQ
36

Let's say that you are new to Eclipse, but have some existing projects with file system layouts that cannot be changed. Perhaps you have other tools or build processes that require your projects to be laid out in a certain way. Because Eclipse also has expectations about how projects are laid out on disk, you can run into problems when you try to get started in Eclipse with your existing projects.

In release 2.1, Eclipse introduced the notion of *linked resources* to help deal with problems like this. Linked resources can refer to files or folders anywhere in your file system, even inside other Eclipse projects. Using linked resources, you can cobble together a project from files and folders that are scattered all over your file system. The link descriptions are stored in the file called `.project` inside your project content area. If you share this file with a repository, other users will be able to load the project and get all the links reconstructed automatically in their workspace. If you do not want to hard-code particular file system paths, you can define linked resources relative to workspace path variables. Path variables can be added or changed from the **Workbench > Linked Resources** preference page.

For more information on using linked resources, see the good general introduction in the *Workbench User Guide*, under **Concepts > Workbench > Linked resources**. The *Java Development User Guide* also has an excellent tutorial that helps you get started with various types of project configurations. Look under **Getting Started > Project configuration tutorial**. Information on how to define linked resources programmatically is found in the *Platform Plug-in Developer Guide*, under **Programmer's Guide > Resource and workspace API > Linked Resources**.

What is new in Eclipse 3.0?

Attempting to enumerate all of new features and APIs in Eclipse 3.0 would be futile. The past year or so of development has focused on more than 50 major features of the Eclipse 3.0 plan, not to mention addressing more than 5,000 bugs and feature requests, according to a quick query of the Eclipse Bugzilla. The best place to get an overview of major new changes in Eclipse 3.0 is to read through all the *New and Noteworthy* documents included with each milestone build.

To give you a quick summary, the development of Eclipse 3.0 has centered on the following major themes:

- *User experience*. This theme deals with all aspects of the end user experience, especially for new users, the so-called out-of-box experience. This theme also focuses on UI scalability, affordances, improved file-encoding support, key bindings, editor management, text editor presentation, workspace selection, and the introduction of an SWT browser widget.

- *Responsive UI*. This involves identifying and reducing the number of places where users are forced to wait when using Eclipse. Major work on this theme included the introduction of an Eclipse concurrency architecture and tackling the performance gap in Eclipse between Windows and other platforms, such as Linux GTK, QNX, and Mac.

- *Rich client platform*. The Eclipse APIs have been reorganized to better support development of applications outside the development tools domain. Work on this theme also included a new infrastructure for storing user settings and support for dynamic installation and removal of plug-ins.

- *Extended Java family*. This theme deals only with the Java development tools subproject. Work in this area focused on opening up the JDT APIs to better support Java-like source files, such as Java Server Pages (JSPs) and SQLj. This included opening up the refactoring and Java search infrastructure to facilitate participation by third-party plug-ins.

FAQ 38 *Is Eclipse 3.0 going to break all of my old plug-ins?*
The Eclipse 3.0 plan (http://eclipse.org/development/plan)

Is Eclipse 3.0 going to break all of my old plug-ins?

No. Many rumors and discussions circulated during the development of Eclipse 3.0 about how compatible it would be with plug-ins written from Eclipse 2.1 or earlier. Clearly, in the large community of Eclipse plug-in writers, many would be greatly inconvenienced by any breaking changes to existing API. On the other hand, rigidly maintaining API across all releases can be a great barrier to ongoing innovation in the platform. Eventually, a balance was struck that allowed for some well-justified breaking changes, while also providing a compatibility story to allow old plug-ins to continue running on Eclipse 3.0. What does this mean if you have written plug-ins targeting older versions of the platform?

If you do not want to take advantage of new capabilities in Eclipse 3.0, you don't need to do anything. The platform guarantees 99 percent binary compatibility with older versions of Eclipse. Thus, most old plug-ins that used only legal API in previous releases will continue working when installed in Eclipse 3.0. If you find cases in which this is not true, you are encouraged to enter bug reports so that the compatibility support can be fixed.

So far it sounds too easy, right? Well, as the saying goes, "nothing ventured, nothing gained." If you do want to take advantage of new Eclipse 3.0 API, you will need to do some work to port your plug-in to 3.0. In most cases, the amount of work required is minimal, and the Eclipse plug-in development tools provide utilities for automatically migrating your plug-in manifest file for 3.0. All the required migration is carefully described in the *Eclipse 3.0 Porting Guide*, found in the *Platform Plug-in Developer Guide* in the Eclipse help system. If you find that your old code is not compiling or running when being developed against Eclipse 3.0, consult the guide to see what changes might have affected you.

FAQ 39 *How do I prevent my plug-in from being broken when I update Eclipse?*

How do I prevent my plug-in from being broken when I update Eclipse?

Eclipse makes a careful distinction between published APIs and internal implementation details. The APIs are designed to reduce coupling between plug-ins to a small, stable interface. This insulates clients of the interface from being affected by implementation changes, and it allows the plug-in that publishes the interface to continue to innovate and grow without breaking existing clients. If your plug-in uses only published API and carefully follows the API contracts defined in the API javadoc, your plug-in should continue to work after migrating to a new Eclipse release.

In the Eclipse Platform, the API of a plug-in includes all public classes and interfaces that do not have the word *internal* in their package names and all public and protected methods in those classes and interfaces. The API also includes all extension points that are not explicitly described as for internal use only in their documentation; there is only a small handful of such internal extension points.

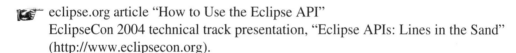 eclipse.org article "How to Use the Eclipse API"
EclipseCon 2004 technical track presentation, "Eclipse APIs: Lines in the Sand" (http://www.eclipsecon.org).

Chapter 3. Java Development in Eclipse

The topic of how to use Eclipse for typical Java development is beyond the scope of this FAQ list. We focus more on the issues Eclipse users may run into when developing new plug-ins for the platform. Also, as a plug-in developer, you need to be familiar with the ways in which Eclipse is used. To achieve seamless integration with the platform, your plug-in must respect common usage patterns and offer the same level of functionality that users of your plug-in have come to expect from the platform. This chapter focuses on user-level issues of interest to plug-in developers as users or as enablers for other users of the platform.

For a comprehensive guide to using Eclipse, refer to other books such as *The Java Developer's Guide to Eclipse* by Sherry Shavor et al. (Addison-Wesley, 2003).

☞ **FAQ 17** *What books have been written on Eclipse?*

FAQ
40

How do I show/hide files like `.classpath` in the Navigator?

Use the menu for Navigator: the small triangle in the Navigator title bar. Select **Filters...** and check the type of files you want to hide. This technique also applies to the JDT's Package Explorer.

If your plug-in must store metadata in the project content area, consider adding a filter to this list, using the `org.eclipse.ui.ide.resourceFilters` extension point. The filter specifies a file name pattern and a Boolean attribute specifying whether the filter should be on by default. As an example, the Java development tools add a filter using this mechanism to hide Java class files generated by the compiler.

☞ **FAQ 46** *How do I hide referenced libraries in the Package Explorer?*

How do I link the Navigator with the currently active editor?

The Navigator provides a view of the workspace and shows resources available on the file system. From the Navigator, files can be opened in an editor. When multiple editors are opened, it can be difficult to keep track of where the related resources are in the Navigator. For this reason, the Navigator has support to synchronize its tree view with the currently edited resource.

To link resources between the Navigator and the editors in the workbench, locate the **Link** button in the Navigator toolbar at the top of its UI. The **Link** button is an icon with two arrows pointing to each other. Move the mouse over it; hover help should read Link with Editor. This technique also applies to the JDT's Package Explorer.

If you are creating views with input linked to the selection in other views or editors, consider introducing a similar link option in your view's toolbar. The platform has been grappling with this issue of view linking for years, and we have found that letting the user decide is the only viable option. A view that always links its input will usually cause the user to lose context, as the view continually jumps around, scrolls, and changes its selection. Very few users will leave linking turned on all the time but will instead toggle it on and off again to find the item they are currently editing.

 FAQ 46 *How do I hide referenced libraries in the Package Explorer?*

How do I use the keyboard to traverse between editors?

The keyboard can be used in several ways to traverse between editors.

- A pop-up list of all open editors in most recently used order will be shown when you press Ctrl+F6 and don't release the Ctrl key. Move backward in this list using Ctrl+Shift+F6.

- Create new key bindings for the **Next Editor** and **Previous Editor** commands in the **Workbench > Keys** preference page, under the **Window** category. Many users find that binding these commands to Ctrl+` and Ctrl+Shift+` (the key directly above Tab on U.S.-English keyboards) makes editor switching much like the Alt+Tab and Alt+Shift+Tab that many window managers use to switch applications.

- Use Alt+Left and Alt+Right—or click the **Forward** and **Back** buttons in the toolbar—to move around in the editor navigation history, much as you would in a Web browser.

- Press Ctrl+Shift+E to open a dialog of all open editors, type the first letter of the editor input name to pick the editor of choice from the list, and press Enter. This is a quick way to get random access in a large group of open editors.

- Press Ctrl+E (Eclipse 3.0 only) to open a drop-down list of open editors when the tabs do not fit on the screen. Start typing the editor name in this list to pick the editor you want to activate.

- Press Alt+F to open the file menu; then press the number of the editor of choice from the editor history list at the bottom of the menu. This is the easiest way to jump quickly to an editor that has recently been closed.

- Press Ctrl+Shift+R to open the Open Resource dialog and find your editor in the list (or Ctrl+Shift+T for Java types). This can be used to switch to an editor whether or not it is already open.

This seemingly long list of choices has probably been the most hotly debated usability issue in Eclipse over the years. Attempts to change or remove any of these features in the past have resulted in passionate criticism, with everyone having a favorite technique for navigating the environment. The lesson for plug-in developers? Sometimes, you have to provide more than one way to do the same thing. Always keep keyboard-only users—and this includes visually impaired users—in mind. The Eclipse team has been known to have mouse-free days, when mice are unplugged to make sure that everything in the environment is accessible without a mouse.

FAQ 48 *What editor keyboard shortcuts are available?*
FAQ 50 *How do I open a type in a Java editor?*

FAQ
43

How can I rearrange Eclipse views and editors?

Eclipse allows you a great deal of flexibility in how the views and editors are presented in the workbench. With the mouse, views can be docked as fast views in toolbars, grouped together in stacks, and dragged around to different areas. Any view can also be maximized by double-clicking its title bar or pressing Ctrl+M, or it can be minimized to show only its title bar.

With editors, you can likewise resize or organize in a number of ways. All editors must be grouped together in one area, but they can be split horizontally or vertically within that area to show multiple editors simultaneously. Editors can also be maximized, by double-clicking the title bar or pressing Ctrl+M, or minimized to show only its title bar.

Many of these actions can be mapped to a key binding from the **Workbench > Keys** preference page. Look at the commands in the **Window** category to see what commands can be bound to your own key sequences. Most part-manipulation commands are also found in the part context menu, accessible by pressing Alt+− (Alt+minus).

FAQ
44

Why doesn't my program start when I click the Run button?

Eclipse is not only a Java development environment. To deal with everything that can be launched with it—Java programs, JUnit tests, Enterprise JavaBeans (EJBs), even Eclipse itself—Eclipse defines the concept of *launch configurations*. When you click the **Run** button, click on **Java Application**, fill out the details, and click **Run**. The next time, your program will be launched automatically when you click the **Run** button (or press Ctrl+F11). To alter your launch configuration or to create a new one, select the **Run...** menu option, in the **Run** button drop-down menu. Alternatively, you can edit a launch configuration by holding down Ctrl and clicking on the launch you want to edit in the **Run** or **Debug** button drop-down list.

The other **Run** button—the one with the toolbox—is for launching external development tools and scripts, such as Ant, from within Eclipse. Generally, this icon is for launching tools that operate on the resources in your workspace rather than for launching programs you are building in your workspace.

☞ **FAQ 313** *What is a launch configuration?*
FAQ 317 *How do I add my own external tools?*

How do I turn off autobuilding of Java code?

FAQ
45

JDT uses the autobuild facilities provided by the platform. If a resource changes, the platform checks the project description file (see `.project` in your projects). When the file contains a reference to the Java builder, the builder gets notified of the change and will then compile the Java source file and its dependents. The following project description file snippet shows that the Java builder is associated with the project:

```
<buildSpec>
    <buildCommand>
        <name>org.eclipse.jdt.core.javabuilder</name>
        <arguments>
        </arguments>
    </buildCommand>
</buildSpec>
```

If a workspace gets large—say, tens of thousands of files—the process of checking each project, activating all registered builders, and discovering whether anything needs to be rebuilt owing to a single resource save may have a considerable impact on the responsiveness of the workbench. In these situations, autobuild can be turned off through **Window > Preferences > Workbench > Perform build automatically on resource modification**.

Even for smaller workspaces, turning off autobuilding may be a useful feature. For instance, when importing a large number of plug-ins from CVS, it may make sense to turn off autobuilding first. After all files are checked out, autobuilding is turned on again, and all pending builds are run in one swoop.

☞ **FAQ 292** *Where can I find information about writing builders?*
FAQ 325 *How do I implement an Eclipse builder?*

FAQ 46

How do I hide referenced libraries in the Package Explorer?

Use the menu for Package Explorer: the small triangle in the explorer's title bar. Select **Filters...** and uncheck **Referenced Libraries**.

 FAQ 40 *How do I show/hide files like* `.classpath` *in the Navigator?*

FAQ 47

Where do my `.class` files disappear to?

If you use the context menu on a project to inspect the project's properties, the **Java Build Path** page will have a field for the **Default output folder**. The initial value is the `bin` directory directly under your project. Similarly, the **Source** tab provides access to the location of your source input folder(s).

The Java perspective filters out the output folder from the Package Explorer. If you like, you can use the Navigator view to browse the output folder.

FAQ 48

What editor keyboard shortcuts are available?

Table 3.1 lists some frequently used but perhaps lesser-known keyboard shortcuts in the context of Java editing.

See **Help > Help Contents > Java Development User Guide > Reference > Java Development tools (JDT) Basics > JDT Actions** for a list of keyboard shortcuts provided by the Java development tools.

See the **Workbench > Keys** preference page to reassign shortcuts or assign shortcuts to common actions.

Shortcut	Action
Alt+Left Alt+Right	Navigate in the editor history.
Ctrl+Shift+P	Go to matching bracket.
Ctrl+Shift+Up Ctrl+Shift+Down	Go to previous/next member.
Ctrl+L	Go to a given line in the editor.
Ctrl+S	Save current editor and build.
Ctrl+, Ctrl+.	Go to previous/next result/error.
Ctrl+Alt+H	Open call hierarchy on a method.
Alt+Up Alt+Down	Move current selection up or down.
Ctrl+E	Switch to another editor.
F3 F4	Open declaration or type hierarchy.
Ctrl+T Ctrl+F3	Pop-up type hierarchy or structure.
Ctrl+Shift+T	Open a type declaration.
Ctrl+Space	Content Assist.
Alt+Shift+M	Extract selection into method.
Alt+Shift+R	Rename currently selected element.
Ctrl+F Ctrl+I Ctrl+K	Find, incremental find, find again.
Ctrl+H	Open search dialog.
Ctrl+Shift+/ Ctrl+Shift+\	Comment/uncomment selection.
Ctrl+M	Maximize/minimize current editor.
Ctrl+Shift+M Ctrl+Shift+O	Add/organize imports.
F11 Ctrl+F11	Debug/run most recent launch.

Table 3.1 Frequently used JDT keyboard shortcuts

How do I stop the Java editor from showing a single method at once?

Activate the editor area, and then click the toolbar button labeled **Show Source of Selected Element Only**.

People sometimes click this button by accident and end up stuck in a state in which the Java editor will show only a single method or field at once. This feature of the Java editor makes it much easier to work in large Java files. By focusing on a single method at once, you have a much less cluttered editor area. Note that you can still view the entire file when in this state by deselecting the selected element in the Outline view. Smalltalkers will recognize this as one of the many innovations Eclipse inherited from its non file-centric Smalltalk IDE ancestors.

How do I open a type in a Java editor?

Opening a given type in an editor can be done in many ways.

- If you see the type in your editor, move the caret inside the name, or select the type and press F3. This works inside javadoc comments.

- Hold down the Ctrl key and move the mouse around inside a Java editor. You will notice types turning into hyperlinks: blue underlined names, just like in a Web browser.

- To open a dialog with a list of available types, press Ctrl+Shift+T.

- To open its type hierarchy, select a type in a Java editor, and press F4.

- To open a type hierarchy on any type, press Ctrl+Shift+H.

- To quickly navigate to a given type in the Package Explorer, give focus to the tree, and start typing the name of the type. The Explorer will automatically scroll to the type, assuming that the type is visible and has not been filtered out of the view. This works in Windows only.

Note that when opening a type hierarchy, there is a preference on the **Java** preference page to open the type in a new type hierarchy perspective versus simply opening a view. This is useful in conjunction with the preference to open perspectives in a new window on the **Workbench > Perspectives** preference page. This allows you to browse a hierarchy without cluttering and losing context in the editors and views in your main window.

☞ **FAQ 42** *How do I use the keyboard to traverse between editors?*

How do I control the Java formatter?

FAQ 51

By activating **Window > Preferences > Java > Code Formatter**, you can create a new formatting profile. The choices for the various layout characteristics show the depth and breadth of the JDT code formatter. Full control exists over indentation, placement of braces, whitespace, blank lines, control statements, line wrapping, and comments. With the code formatter preference settings, a profile can easily be customized, saved, and shared with a team of developers to maintain a consistent company style.

How do I choose my own compiler?

FAQ 52

The JDT compiler is tightly integrated with the rest of the JDT. Extracting the compiler out of the JDT and properly integrating a different compiler is not trivial. A quick approach is to disable the Java builder from the project's **Builders** property page, and replace it with an Ant task that calls `javac` or another compiler. However, we strongly advise you to go with the installed compiler. It knows exactly how to interact with the rest of Eclipse—for instance, by assisting in the creation of tasks, quick fixes, and source decorators. It is one of the fastest, most complete Java compilers available. Finally, the JDT compiler can generate class files even when the source contains compilation errors.

By activating **Window > Preferences > Java > Compiler**, you have full control over the reporting style of the compiler, severity of error conditions, what to do with unused code, and how to treat javadoc comments.

Using the Preference page, you can also select the JDK compliance level of the compiler, the version of generated class files, and whether the compiler should generate debugging symbols.

 FAQ 316 *Why can't my Ant build find* `javac?`

FAQ
53

What Java refactoring support is available?

In the Java perspective, a menu called **Refactor** is enabled. It contains all possible refactoring operations currently implemented by the JDT. All operations are listed, even though they may not be applicable to the current selection. When a given element is selected in the Java editor, the context menu will show the refactoring operations that are specifically applicable to the selection. Refer to the **Help > Help Contents > Java Development User Guide > Refactoring support** for a comprehensive discussion on what refactoring techniques are available, how to preview a refactoring, and how to undo/redo refactorings.

It is important to realize the existence of the underlying mechanisms that allow for refactoring. For instance, when a given method is being renamed, all source files that have a reference to the method will have to be visited and their reference to the renamed method changed. The only way to do these kinds of refactorings in a scalable and manageable way is by using an underlying model of the Java source being refactored. Such a model is commonly referred to as a Document Object Model (DOM).

Frequent refactorings for which you may want to remember the keyboard shortcuts are **rename** with shortcut Alt+Shift+R and **extract method** with shortcut Alt+Shift+M. You can create or change key bindings for all refactorings from the **Workbench > Keys** preference page.

 FAQ 340 *How do I support refactoring for my own language?*
IBM developerWorks article on refactoring (http://ibm.com/developerworks)

How can Content Assist make me the fastest coder ever?

When extending Eclipse, plug-in authors are confronted with an overwhelming selection of API to choose from. In the good old days, books could be published with API references, and programmers could study the material and recite the proper incantations to drive the relatively simple APIs. With modern APIs, this is no longer possible. There simply is too much to read and remember. Content Assist to the rescue!

Content Assist can take the guesswork out of coding in a number of ways:

- *Finding a given type.* Assume that you are writing some code and want to use a button in your UI. You start typing the letter "B" and don't remember the rest of the word. Simply press Ctrl+Space, and the Java tooling will present you with a list of all types that start with the letter "B." The list starts with `Boolean`. Keep typing, and the list narrows down. After typing `But`, you get to choose between `java.awt.Button` and `org.eclipse.swt.widgets.Button`. Choose the one you like, and the editor inserts the class *and* inserts an import statement for the class at the same time.

- *Finding a given field or method.* After typing a dot after a certain expression, Content Assist will suggest all possible fields and methods applicable to the expression's result type. This functionality is very useful for discovering what operations can be applied to a given object. Combined with pervasive use of getters and setters, browsing an API is really simple. For the `Button` example, continuations for `get` show all attributes that can be obtained from a button. The ones starting with `set` show the attributes that can be modified. Another frequent prefix used while writing plug-ins is `add` to add event listeners. Having Content Assist at your fingertips definitely improves coding speed by combining intuition with content-assisted browsing.

- *Entering method parameter values.* When entering Ctrl+Space after the "(" for a method call, Content Assist will provide the expected type name for each parameter. When you advance to the next parameter—by pressing a comma—the Content Assist hints move along with you. This is especially useful for overloaded methods with ambiguous signatures and for methods with many parameters.

- *Overriding inherited methods.* Invoke Content Assist when the cursor is between method declarations. Proposals will be shown for all possible methods that can be overridden from superclasses.

- *Generating getters and setters.* Between two method declarations, type `get`, and invoke Content Assist. Proposals will be shown for creating accessor methods for any fields in the class that do not yet have an accessor. The same applies for generating setter methods by invoking Content Assist on the prefix `set`.

- *Creating anonymous inner classes.* Eclipse likes loose coupling and hence works a lot with listeners that are registered on demand. The listeners implement a given interface with methods that are called when the event of interest happens. Typical usage is to declare an anonymous inner class, as in this example:

```
button.addSelectionListener(new SelectionAdapter() {
    public void widgetSelected(SelectionEvent e) {
        // do something here
    }
});
```

Here is how an experienced Eclipse user might enter that code using Content Assist.

```
but<Ctrl+Space> select 'button'
.add<Ctrl+Space> select 'addSelectionListener'
new Sel<Ctrl+Space> select 'SelectionAdapter'
() { <Ctrl+Space> select 'widgetSelected'
```

Note that Content Assist is also available inside javadoc comments and can help when declaring fields and can assist with named local variables and method arguments. In **FAQ 336** we explain how Content Assist is implemented in Eclipse.

Also note that Content Assist can be fully customized from the **Java > Editor** preference page.

FAQ 55 *How can templates make me the fastest coder ever?*
FAQ 336 *How do I add Content Assist to my language editor?*

How can templates make me the fastest coder ever?

The Eclipse editor framework has excellent support for templates, and we don't mean the C++ kind.

In Eclipse, templates are fragments of code that can be inserted in an editor to ease the entering of repetitive code. Code templates are accessed and used in the same way as Content Assist. In the following example, we entered **for**, then pressed Ctrl+Space. We chose **iterate over array with temporary value** and pressed the Tab key to advance to the first variant in the inserted template (Figure 3.1). When we enter a new name for the index variable, all occurrences in the template are automatically changed also.

```
*TemplateSample.java

public class TemplateSample {
    public static void main(String[] args) {
        for (int arg = 0; arg < args.length; arg++) {
            String string = args[arg];

        }
    }
}
```

Figure 3.1 After inserting the `for` loop template

Another powerful, and quite useful, example is the following: Select a couple of statements, press Ctrl+Space and select **try catch block** to encapsulate the current selection with an exception handler.

New templates can also be defined. Templates can be imported and exported, allowing them to be shared among multiple developers in a team.

See **Window > Preferences > Java > Editor > Templates** and press F1 for relevant help on this topic.

☞ **FAQ 54** *How can Content Assist make me the fastest coder ever?*

What is a Quick Fix?

Whenever it detects an error, the Java editor highlights the error using a wavy red line under the offending code and a marker in the left editor margin. Moving the mouse over the underlined code or the marker will indicate the error. The marker can be selected with the left mouse to activate the Quick Fix pop-up, indicating actions that can be undertaken to repair the error. Alternatively, pressing Ctrl+1 will activate Quick Fix from the keyboard.

Quick Fixes can be used to make typing much faster. Let's assume that you are using Eclipse to rewrite Deep Blue and are writing variation 128839. At some point during editing, you need access to the Rook class. You have not yet written a declaration for Rook, so when you use it in your code, a problem marker will indicate the nonexistence of the type. The marker is normally a simple red cross to indicate an error. If a Quick Fix is available, a small light bulb is shown on top of the error marker.

The JDT can detect syntax errors but is also smart enough to guess what you could do to correct the problem. As can be seen in Figure 3.2, the JDT can create the class for us with a single mouse click.

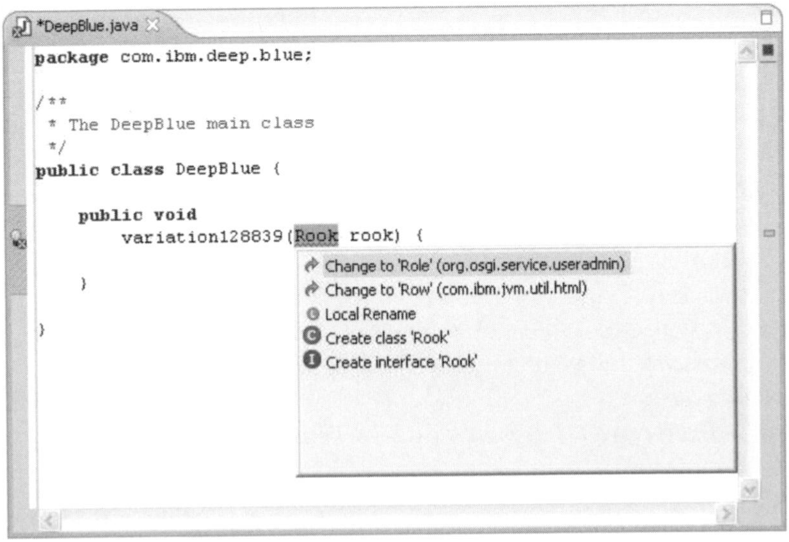

Figure 3.2 Quick Fix suggestions

A major tenet of Extreme Programming is to write test cases first. In other words, use cases are specified first; then the implementation is provided. Quick Fixes help in this process. For instance, we start using our `Rook` class as if it has a `move` method. Of course, the editor will complain and place a marker next to the reference to the nonexistent method. However, the editor also guesses what we want to do with the method (Figure 3.3).

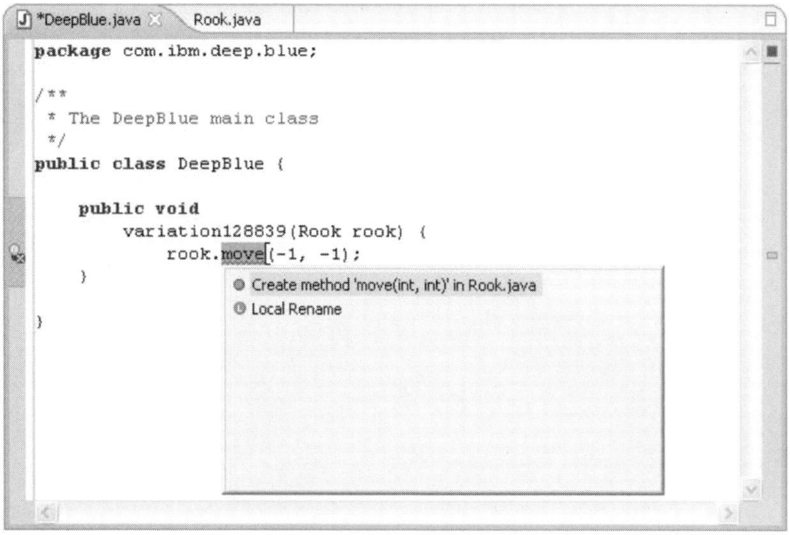

Figure 3.3 Quick Fix guesses

In a similar fashion, Quick Fixes can be used to add fields to classes, add parameters to methods, help with unhandled exceptions, and generate local variable declarations. Quick Fixes are designed to allow you to continue the creative process of designing API while using it, a major component of Extreme Programming.

A full list of available Quick Fixes is given at **Help > Help Contents > Java Development User Guide > Concepts > Quick Fix**. Updating quick fixes as you type can be computationally intensive, so you can turn this off via **Window > Preferences > Java > Editor > Annotations > Analyze annotations while typing**.

FAQ 339 *How do I implement Quick Fixes for my own language?*

How do I profile my Java program?

Eclipse has built-in support for launching applications and for debugging Java applications but no inherent support for profiling. However, support for profilers can be implemented by using a special launch configuration. Commercial products, such as WebSphere Studio Application Developer, do this by adding profiling support to their set of plug-ins. Much of this work is being standardized and moved down into the open source Eclipse subproject called Hyades.

A couple of individual profiler projects and products are under way. The Eclipse Colorer profiler with elaborate reporting views may be of interest to people who want to experiment with profiling Java code from Eclipse. This profiler can be downloaded under the CPL from SourceForge.

See **FAQ 314** for a discussion of how profilers are implemented.

 FAQ 314 *When do I use a launch delegate?*
Eclipse Profiler (http://eclipsecolorer.sourceforge.net/index_profiler.html)

How do I debug my Java program?

If you know how to run your Java program, you can debug it. Assuming that you just ran your Java program, press F11, and the most recently executed launch configuration will be launched under control of the Eclipse Java debugger. Breakpoints can be set in any Java editor by double-clicking in the left margin of the editor or by using the context menu in the left margin to toggle the breakpoint on this line.

Because it is a Java program, Eclipse can also be debugged in a similar fashion. F11 also honors runtime workbenches and allows debugging in exactly the same way. In combination with hot code replace, plug-in development can be done in a very incremental fashion: Run an inner Eclipse using the debugger, fix the code of your plug-ins, and continue using the inner Eclipse with the new code without even restarting the inner workbench. You gotta see it to believe it!

 FAQ 60 *What is hot code replace?*

How do I find out the command-line arguments of a launched program?

In the Debug view, use the context menu on the process in question, and select **Properties....** From this dialog you can see the exact command line that was passed to the JVM. If you launched in debug mode, there will be some extra command-line arguments that instruct the JVM to run in debug mode. To show the Debug view, you can use **Window > Show View > Debug > Debug**.

What is hot code replace?

Hot code replace (HCR) is a debugging technique whereby the Eclipse debugger transmits new class files over the debugging channel to another VM. In the case of Eclipse development, this also applies to the VM that runs the runtime workbench. The idea is that you can start a debugging session on a given runtime workbench and change a Java file in your development workbench, and the debugger will replace the code in the receiving VM while it is running. No restart is required, hence the reference to "hot."

HCR has been specifically added as a standard technique to Java to facilitate experimental development and to foster iterative trial-and-error coding. HCR only works when the class signature does not change; you cannot remove or add fields to existing classes, for instance. However, HCR can be used to change the body of a method. HCR is reliably implemented only on 1.4.1 VMs and later, or using any version of the IBM J9 VM. J9 is available in IBM products such as Websphere Studio Device Developer.

☞ The WSDD Web site (http://ibm.com/software/wireless/wsdd/)

How do I set a conditional breakpoint?

First, set a breakpoint at a given location. Then, use the context menu on the breakpoint in the left editor margin or in the Breakpoints view in the Debug perspective, and select the breakpoint's properties. In the dialog box, check **Enable Condition**, and enter an arbitrary Java condition, such as `list.size()==0`. Now, each time the breakpoint is reached, the expression is evaluated in the context of the breakpoint execution, and the breakpoint is either ignored or honored, depending on the outcome of the expression.

Conditions can also be expressed in terms of other breakpoint attributes, such as hit count.

How do I find all Java methods that return a `String`?

The JDT contributes to the search framework by adding a **Java Search** tab to the Search dialog (activated with the **Search** menu or by pressing Ctrl+H. Methods can be searched for by name and return type. The first word you enter in the Search dialog is interpreted as the method name, and the second word is interpreted as the method's return type. By specifying `* String` and checking **Method** and **Declarations**, you will find all methods with a `String` return value (Figure 3.4).

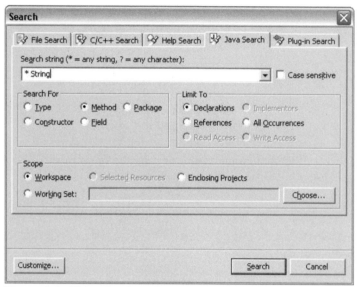

Figure 3.4 Using the **Java Search** tab

📇 **FAQ 278** *How do I write a Search dialog?*

What can I view in the Hierarchy view?

The Hierarchy view shows types, their subtypes, and their supertypes. In Figure 3.5, we pressed Ctrl+Shift+H and entered `Button`. This shows the inheritance hierarchy of `Button`.

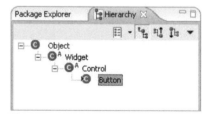

Figure 3.5 Inheritance hierarchy of `Button`

To see the full inheritance hierarchy of another type in the hierarchy, use the **Focus On** command in the context menu. For example, to see the inheritance hierarchy of `Widget`, select `Widget` and choose **Focus On 'Widget'** from the context menu (Figure 3.6).

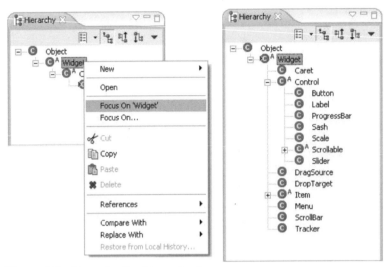

Figure 3.6 Changing the hierarchy focus

You can select any package, type, or method in the various Java views and open it in the Hierarchy view from the context menu. You can also select a working set in the Hierarchy view to limit the displayed elements to a particular portion of the workspace.

FAQ 64

How do I add an extra library to my project's classpath?

Open the context menu on the project, and select **Properties > Java Build Path > Libraries**. From here, you can add JAR files to the build path, whether they are inside your workspace or not. You can also add a *class folder*, a directory containing Java class files that are not in a JAR. Note that plug-in development has more restrictions on where build path entries can come from. For plug-in projects, you should always let the plug-in development tools organize your build path for you. Simply select the `plugin.xml` file, and choose **PDE Tools > Update Classpath** from the context menu.

 FAQ 67 *How do I set up a Java project to share in a repository?*
FAQ 77 *When does PDE change a plug-in's Java build path?*
FAQ 104 *What is the classpath of a plug-in?*

What is the advantage of sharing the `.project` file in a repository?

The `.project` file contains important information about your project, including what kind of project it is, what builders it contains, and what linked resources are attached to it. It is generally advisable to store this file in your code repository or to include the file if you zip the project up to give to a colleague. This will allow another user who is importing or loading the project to obtain this important information. If you don't, the project will appear in the other user's workspace as a simple project, with no builders or linked resources. Similarly, other plug-ins store important project metadata in the project content area, typically with a leading period on the file name. For example, the Java development tools store the project's build path in a file called `.classpath`. Plug-ins put their metadata in the project content area for a reason: to allow this information to be exported and loaded into other workspaces.

 FAQ 67 *How do I set up a Java project to share in a repository?*

What is the function of the `.cvsignore` file?

To exclude resources from management under CVS version control, a `.cvsignore` file can be placed in the parent folder of a resource. Each folder has to specify its own `.cvsignore` file as there is no logic for path-relative resource specification.

The Navigator has UI support for CVS exclusion in its context menu for any resource in a project. Follow **Team > Add to .cvsignore** to the dialog that allows selection based on the name of the resource, a wildcard, or a custom pattern to match multiple resources.

The `.cvsignore` file is not an Eclipse invention. Its syntax is defined by CVS, and the Eclipse team plug-ins simply pass the file on to CVS when sharing a project.

 The CVS manual (http://www.cvshome.org)

FAQ
67

How do I set up a Java project to share in a repository?

A number of steps are needed to get a Java project properly set up to share with teammates in a repository.

1. Make sure that the `.project` and `.classpath` files are under version control. These files must be stored in the repository so that other users checking out the projects for the first time will get the correct type of project and will get the correct Java build path.

2. Avoid absolute paths in your `.project` and `.classpath` files. If you are using linked resources, make sure that they are created using *path variables* (see the **Workbench > Linked Resources** preference page). If your project has references on its build path to external libraries, make sure that they are specified using a classpath variable (see the **Java > Build Path > Classpath Variables** preference page).

3. Make sure that the Java builder's output directory (conventionally called `bin`) is not under version control. In CVS, you can do this by creating a `.cvsignore` file in the project root directory containing the name of the output directory.

 FAQ 65 *What is the advantage of sharing the* `.project` *file in a repository?*
FAQ 66 *What is the function of the* `.cvsignore` *file?*

FAQ
68

Why does the Eclipse compiler create a different `serialVersionUID` from javac?

You may discover that serializable classes compiled with Eclipse are not compatible with the same classes compiled using javac. When classes compiled in Eclipse are written to an object stream, you may not be able to read them back in a program that was compiled elsewhere. Many people blame this on the Eclipse compiler, assuming that it is somehow not conforming properly to spec. In fact, this can be a problem between any two compilers or even two versions of a compiler provided by the same vendor.

If you need object serialization, the *only* way to be safe is to explicitly define the serialVersionUID in your code:

```
class MyClass implements Serializable {
    public static final long serialVersionUID = 1;
}
```

Then, whenever your class changes shape in a way that will be incompatible with previously serialized versions, simply increment this number.

If you don't explicitly define a serialVersionUID, the language requires that the VM generate one, using some function of all field and method names in the class. The problem is, the compiler generates some *synthetic* methods that you never see in your source file, and there is no clear specification for how these synthetic method names are generated. Any two compilers are likely to generate different method names, and so the serialVersionUID will be different. Bottom line: Always define the serialVersionUID explicitly in your source files.

Chapter 4. Plug-In Development Environment

This book is all about extending the Eclipse Platform. The main instrument for extending the platform is a *plug-in*. Plug-ins solidify certain crucial design criteria underlying Eclipse. Special tooling has been developed as part of Eclipse to support the development of plug-ins. This set of plug-ins is called the Plug-in Development Environment; or PDE. The PDE tools cover the entire lifecycle of plug-in development, from creating them using special wizards to editing them to building them to launching them to exporting and sharing them.

This chapter describes the mechanics of plug-in development, such as creating plug-ins, features, and update sites, and introduces the PDE tooling. We go into much more depth about what plug-ins are in later FAQs. If you want to jump ahead, we suggest that you first visit **FAQ 94**.

How do I create a plug-in?

FAQ
69

The simplest way to develop and maintain a plug-in is to use the special wizards and editors the PDE provides. Using a wizard, you can generate basic plug-ins with a few mouse clicks. After some practice, you can create an extension to Eclipse, and even launch it in a runtime workbench, in under a minute. A lot of XML and Java code is automatically generated for you.

Select **File > New > Other... >Plug-in Development > Plug-in Project > Next** and choose a suitable name for your plug-in. Most Eclipse plug-in names start with org.eclipse, but you can choose any suitable name here. Accept all the defaults following in the next wizard pages by clicking **Next** until you get to the wizard page shown in Figure 4.1.

Using one of the provided code templates will get you going quickly. Once it is generated, you can edit the generated plug-in code by using the special PDE Manifest Editor that has various editors with both visual and textual views of the underlying XML.

Using the combination of PDE code wizards and editors, you can quickly generate and maintain plug-in code. Once you get more experienced, you will

learn how to travel down into the XML code that describes your plug-in and
directly influence the behavior for your plug-in to do more advanced tasks.

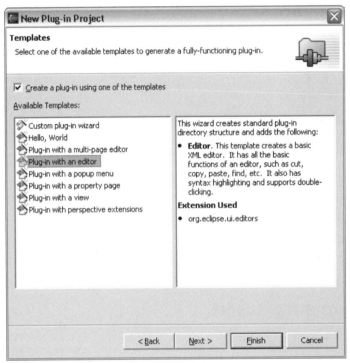

Figure 4.1 PDE wizard page

We advise using wizards as much as possible to develop or maintain your
plug-ins. However, at the same time, wizards will take you only so far. At some
point, you have to dive in and modify or enhance the generated code to make the
plug-ins fit your own needs. Luckily, the PDE allows you to smoothly transition
between wizards, graphical editors, and full-text editors of plugin.xml files.
Changes in one view are reflected in the other, and plug-in authors can jump
back and forth between textual and visual editing forms.

We also recommend checking out the new Cheat Sheet support added in Eclipse
3.0, see **Help > Cheat Sheets...**, for an excellent step-by-step- guide to
developing plug-ins.

FAQ 70 *How do I use the plug-in Manifest Editor?*
FAQ 94 *What is a plug-in?*

How do I use the plug-in Manifest Editor?

The plug-in Manifest Editor (Figure 4.2) is used to edit the XML description contained in the `plugin.xml` file. The editor is activated by double-clicking the `plugin.xml` file in the Navigator.

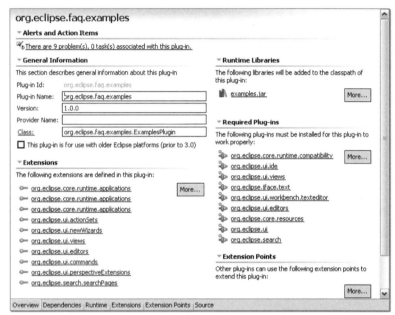

Figure 4.2 Plug-in Manifest Editor

The editor consists of six different editor panes. The **Overview** pane gives a summary of the plug-in's configuration and links to the other editor panes. For instance, clicking on **More...** in the **Extensions** section takes you to the **Extensions** editor pane. The first five editors provide visual access to the underlying XML text shown in the **Source** pane.

Press F1 at any time to get specific help on how to use the page you are currently in.

**FAQ
71**

Why doesn't my plug-in build correctly?

It is important to realize that a plug-in consists of a manifest description written in XML and an independent implementation written in Java. The `plugin.xml` file defines the prerequisite plug-ins and effectively defines the classpath for your own plug-in classes. A typical build problem is caused by a change to the build classpath, often indirectly owing to a change to the `plugin.xml` file. This may happen when you extract a plug-in out of CVS, for instance. The classpath settings are copied from the CVS repository but were put there by someone who may have had a different installation location for Eclipse. Be careful, as the classpath consists mainly of hard-coded file system locations.

To recompute the classpath, use the context menu on your project: **PDE Tools > Update Classpath**. This will instruct PDE to look at your `plugin.xml` file and construct a build classpath specific to your Eclipse installation and workspace contents.

If your plug-in relies on other broken plug-ins in your workspace, your plug-in may not be able to build itself. Start with the offending plug-in and work your way up the dependency hierarchy to find the problem. When all else fails, try **Project >Clean...** to force everything to be rebuilt from scratch.

 FAQ 67 *How do I set up a Java project to share in a repository?*
FAQ 104 *What is the classpath of a plug-in?*

**FAQ
72**

How do I run my plug-in in another instance of Eclipse?

You can easily run plug-ins in another instance of Eclipse by selecting **Run > Run As > Run-time Workbench**. This will launch a new workbench on the same Java runtime as your development workbench, with all plug-ins in your current workspace enabled, and starting in a special runtime workspace.

Another way of running your plug-in for the first time is by selecting the **Overview** tab of the plug-in Manifest Editor and clicking the link to **Run-time Workbench**.

After you close the runtime workbench, select **Run...** to edit the launch configuration for your runtime workbench. In the Launch Configuration Editor, you can select a logical name for this plug-in test scenario, which is useful when you want to experiment with multiple scenarios.

The Launch Configuration Editor also lets you choose which plug-ins to enable from your workspace and, in the case of conflicts with already installed plug-ins, which one to choose. Furthermore, you can choose which JRE to launch with, if you want or need to experiment with different VMs.

Finally, the editor allows you to specify special arguments, such as commands to increase the Java heap size available or to enable a special profiling library, to the VM.

Once you have launched a runtime workbench, pressing Ctrl+F11 will run it again, and F11 will launch the Eclipse debugger to debug your runtime workbench.

☞ **FAQ 313** *What is a launch configuration?*

What causes my plug-in to build but not to load in a runtime workbench?

FAQ 73

Here is a typical scenario for a new user: You are writing a plug-in that extends plug-in XYZ. To get it to compile, you add a reference to the JAR file for plug-in XYZ to your project's build path either from the **Java Build Path** property page or by editing the `.classpath` file. When you launch a runtime workbench, the following surprising error is reported: **java.lang.NoClassDefFoundError: XYZ.SomeClass**. Do not start looking in the **Plug-ins and Fragments** tab in the launch configuration for the runtime workbench. That tab influences only which plug-ins are used for your runtime workbench and whether they are loaded from the workspace or from the Eclipse install directory.

Instead, start looking in the plug-in manifest. Edit the `plugin.xml` file and ensure that XYZ is mentioned as a required plug-in. Then, save the `plugin.xml` file. This will update the project's build path automatically.

Never manually edit the `.classpath` file when you are writing a plug-in. The plug-in Manifest Editor simply overwrites any changes you make to it. Not very civilized, but that is the way it works.

 FAQ 64 *How do I add an extra library to my project's classpath?*
FAQ 74 *My runtime workbench runs, but my plug-in does not show. Why?*
FAQ 77 *When does PDE change a plug-in's Java build path?*

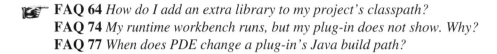

My runtime workbench runs, but my plug-in does not show. Why?

FAQ 69 contains instructions for writing plug-ins in Eclipse. **FAQ 71** tells you what to do if your plug-in has problems building. **FAQ 72** explains how to run a plug-in in another instance of Eclipse. Despite all these instructions, in some cases, your plug-in builds fine and the runtime workbench launches but your plug-in still does not show. Various configuration-related things could be wrong.

* The plug-in may not be selected in the launch configuration. (See **FAQ 72** for instructions on how to select plug-ins.)

* Your plug-in may rely on other plug-ins not enabled in your current launch configuration. Check the error log. (See **FAQ 27** for messages referring to your plug-in.)

* If your plug-in contributes an action to the toolbar and it does not show or if a menu option does not appear, your plug-in may still be activated. The workbench does not automatically add toolbar and menu items to every perspective. Run **Window > Customize Perspective** and verify whether your contribution is enabled for the current perspective.

* Your plug-in may not show because it is not yet needed. If all your plug-in does is contribute a view, you may need to show it explicitly by using **Window > Show View > Other...**. If your plug-in contributes an editor for a particular type, you may need to configure the file association; see **Window > Preferences > Workbench > File Associations**.

- Your plug-in may throw an exception in its static initializer or in its plug-in class instance initializer. Again, consult the log file for error messages involving your plug-in.

☞ **FAQ 73** *What causes my plug-in to build but not to load in a runtime workbench?*

How do I add images and other resources to a runtime JAR file?

A plug-in is built using an Ant build script called `build.xml`. You create this script from a `plugin.xml` file by choosing from the context menu **Create Ant Build File**. When it runs the build script, Ant includes settings from the `build.properties` file. Open that file in an editor, and add an entry for the `bin.includes` variable. Add a pattern such as **images/*.gif** to add all GIF files in the images directory.

Then, rerun the Ant build script to generate a runtime JAR including the resources you just specified. Check to see whether the created JAR includes the resources you intended.

☞ **FAQ 76** *Can I add icons declared by my* `plugin.xml` *in the runtime JAR?*

Can I add icons declared by my `plugin.xml` in the runtime JAR?

No. Statically declared plug-in icons are not meant to be in the runtime JAR because Eclipse wants to load plug-ins lazily. In other words, during loading of the platform, the platform loader reads only the `plugin.xml` file and will use the icons that are declared there. Only when the plug-in is really needed is the JAR opened; the class loader starts loading classes, and the plug-in is activated.

The structure of a plug-in roughly looks like this:

```
plugin.xml          // used by platform loader
icons/
    delete.gif      // icons used in the toolbar, and so on.
    create.jpg
code.jar            // jar (class files + resources)
```

Plug-in activation is a process that requires considerable memory and central processing unit (CPU) cycles. To speed up load time of the platform, opening the runtime JAR is avoided for as long as possible.

Of course, images included in a runtime JAR can be used by plug-in code using standard Java resource-loading techniques, such as `getResource` on a given Java class or by using a class loader.

☞ **FAQ 75** *How do I add images and other resources to a runtime JAR file?*
FAQ 101 *When does a plug-in get started?*

FAQ 77

When does PDE change a plug-in's Java build path?

Whenever you add dependent plug-ins in the Manifest Editor, the underlying classpath has to be updated to give you access to the classes defined by the plug-in in question. When you save the `plugin.xml` file, the editor will also update the Java build path: the `.classpath` file.

In Eclipse 3.0, the PDE uses a special classpath entry called a *classpath container* to avoid having to directly modify the `.classpath` file every time your plug-in's dependencies change. During builds, this classpath container resolves to the set of dependencies specified in the `plugin.xml` file.

Regardless of whether classpath containers are used, it makes little sense to edit the `.classpath` file by hand or to make changes directly to the **Java Build Path** property page for plug-in projects. Any changes you make there will be silently overwritten the next time you save the Manifest Editor.

☞ **FAQ 71** *Why doesn't my plug-in build correctly?*
FAQ 104 *What is the classpath of a plug-in?*

What is a PDE JUnit test?

FAQ
78

PDE JUnit tests are used to write unit tests for your plug-ins. The tests themselves look exactly like any other JUnit test, organized into `TestCase` subclasses, one test per method, with `setUp` and `tearDown` methods for creating and discarding any state required by the test.

The difference with PDE JUnit tests is in how they are executed. Instead of using the standard JUnit class `TestRunner`, PDE JUnit tests are executed by a special test runner that launches another Eclipse instance in a separate VM—just like a runtime workbench—and executes the test methods within that workbench. This means your tests can call Eclipse Platform API, along with methods from your own plug-in, to exercise the functionality you want to test.

PDE JUnit tests are launched by selecting your test class and pressing **Run > Run As > JUnit Plug-in Test**. On the **Arguments** tab of the launch configuration dialog, you can choose what Eclipse application will be used to run your tests. By default, the Eclipse IDE workbench is used. If you are not testing user-interface components, you can choose **[No Application] – Headless Mode**. If you have written your own Eclipse application—such as a rich client application—you will need to write your own test runner application as well.

 FAQ 72 *How do I run my plug-in in another instance of Eclipse?*
FAQ 359 *What is JUnit?*

Where can I find the Eclipse plug-ins?

FAQ
79

The easiest way to get plug-ins from Eclipse into your workspace is by invoking **File > Import > External Plug-ins and Fragments** and selecting the ones you are interested in loading. You can choose either to load all of the source, allowing you to hack on it, or to import binary plug-ins for the purpose of browsing and searching.

You can also load the latest Eclipse source from the Eclipse CVS repository. The access info is

```
:pserver:anonymous@dev.eclipse.org:/home/eclipse
```

In other words, go to the CVS Repository Exploring perspective and add a new repository location with host `dev.eclipse.org`, repository path `/home/eclipse`, and user name `anonymous`; a password is not required. Once you see the repository location in the CVS Repositories view, browse it by going into HEAD and select the project you are interested in. Use the context menu on a project to check it out into your current workspace.

Loading plug-ins into your workspace can result in build path problems for both newly loaded plug-ins and existing plug-ins in your workspace. When the plug-in you just checked out relies on other plug-ins that are not yet in your workspace, you are bound to get many complaints, such as those in Figure 4.3.

	✓	!	Description	Resource	In Folder	Location
⊗			Missing required Java project: org.apache.xerces.	org.eclipse.pde.ui		Build path
⊗			Missing required Java project: org.eclipse.ant.core.	org.eclipse.pde.ui		Build path
⊗			Missing required Java project: org.eclipse.ant.ui.	org.eclipse.pde.ui		Build path
⊗			Missing required Java project: org.eclipse.core.boot.	org.eclipse.pde.ui		Build path
⊗			Missing required Java project: org.eclipse.core.resources.	org.eclipse.pde.ui		Build path
⊗			Missing required Java project: org.eclipse.core.runtime.	org.eclipse.pde.ui		Build path
⊗			Missing required Java project: org.eclipse.debug.core.	org.eclipse.pde.ui		Build path
⊗			Missing required Java project: org.eclipse.debug.ui.	org.eclipse.pde.ui		Build path

Figure 4.3 Build path problems

To fix references to missing plug-ins, either add the missing plug-ins to your workspace or refer to plug-ins in your base Eclipse installation. The latter is much easier; simply run **PDE Tools > Update Classpath...** from the project's context menu. However, remember that when checking out from CVS, you are obtaining bleeding-edge contents that committers may have modified minutes earlier. If you mix plug-ins from different builds of Eclipse, such as some from CVS and some from your Eclipse install, incompatibilities may be insurmountable. Your best bet is to make sure that all plug-ins in your workspace are from the same Eclipse build.

It may be a struggle to keep your workspace error free when you bring in only portions of the Eclipse Platform. Eclipse can become just as confused as you. When all else fails, run **Update Classpath...** on all plug-ins in your workspace. Running **Project > Clean...** to completely discard all build states and force a fresh build may also help.

☞ **FAQ 77** *When does PDE change a plug-in's Java build path?*

How do I find a particular class from an Eclipse plug-in?

FAQ
80

Suppose that you ask a question on the Eclipse newsgroup, and someone answers, "That's easy; just look at `JavaAnnotationImageProvider`." You are left scratching your head, wondering how to find that particular needle in the Eclipse haystack. Once you are familiar with searching for things in Eclipse, you too will come to realize that package names are rarely needed when browsing for information in the Eclipse source.

The first thing you need to do is set up your workspace so that all Eclipse plug-ins are found by the Java search engine. This can be accomplished by loading all the Eclipse plug-ins into your workspace, but this quickly results in a cluttered workspace in which it is difficult to find your own projects. There is an easier approach to adding Eclipse plug-ins to the Java search engine's index.

1. Open the Plug-in Development perspective.
2. Activate the Plug-ins view.
3. Select all plug-ins in the view.
4. From the context menu, select **Add to Java Search**.

Once you have done this, switch back to the Java perspective and use **Navigate > Open Type** (or press Ctrl+Shift+T) and start typing the name of the class or interface you are looking for. You will now be able to quickly open an editor on any Java type in the Eclipse Platform.

In case you are curious, this works by creating in your workspace a Java project called External Plug-in Libraries. This project will have all the Eclipse plug-ins you selected on its build path, which ensures that they will be consulted by the Java search engine when searching for and opening Java types. You can use a similar technique to add other Java libraries to the search index. Simply add the JARs you want to be able to search to the build path of any Java project in your workspace, and they will automatically be included in the search.

 FAQ 50 *How do I open a type in a Java editor?*
FAQ 79 *Where can I find the Eclipse plug-ins?*

Why do I get a "plug-in was unable to load class" error when I activate a menu or toolbar action?

It is possible to get the following error message on the console:

```
Could not create action delegate for id: sample.Action
Reason:
    Plug-in sample was unable to load class sample.Action.
```

The most likely reason is that an exception was thrown in the static initializer for a class declared by the offending plug-in. Check the `.log` file to see whether that indeed happened. The Eclipse Platform loader will not load a plug-in when exceptions are thrown during the initialization of the Java classes that make up the plug-in. Another common reason for this error is the lack of an appropriate constructor for the class being loaded. Most classes declared in extension points must have a public zero-argument constructor. Check the extension point documentation to see what constructor is required for the classes that you declare in an extension.

What is the use of the `build.xml` file?

The `build.xml` file is an Ant script that is created by the PDE to take your plug-in components and combine them into a deployable format. This file compiles and archives your plug-in source code into a single JAR file. The `build.properties` file controls what goes into your plug-in distribution.

The `build.xml` file can be created by using the context menu on `plugin.xml` and selecting **PDE Tools > Create Ant Build File**.

Ant build files are low-level mechanisms to package up plug-ins. A much easier way to share and deploy plug-ins is to create a feature for your plug-in and then an update site. The Update Site Editor has a very handy button, **Build All...**, that will create the `build.xml` behind the scenes, run it, and collect all the output without cluttering your plug-in and feature projects.

FAQ 84 *When is the* `build.xml` *script executed?*
FAQ 89 *How do I create a feature?*
FAQ 92 *How do I create an update site (*`site.xml`*)?*
FAQ 315 *What is Ant?*

FAQ 83

How do I prevent my `build.xml` file from being overwritten?

Normally, you can use the `build.xml` file that is automatically generated for you, based on your plug-in manifest and the contents of your `build.properties` file. However, in some situations, you might want to customize your own plug-in build script. To prevent PDE from deleting your custom build script, open `build.properties` for your plug-in and check **This plug-in uses a custom build script**.

 FAQ 82 *What is the use of the* `build.xml` *file?*

FAQ 84

When is the `build.xml` script executed?

The build script for a plug-in is executed when you manually run the context menu command **Run Ant...** on a `build.xml` file. The build script is also executed when you export your plug-in project or when you click **Build All...** in the Update Site Editor.

 FAQ 82 *What is the use of the* `build.xml` *file?*
FAQ 92 *How do I create an update site (*`site.xml`*)?*

How do I declare my own extension point?

Declaring an extension point is arguably one of the more difficult and less documented and supported tasks in Eclipse. Most plug-in writers simply copy an extension point schema from others to get an approximation of what they need.

Adding an extension point can be done with some PDE support by following these steps.

1. Edit your `plugin.xml` using the Manifest Editor. Select the **Extension Points** tab, and click **Add...**.

2. Now stop for a minute. Think up a good name and an equally descriptive ID for your extension point. Don't choose too lightly. These two names are part of your plug-in API. The ID is one word without dots; your plug-in ID will be prepended to it. When in doubt, press F1 to get help.

3. Choose a name for your schema. This file name is private to you, so you can choose any name you like. Check the box to edit the schema. Click **Finish** to launch the PDE Schema Editor to edit the schema.

4. Click **New Element**; in the properties view, change the name to the extension element you want your clients to fill in.

5. Add a new attribute to this element, and call it **id**. Change the value of **Use** to **Required**. In the Properties view, click the **Clone this attribute** button in the local toolbar.

6. Rename the clone to **name**. Clone it.

7. Rename the second clone to **class**. Change the **kind** to **java**.

8. Choose the interface your contributors need to implement or the class they need to subclass. Note that it is generally better to provide a superclass, as this allows you greater flexibility in extending the API in the future without breaking existing implementations. Choose a descriptive name that captures the meaning of the collaboration between you and your contributors.

9. In the **Based On** property, enter the name of the interface/class to create an executable extension from.

That's it. You now have defined a new extension that others can contribute to. Look around in the editor and add descriptions, documentation, and example code where appropriate.

If you want to customize the extension with more attributes, read **Help > Help Contents... > PDE Guide > Extension Point Schema > Extension point schema editor**.

☞ **FAQ 98** *What are extensions and extension points?*
FAQ 99 *What is an extension point schema?*

How do I find all the plug-ins that contribute to my extension point?

FAQ
86

Assuming that you used an element attribute named `class` to encode the name of the class that your contributors have to provide, you can obtain a list of all the plug-in classes that contribute to your extension point by using the following piece of code:

```
IExtensionRegistry reg = Platform.getExtensionRegistry();
IExtensionPoint ep = reg.getExtensionPoint(extensionID);
IExtension[] extensions = ep.getExtensions();
ArrayList contributors = new ArrayList();
for (int i = 0; i < extensions.length; i++) {
   IExtension ext = extensions[i];
   IConfigurationElement[] ce =
      ext.getConfigurationElements();
   for (int j = 0; j < ce.length; j++) {
      Object obj = ce[j].createExecutableExtension("class");
      contributors.add(obj);
   }
}
```

From a given extension point, it is straightforward to get a list of extensions that contribute to it. For each extension, we create an executable extension using the value of the `class` property. We save all the executable extensions in an array list and return it.

Why is the interface for my new extension point not visible?

When you declare a new extension point and a corresponding interface to implement, plug-ins that contribute to your extension point sometimes cannot see your interface. The reason is that your interface may not match the export tag' regular expression in your plug-in's runtime library tag. If your interface is called `com.xyz.MyInterface`, your `plugin.xml` should look like this:

```
<runtime>
    <library> name="sample.jar">
        <export name="com.xyz.MyInterface"/>
    <library>
<runtime>
```

Multiple export tags can be used, in addition to wildcards. The default tag set by the PDE is "*", indicating that all types in the JAR should be exported.

Can my extension point schema contain nested elements?

Yes. The extension point schema supports top-level elements with attributes. Each attribute can refer to another element in the schema. The Schema Editor has a difficult job indicating this, but the nesting can be observed in Figure 4.4 that shows an example that uses the `org.eclipse.ui.actionSets` extension point. The schema for this extension point explicitly defines the grammar rules for nesting one or more menus and actions into one action set (Figure 4.5). A similar hierarchy can be used for your own extension point schemas.

Figure 4.4   Nested elements in extension point schema

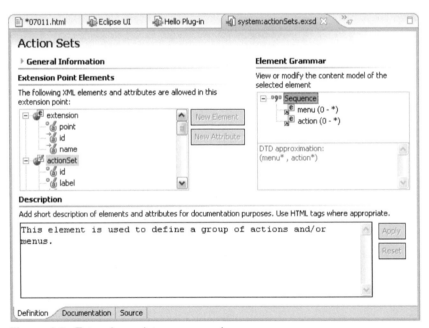

Figure 4.5   Extension point grammar rules

☞ **FAQ 99** *What is an extension point schema?*

How do I create a feature?

Select **File > New > Other... > Plug-in Development > Feature Project**, and choose the plug-ins you want to add.

One important caveat is that in order for features to be installable using an update site, you have to specify a license agreement. Open the Feature Editor on your `feature.xml` file, select the **Information** tab, and enter the license text under the **License Agreement** section. For testing, a simple **CPL 1.0** will do.

 FAQ 92 *How do I create an update site (`site.xml`)?*

How do I synchronize versions between a feature and its plug-in(s)?

A version can be forced from a feature into its dependent plug-ins and fragments as follows.

1. Open the Manifest Editor on the `feature.xml` file.
2. Enter a new version, making it a higher number than the old version.
3. Click **Versions...**.
4. Choose **Force feature version into plug-in and fragment manifests**.
5. Save the `feature.xml` file.

To build the feature, we strongly advise that you create an update site project, add and publish this feature to it, and click the **Build All...** button. (Press F1 in the Manifest Editor for more online help.)

 FAQ 92 *How do I create an update site (`site.xml`)?*

What is the Update Manager?

The Update Manager allows you to find new plug-ins on your machine, your network, or the Internet, compare new plug-ins to your configuration, and install only those that are compatible with your current configuration. The Update Manager thinks in terms of *features*, a logical group of related plug-ins, and also provides support for managing configurations to undo a given installation or to automatically update all the features currently installed in your Eclipse configuration.

Before plug-ins can be installed by the Update Manager, they need to be collected into a feature. The feature itself has to be published using an update site.

The Update Manager is invoked by **Help > Software Updates**.

 FAQ 69 *How do I create a plug-in?*
FAQ 89 *How do I create a feature?*
FAQ 237 *What is the purpose of activities?*
eclipse.org article "How to Keep Up to Date"

How do I create an update site (`site.xml`)?

Select **File > New > Other... > Plug-in Development > Update Site Project**. Open the Update Site Editor and add the features you want to publish. A site can contain multiple categories of features, and we added one for this example. After adding a feature, it has to be explicitly published (Figure 4.6).

Click **Build All** to build all features and plug-ins recursively required for this update site. The result is an update site that is ready to be used in your Navigator (Figure 4.7).

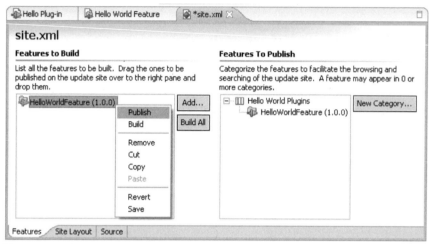

Figure 4.6 Creating an update site

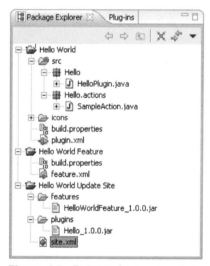

Figure 4.7 Building features and plug-ins for an update site

You can simply drag the contents of the Hello World Update Site project to an file transfer protocol (FTP) client to publish at a Web site. Alternatively, you can even test out the update site directly by selecting **Help > Software Updates > Find and Install... > Search for new features to install > Add Local Site...** and finding the workspace project on your local file system.

Why does my update site need a license?

When installing a feature using the Update Manager, you may run into a cryptic message that this feature will invalidate the current configuration. When you click **Details...**, the reason is indicated: A license agreement is missing for the feature. A feature must have a license before it can be shared with others on an update site.

For each feature published through your update site, edit the feature.xml file and enter a license agreement. Then, in the site.xml editor, click **Build All** again to rebuild the features.

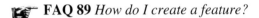 **FAQ 89** *How do I create a feature?*

Part II. The Rich Client Platform

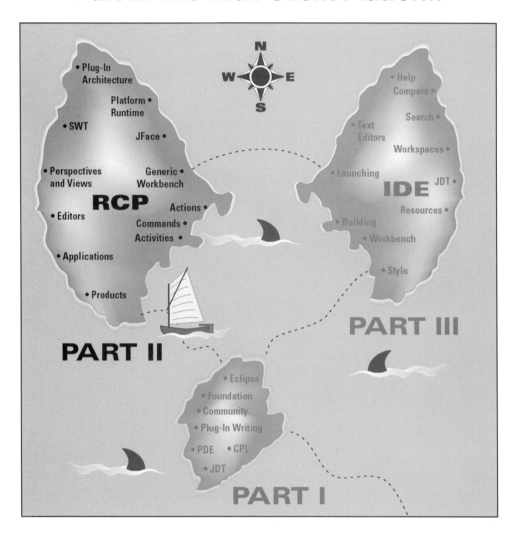

Chapter 5. All about Plug-Ins

Part I discussed the Eclipse ecosystem: how to run it, how to use it, and how to extend it. In this chapter, we revisit the topic of plug-ins and lay the groundwork for all plug-in development topics to be discussed in later chapters. This chapter answers questions about the core concepts of the Eclipse kernel, including plug-ins, extension points, fragments, and more. All APIs mentioned in this chapter are found in the `org.eclipse.core.runtime` plug-in.

What is a plug-in?

FAQ
94

In retrospect, *plug-in*, perhaps wasn't the most appropriate term for the components that build up an Eclipse application. The term implies the existence of a socket, a monolithic machine or grid that is being plugged into. In Eclipse, this isn't the case. A plug-in connects with a universe of other plug-ins to form a running application. The best software analogy compares a plug-in to an object in object-oriented programming. A plug-in, like an object, is an encapsulation of behavior and/or data that interacts with other plug-ins to form a running program.

A better question in the context of Eclipse is, What isn't a plug-in? A single Java source file, `Main.java`, is not part of a plug-in. This class is used only to find and invoke the plug-in responsible for starting up the Eclipse Platform. This class will typically in turn be invoked by a native executable, such as `eclipse.exe` on Windows, although this is just icing to hide the incantations required to find and launch a Java virtual machine. In short, just about everything in Eclipse is a plug-in.

More concretely, a plug-in minimally consists of a *plug-in manifest file*, `plugin.xml`. This manifest provides important details about the plug-in, such as its name, ID, and version number. The manifest may also tell the platform what Java code it supplies and what other plug-ins it requires, if any. Note that everything except the basic plug-in description is optional. A plug-in may provide code, or it may provide only documentation, resource bundles, or other data to be used by other plug-ins.

A plug-in that provides Java code may specify in the manifest a concrete subclass of `org.eclipse.core.runtime.Plugin`. This class consists mostly of convenience methods for accessing various platform utilities, and it may also implement `startup` and `shutdown` methods that define the lifecycle of the plug-in within the platform.

 FAQ 96 *What is the plug-in manifest file (`plugin.xml`)?*
FAQ 98 *What are extensions and extension points?*

FAQ
95

Do I use *plugin* or *plug-in*?

That depends. Those with a slavish devotion to the dictates of the English language—copy editors, English teachers, and automatic spellcheckers—will insist that because "plugin" is not a recognized word, the hyphenated plug-in is required. Others—writers, hackers, and the general public—recognize that language is an organic structure that must adapt and evolve to remain relevant. This latter group welcomes the introduction of new words into the lexicon and, thus, will happily adopt the new word *plugin*. While we use *plug-in* in this book, here is a more practical answer: If you are searching in the documentation, use plug-in. If you are grepping or writing code, use plugin. If you do not think *grepping* is a word, you are a lost cause.

FAQ
96

What is the plug-in manifest file (`plugin.xml`)?

The plug-in manifest file, `plugin.xml`, describes how the plug-in extends the platform, what extensions it publishes itself, and how it implements its functionality. The manifest file is written in XML and is parsed by the platform when the plug-in is loaded into the platform. All the information needed to display the plug-in in the UI, such as icons, menu items, and so on, is contained in the manifest file. The implementation code, found in a separate Java JAR file, is loaded when, and only when, the plug-in has to be run. This concept is referred to as *lazy loading*. Here is the manifest file for a simple plug-in:

```
<?xml version="1.0" encoding="UTF-8"?>
<?eclipse version="3.0"?>
<plugin id="com.xyz.myplugin" name="My Plugin"
    class="com.xyz.MyPlugin" version="1.0">
    <runtime>
        <library name="MyPlugin.jar"/>
    </runtime>
    <requires>
```

```
      <import plugin="org.eclipse.core.runtime"/>
   </requires>
</plugin>
```

The processing instructions at the beginning specify the XML version and character encoding and that this plug-in was built for version 3.0 of the Eclipse Platform. The `plugin` element specifies the basic information about the plug-in, including, in this case, the optional `class` attribute to specify an instance of the `Plugin` class associated with this plug-in. Because it contains a subclass of `Plugin`, this plug-in must include a `runtime` element that specifies the JAR file that contains the code and a `requires` element to import the `org.eclipse.core.runtime` plug-in where the superclass resides. The manifest may also specify *extensions* and *extension points* associated with the plug-in. Of all this, only the `plugin` element with the `id`, `name`, and `version` attributes are required.

FAQ 94 *What is a plug-in?*
FAQ 98 *What are extensions and extension points?*
FAQ 101 *When does a plug-in get started?*

How do I make my plug-in connect to other plug-ins?

FAQ
97

Like members of a community, plug-ins do not generally live in isolation. Most plug-ins make use of services provided by other plug-ins, and many, in turn, offer services that other plug-ins can consume. Some groups of plug-ins are tightly related, such as the group of plug-ins providing Java development tools—the JDT plug-ins—and other plug-ins, such as SWT, stand-alone without any awareness of the plug-ins around them. Plug-ins can also expose a means for other plug-ins to customize the functionality they offer, just as a handheld drill has an opening that allows you to insert other attachments such as screwdrivers and sanders. When designing a plug-in, you need to think about what specific plug-ins or services it will need, what it will expose to others, and in what ways it wants to allow itself to be customized by others.

To rephrase all this in Eclipse terminology, plug-ins define their interactions with other plug-ins in a number of ways. First, a plug-in can specify what other plug-ins it *requires*, those that it absolutely cannot live without. A UI plug-in will probably require the SWT plug-in, and a Java development tool will usually require one or more of the JDT plug-ins. Plug-in requirements are specified in the *plug-in manifest file* (plugin.xml). The following example shows a plug-in that requires only the JFace and SWT plug-ins:

```
<requires>
   <import plugin="org.eclipse.jface"/>
   <import plugin="org.eclipse.swt"/>
</requires>
```

Your plug-in can reference *only* the classes and interfaces of plug-ins it requires. Attempts to reference classes in other plug-ins will fail.

Conversely, a plug-in can choose which classes and interfaces it wants to expose to other plug-ins. Your plug-in manifest must declare what libraries (JARs) it provides and, optionally, what classes it wants other plug-ins to be able to reference. This example declares a single JAR file and exposes classes only in packages starting with the prefix com.xyz.*:

```
<runtime>
   <library name="sample.jar">
     <export name="com.xyz.*"/>
   </library>
</runtime>
```

Finally, a plug-in manifest can specify ways that it can be customized (*extension points*) and ways that it customizes the behavior of other plug-ins (*extensions*).

 FAQ 96 *What is the plug-in manifest file (plugin.xml)?*
FAQ 98 *What are extensions and extension points?*
FAQ 104 *What is the classpath of a plug-in?*

What are extensions and extension points?

A basic rule for building modular software systems is to avoid tight coupling between components. If components are tightly integrated, it becomes difficult to assemble the pieces into different configurations or to replace a component with a different implementation without causing a ripple of changes across the system.

Loose coupling in Eclipse is achieved partially through the mechanism of extensions and extension points. The simplest metaphor for describing extensions and extension points is electrical outlets. The outlet, or socket, is the extension point; the plug, or light bulb that connects to it, the extension. As with electric outlets, extension points come in a wide variety of shapes and sizes, and only the extensions that are designed for that particular extension point will fit.

When a plug-in wants to allow other plug-ins to extend or customize portions of its functionality, it will declare an extension point. The extension point declares a contract, typically a combination of XML markup and Java interfaces, that extensions must conform to. Plug-ins that want to connect to that extension point must implement that contract in their extension. The key attribute is that the plug-in being extended knows nothing about the plug-in that is connecting to it beyond the scope of that extension point contract. This allows plug-ins built by different individuals or companies to interact seamlessly, even without their knowing much about one another.

The Eclipse Platform has many applications of the extension and extension point concept. Some extensions are entirely *declarative*; that is, they contribute no code at all. For example, one extension point provides customized key bindings, and another defines custom file annotations, called *markers*; neither of these extension points requires any code on behalf of the extension.

Another category of extension points is for overriding the default behavior of a component. For example, the Java development tools include a code formatter but also supply an extension point for third-party code formatters to be plugged in. The resources plug-in has an extension point that allows certain plug-ins to replace the implementation of basic file operations, such as moving and deletion.

Yet another category of extension points is used to group related elements in the user interface. For example, extension points for providing views, editors, and wizards to the UI allow the base UI plug-in to group common features, such as putting all import wizards into a single dialog, and to define a consistent way of presenting UI contributions from a wide variety of other plug-ins.

FAQ 85 *How do I declare my own extension point?*
FAQ 94 *What is a plug-in?*
FAQ 96 *What is the plug-in manifest file (`plugin.xml`)?*
FAQ 97 *How do I make my plug-in connect to other plug-ins?*
FAQ 99 *What is an extension point schema?*
Go to **Platform Plug-in Developer Guide > Programmer's Guide > Platform architecture**

What is an extension point schema?

Each extension point has a *schema* file that declares the elements and attributes that extensions to that point must declare. The schema is used during plug-in development to detect invalid extensions in the `plugin.xml` files in your workspace and is used by the schema-based extension wizard in the plug-in Manifest Editor to help guide you through the steps to creating an extension. Perhaps most important, the schema is used to store and generate documentation for your extension point. The schema is *not* used to perform any runtime validation checks on plug-ins that connect to that extension point. In fact, extension point schema files don't even need to exist in a deployed plug-in.

The exact format of the schema file is an implementation detail that you probably don't want to become familiar with. Instead, you should use the graphical schema editor provided by the Plug-in Development Environment.

 FAQ 85 *How do I declare my own extension point?*
FAQ 88 *Can my extension point schema contain nested elements?*
FAQ 98 *What are extensions and extension points?*

How do I find out more about a certain extension point?

To find out more about a given extension point, try the following.

- Consult **Platform Plug-in Developer Guide > Reference > Extension Points Reference**. Here you will find the official documentation for all extension points, including extension point schema descriptions and examples.

- While adding a plug-in in the PDE Manifest Editor, click the **Details** button (Figure 5.1). It will take you to the page discussed above.

- Perform **Search > Plug-in Search** (the keyboard shortcut is Ctrl+H). You can search for a given extension point and also find all contributors to a given extension point. This gives you valuable access to examples of how the rest of the platform uses that extension point.

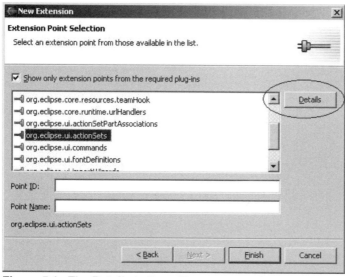

Figure 5.1   The **Details** button with more extension point information

When does a plug-in get started?

A plug-in gets started when the user needs it. In UI design, an often cited rule is
that the screen belongs to the user. A program should not make changes on the
screen that the user didn't somehow initiate. Making users feel that they are in
control of what is happening builds their confidence in the UI and results in a
much pleasanter user experience. This rule is followed by the Eclipse UI, but the
underlying principle has been applied to a much broader scope. In Eclipse, one of
the goals is to have the screen, the CPU, and the memory footprint belong to the
user; that is, the CPU should not be doing things the user didn't ask it to do, and
memory should not be bloated with functions that the user may never need.

This principle is enforced in the Eclipse Platform through lazy plug-in activation.
Plug-ins are activated only when their functionality has been explicitly invoked
by the user. In theory, this results in a relatively small start-up time and a
memory footprint that starts small and grows only as the user begins to invoke
more and more functionality.

The extension point mechanism plays an important role in lazy activation. Each
plug-in can be viewed as having a *declarative* section and a code section. The
declarative part is contained in the `plugin.xml` file. This file is loaded into a
registry when the platform starts up and so is always available, regardless of

whether a plug-in has started. This allows the platform to present a plug-in's functionality to the user without going through the expense of loading and activating the code segment. Thus, a plug-in can contribute menus, actions, icons, editors, and so on, without ever being loaded. If the user tries to run an action or open a UI element associated with that plug-in, only then will the code for that plug-in be loaded.

To get down to specifics, a plug-in can be activated in three ways.

1. If a plug-in contributes an *executable extension*, another plug-in may run it, causing the plug-in to be automatically loaded. For more details, read the API javadoc for `IExecutableExtension` in the `org.eclipse.core.runtime` package.

2. If a plug-in exports one of its libraries (JAR files), another plug-in can reference and instantiate its classes directly. Loading a class belonging to a plug-in causes it to be started automatically.

3. Finally, a plug-in can be activated explicitly, using the API method `Platform.getPlugin()`. This method returns a fully initialized plug-in instance.

In all these cases, if the plug-in contributes a runtime plug-in object (subclassing `org.eclipse.core.runtime.Plugin`), its class initializer, constructor, and `startup` method will be run before any other class in the plug-in gets loaded. Of course, if the plug-in's constructor or `startup` method references any of its own classes, they will be loaded and, possibly, instantiated before the plug-in is fully initialized.

It is a common misconception that adding a plug-in to your `requires` list will cause it to be activated before your plug-in. This is *not true*. Your plug-in may very well be loaded and used without plug-ins in your `requires` list ever being started. Never assume that another plug-in has been started unless you know you have referenced one of its classes or executed one of its extensions.

To play along with the rule of lazy activation, plug-in writers should follow some general rules.

- Do an absolute minimum of work in your `Plugin.startup` method. Does the code in your `startup` method need to be run immediately? Do you need to load those large in-memory structures right away? Consider deferring as much work as possible until it is needed.

- Avoid referencing other plug-ins during your `Plugin.startup`. This can result in a sequence of cascading plug-in activations that ends up loading large amounts of unneeded code. Load other plug-ins—either through executable extensions or by referencing classes—only when you need them.

- When defining extension points, make the extension *declarative* as much as possible. Keep in mind that extensions can contribute text strings, icons, and simple logic statements via `plugin.xml`, allowing you to defer or possibly completely avoid plug-in activation.

☞ **FAQ 96** *What is the plug-in manifest file (`plugin.xml`)?*
FAQ 182 *Can I activate my plug-in when the workbench starts?*

Where do plug-ins store their state?

FAQ
102

Plug-ins store data in two standard locations. First, each plug-in has its own install directory that can contain any number of files and folders. The install directory must be treated as read-only, as a multi-user installation of Eclipse will typically use a single install location to serve many users. However, your plug-in can still store read-only information there, such as images, templates, default settings, and documentation.

The second place to store data is the plug-in state location. Each plug-in has within the user's workspace directory a dedicated subdirectory for storing arbitrary settings and data files. This location is obtained by calling the method `getStateLocation` on your `Plugin` instance. Generally, this location should be used only for cached information that can be recomputed when discarded, such as histories and search indexes. Although the platform will never delete files in the plug-in state location, users will often export their projects and preferences into a different workspace and expect to be able to continue working with them.

If you are storing information that the user may want to keep or share, you should either store it in a location of the user's choosing or put it in the preference store. If you allow the user to choose the location of data, you can always store the location information in a file in the plug-in state location.

Plug-ins can store data that may be shared among several workspaces in two locations. The *configuration location* is the same for all workspaces launched on a particular configuration of Eclipse plug-ins. You can access the root of this location by using getConfigurationLocation on Platform. The *user location* is shared by all workspaces launched by a particular user and is accessed by using getUserLocation on Platform.

Here is an example of obtaining a lock on the user location:

```
Location user = Platform.getUserLocation();
if (user.lock()) {
   // read and write files
} else {
   // wait until lock is available or fail
}
```

Note that these locations are accessible to all plug-ins, so make sure that any data stored here is in a unique subdirectory based on your plug-in's unique ID. Even then, keep in mind that a single user may open multiple workspaces simultaneously that have access to these areas. If you are writing files in these shared locations, you must make sure that you protect read-and-write access by locking the location.

 FAQ 103 *How do I find out the install location of a plug-in?*
FAQ 111 *What is a configuration?*
FAQ 123 *How do I load and save plug-in preferences?*

**FAQ
103**

How do I find out the install location of a plug-in?

You should generally avoid making assumptions about the location of a plug-in at runtime. To find resources, such as images, that are stored in your plug-in's install directory, you can use URLs provided by the Platform class. These URLs use a special Eclipse Platform protocol, but if you are using them only to read files, it does not matter.

The following snippet opens an input stream on a file called `sample.gif` located in a subdirectory, called `icons`, of a plug-in's install directory:

```
Bundle bundle = Platform.getBundle(yourPluginId);
Path path = new Path("icons/sample.gif");
URL fileURL = Platform.find(bundle, path);
InputStream in = fileURL.openStream();
```

If you need to know the file system location of a plug-in, you need to use `Platform.resolve(URL)`. This method converts a platform URL to a standard URL protocol, such as HyperText Transfer Protocol (HTTP), or file. Note that the Eclipse Platform does not specify that plug-ins must exist in the local file system, so you cannot rely on this method's returning a file system URL under all circumstances in the future.

FAQ 102 *Where do plug-ins store their state?*

What is the classpath of a plug-in?

FAQ
104

Developers coming from a more traditional Java programming environment are often confused by classpath issues in Eclipse. A typical Java application has a global namespace made up of the contents of the JARs on a single universal classpath. This classpath is typically specified either with a command-line argument to the VM or by an operating system environment variable. In Eclipse, each plug-in has its own unique classpath. This classpath contains the following, in lookup order:

- *The OSGi parent class loader.* All class loaders in OSGi have a common parent class loader. By default, this is set to be the Java boot class loader. The boot loader typically only knows about `rt.jar`, but the boot classpath can be augmented with a command-line argument to the VM.

- *The exported libraries of all imported plug-ins.* If imported plug-ins export their imports, you get access to their exported libraries, too. Plug-in libraries, imports, and exports are all specified in the `plugin.xml` file.

- *The declared libraries of the plug-in and all its fragments.* Libraries are searched in the order they are specified in the manifest. Fragment libraries are added to the end of the classpath in an unspecified order.

In Eclipse 2.1, the libraries from the `org.eclipse.core.boot` and `org.eclipse.core.runtime` were also automatically added to every plug-in's classpath. This is not true in 3.0; you now need to declare the runtime plug-in in your manifest's `requires` section, as with any other plug-in.

 FAQ 96 *What is the plug-in manifest file (`plugin.xml`)?*
FAQ 97 *How do I make my plug-in connect to other plug-ins?*
FAQ 105 *How do I add a library to the classpath of a plug-in?*
FAQ 106 *How can I share a JAR among various plug-ins?*
FAQ 107 *How do I use the context class loader in Eclipse?*

How do I add a library to the classpath of a plug-in?

In **FAQ 104**, we explained how the classpath for a plug-in is computed. To access a given library from a plug-in, the library needs to be added to the classpath of the plug-in.

A JAR can be added to the classpath of a plug-in in four ways.

1. The JAR can be added to the boot classpath. This is generally a bad idea, however, as it requires an extra VM argument, and it also affects the classpath of all other installed plug-ins. If the JAR adds types—classes or interfaces—that mask types declared in other plug-ins, you will probably break those other plug-ins. Nonetheless, if you are looking for a quick and dirty hack, this is the easiest approach.

2. The JAR can be added to the declared libraries for a plug-in. This is fine if you don't anticipate a need for other plug-ins also to use that JAR.

3. A new plug-in can be created that is a wrapper for the library; then the new plug-in is added to the list of required plug-ins for all plug-ins that want access to the library.

4. The OSGi parent loader can be changed by setting the
`osgi.parentClassloader` system property on startup. This is also
generally a bad idea, for the same reasons listed for changing the boot
classpath. Valid values for the parent loader property are:

- ◆ `boot`. The Java boot class loader. This is the default OSGi parent
  loader, and has access to all JARs on the VM's boot classpath.

- ◆ `ext`. The Java extension class loader. This class loader has
  access to the JARs placed in the `ext` directory in the JVM's
  install directory. The parent of the extension loader is typically
  the boot class loader.

- ◆ `app`. The Java application class loader. This class loader has
  access to the traditional classpath entries specified by the
  `-classpath` command-line argument. In Eclipse this typically
  includes only the bootstrap classes in `startup.jar`. The parent
  of the application class loader is the extension class loader.

- ◆ `fwk`. The OSGi framework class loader. This is the class loader
  that is responsible for starting the OSGi framework. Typically
  you will not want to use the class loader, as its classpath is not
  strictly specified.

Using a separate plug-in to contain a library is the most powerful approach
because it means that other plug-ins can make use of that library without having
to load your plug-in or add the library to their own classpath explicitly. This
approach is used throughout the Eclipse Project to add third-party libraries, such
as Xerces, Ant, and JUnit.

Of course, because this is Java, there is always a way to load classes outside the
scope of your classpath. You can instantiate your own class loader that knows
how to find the code you need and use that to load other classes. This is a very
powerful mechanism because it can change dynamically at runtime, and it can
even load classes that aren't in your file system, such as classes in a database or
even classes generated on the fly. Manipulating class loaders is a bit outside the
scope of this book, but plenty of information is available in Java programming
books or at the Java Web site (http://java.sun.com).

FAQ 106 *How can I share a JAR among various plug-ins?*
FAQ 109 *What is a plug-in fragment?*

**FAQ
106**

How can I share a JAR among various plug-ins?

Suppose that plug-in *A* and plug-in *B* both use `xmlparser.jar`. In your workspace are two projects (for *A* and *B*), each containing a copy of the `xmlparser.jar` library. This is clearly not ideal: Two copies of the JAR are loaded at runtime, and classes from those JARs will not be compatible with each other, as they are loaded by different class loaders. (You will get a `ClassCastException` if you try to cast a type from one library into a type from the other library.)

Declaring `xmlparser.jar` as an external JAR does not work, as there is no easy way during deployment of your plug-ins to manipulate your plug-in's classpath so that they can see the library. The best way to share libraries is to create a new plug-in that wraps the library you want to share.

Declare a new plug-in, *C*, to contain the library JAR, and make both plug-in *A* and plug-in *B* dependent on plug-in *C*. Make sure that plug-in *C* exports its library so other plug-ins can see it:

```
<runtime>
    <library name="xmlParserAPIs.jar">
        <export name="*"/>
    </library>
</runtime>
```

When you deploy these three plug-ins, they will all share the same library. Note that in some situations, sharing libraries between plug-ins is not possible. If two plug-ins require different or incompatible versions of the same library, they have no choice but to each have a copy of the library.

☞ **FAQ 104** *What is the classpath of a plug-in?*
FAQ 105 *How do I add a library to the classpath of a plug-in?*

How do I use the context class loader in Eclipse?

In Java, each thread can optionally reference a *context class loader*. This loader can be set at any time by an application and is used for loading classes only when it is explicitly requested to do so. Many code libraries, in particular Java Database Connectivity (JDBC) and Xerces, use the context class loader in factory methods to allow clients of the library to specify what class loader to use. Although the context loader is not used by Eclipse itself, you may need to be aware of it when referencing third-party libraries from within Eclipse.

By default, the context loader is set to be the application class loader, which is not used in Eclipse. Because Eclipse has a separate class loader for each installed plug-in, a default class loader generally does not make sense as the context loader for a given thread. If you are calling third-party libraries that rely on the context loader, you will need to set it yourself. The following code snippet sets the context class loader before calling a library. Note that the code politely cleans up afterward by resetting the context loader to its original value:

```
Thread current = Thread.currentThread();
ClassLoader oldLoader = current.getContextClassLoader();
try {
   current.setContextClassLoader(getClass().getClassLoader());
   //call library code here
} finally {
   current.setContextClassLoader(oldLoader);
}
```

☞ **FAQ 104** *What is the classpath of a plug-in?*

Why doesn't Eclipse play well with Xerces?

Many plug-ins in the Eclipse Platform require an XML parser for reading and storing various data in XML format. In particular, the platform uses an XML parser to read each plug-in's `plugin.xml` file during start-up. Because the JDK before 1.4 did not provide an XML parser, Eclipse used to ship with a plug-in containing a Xerces parser. Xerces is one of the two XML parser implementations maintained by the Apache Project.

The first problems began to appear when users tried to start Eclipse using a JDK that also contained an implementation of Xerces. Prior to JDK 1.4, it was common practice to throw a copy of Xerces or Xalan into the JDK's `ext` directory so that it could be used by all applications. Thus, two copies of Xerces were available when Eclipse was starting up, one in the `ext` directory and one in the `org.apache.xerces` plug-in. Because libraries provided by the JDK always appear at the beginning of the runtime classpath, the one in the JDK is always found first. If this copy of Xerces was slightly different from the one the platform expected, various linkage errors or `ClassCastException`s occurred on start-up, often preventing Eclipse from starting up at all. The workaround in this case was pretty straightforward: Omit the `ext` directory from the classpath when starting Eclipse:

```
eclipse -vmargs -Djava.ext.dirs=
```

The situation became worse with JDK 1.4, which added a specification for XML called Java API for XML Processing (JAXP). The exact parser implementation was left unspecified, so each JDK was free to choose its own, as long as it was compliant with the interfaces defined by JAXP. Sun decided to use the Apache Crimson parser, and IBM went with the Apache Xerces parser. Worst of all, because these packages were now part of the standard JDK libraries, there was no easy workaround as there has been for the `ext` problem. The JDK people, realizing that they had messed up by bundling such widely used packages in their JDKs, thereby breaking any application that used slightly different versions of those packages, plan to prefix the implementation package names with a unique prefix to prevent these collisions in the future. However, it was too late to fix this problem for JDK 1.4. The bottom line: You cannot use Eclipse 2.1 or earlier with an IBM 1.4 VM.

For Eclipse 3.0, the problem was solved by tossing out the Xerces plug-in and simply using JAXP for any XML processing. Now at most one Xerces is on the classpath, so there cannot be any collisions. Of course, this means that you need at least JDK 1.4 to run Eclipse 3.0.

What is a plug-in fragment?

Sometimes it is useful to make part of a plug-in optional, allowing it to be installed, uninstalled, or updated independently from the rest of the plug-in. For example, a plug-in may have a library that is specific to a particular operating system or windowing system or a language pack that adds translations for the plug-in's messages. In these situations, you can create a fragment that is associated with a particular host plug-in. On disk, a fragment looks almost exactly the same as a plug-in, except for a few cosmetic differences.

- The manifest is stored in a file called `fragment.xml` instead of `plugin.xml`.
- The top-level element in the manifest is called `fragment` and has two extra attributes—`plugin-id` and `plugin-version`—for specifying the ID and version number of the host plug-in.
- The fragment manifest does not need its own `requires` element. The fragment will automatically inherit the `requires` element of its host plug-in. It can add `requires` elements if it needs access to plug-ins that are not required by the host plug-in.

Apart from these differences, a fragment appears much the same as a normal plug-in. A fragment can specify libraries, extensions, and other files. When it is loaded by the platform loader, a fragment is logically, but not physically, merged into the host plug-in. The end result is exactly the same as if the fragment's manifest were copied into the plug-in manifest, and all the files in the fragment directory appear as if they were located in the plug-in's install directory. Thus, a runtime library supplied by a fragment appears on the classpath of its host plug-in. In fact, a Java class in a fragment can be in the same package as a class in the host and will even have access to package-visible methods on the host's classes. The methods `find` and `openStream` on `Plugin`, which take as a parameter a path relative to the plug-in's install directory, can be used to locate and read resources stored in the fragment install directory.

☞ **FAQ 94** *What is a plug-in?*

Can fragments be used to patch a plug-in?

A common misconception is that a fragment can be used to patch or replace
functionality in its host plug-in. Although this is possible to a certain extent, this
is not what fragments were designed for. A plug-in and its fragments each
contribute a manifest, and each may also contribute native libraries, Java code
libraries, and other resources. At runtime, these contributions are all merged into
a single manifest and a single namespace of libraries and resources. If a fragment
defines the same library as its host, whether the fragment's library will be found
over the host's library is undefined. This makes it impractical to use fragments as
a way of replacing libraries or other resources defined by a plug-in.

Nonetheless, it is possible to design a plug-in so that it allows a portion of its
functionality to be implemented or replaced by a fragment. Let's look at a
notable example of how this is applied in the org.eclipse.swt plug-in. The
SWT plug-in manifest declares a runtime library by using a special
path-substitution variable:

```
<library name="$ws$/swt.jar">
```

When the plug-in manifest is loaded, the platform will substitute the ws
variable with a string describing the windowing system of the currently running
operating system. Each windowing system has a separate SWT plug-in fragment
that will provide this library. For example, when running on windows, ws will
resolve to ws/win32. You can make use of this path-substitution facility in your
own plug-in code by using the Plugin.find methods. The fragment
org.eclipse.swt.win32 supplies the swt.jar library at the path
org.eclipse.swt.win32/ws/win32/swt.jar. Thus, in this case the fragment
will supply a library that was specified by its host plug-in.

The same principle can be used to allow a fragment to provide a patch to a host
plug-in. The host plug-in can specify both its own library and a patch library in
its plug-in manifest:

```
<runtime>
   <library name="patch.jar">
      <export name="*"/>
   </library>
   <library name="main.jar">
      <export name="*"/>
   </library>
</runtime>
```

The host plug-in puts all its code in `main.jar` and does not specify a `patch.jar` at all. When no patch is needed, the `patch.jar` library is simply missing from the classpath. This allows a fragment to be added later that contributes the `patch.jar` library. Because the host plug-in has defined `patch.jar` at the front of its runtime classpath, classes in the patch library will be found before classes in the original library.

This technique is used in Eclipse 3.0 to provide backward-compatibility support for plug-ins based on Eclipse 2.1 or earlier. The plug-in `org.eclipse.ui.workbench` defines a library called `compatibility.jar` at the start of its classpath. When the platform detects a plug-in written prior to Eclipse 3.0, a fragment called `org.eclipse.ui.workbench.compatibility` containing `compatibility.jar` is automatically added to the plug-in's classpath. This library adds back some old API that was moved in Eclipse 3.0. The beauty of this mechanism is that it allows the backward-compatibility support to be added or removed with no impact on the host plug-in.

☞ **FAQ 104** *What is the classpath of a plug-in?*

What is a configuration?

FAQ
111

A configuration is the set of plug-ins available in a particular instance of the Eclipse Platform. A given installation of Eclipse may contain hundreds or even thousands of plug-ins. More than one Eclipse-based application can share this same install location, but they don't always want to use all the same plug-ins. When Eclipse is started, a *configurator* determines what subset of the installed pool of plug-ins will be used for that particular instance of the platform. By default, all installed plug-ins will be in the configuration, but a configuration can be customized to contain different groups of plug-ins. Go to **Help > Software Updates > Manage Configuration** to see and modify what plug-ins are in your configuration.

☞ **FAQ 243** *What is the minimal Eclipse configuration?*

**FAQ
112**

How do I find out whether the Eclipse Platform is running?

If you have a library of code that can be used within both the Eclipse Platform and a stand-alone application, you may need to find out programmatically whether the Eclipse Platform is running. In Eclipse 3.0, this is accomplished by calling `Platform.isRunning`. In 2.1, call `BootLoader.isRunning`. You will need to set up the classpath of your stand-alone application to make sure that the boot or runtime plug-in's library is reachable. Alternatively, you can reference the necessary class via reflection.

You can find out whether an Ant script is running from within Eclipse by querying the state of the variable `eclipse.running`. You can use this information to specify targets that are built only when Ant is invoked from within Eclipse:

```
<target name="properties" if="eclipse.running"/>
```

 FAQ 315 *What is Ant?*

**FAQ
113**

Where does `System.out` and `System.err` output go?

Most of the time, the answer is *nowhere*. Eclipse is simply a Java program, and it acts like any other Java program with respect to its output streams. When launched from a shell or command line, the output will generally go back to that shell. In Windows, the output will disappear completely if Eclipse is launched using the `javaw.exe` VM. When Eclipse is launched using `java.exe`, a shell window will be created for the output.

Because the output is usually lost, you should avoid using standard output or standard error in your plug-in. Instead, you can log error information by using the platform logging facility. Other forms of output should be written to a file, database, socket, or other persistent store. The only common use of standard output is for writing debugging information, when the application is in debug mode. Read up on the platform tracing facility for more information.

☞ **FAQ 121** *How do I use the platform logging facility?*
FAQ 122 *How do I use the platform debug tracing facility?*

How do I locate the owner plug-in from a given class?

FAQ
114

You can't. Some known hacks were used prior to Eclipse 3.0 to obtain this information, but they relied on implementation details that were not strictly specified. For example, you could obtain the class's class loader, cast it to `PluginClassLoader`, and then ask the class loader for its plug-in descriptor. This relied on an assumption about the class loading system that is subject to change and, in fact, has changed in Eclipse 3.0. The correct answer to this question is that there is no way to reliably determine this information. If you are exploiting knowledge of the Eclipse runtime's implementation to obtain this information, expect to be foiled when the runtime implementation changes.

How does OSGi and the new runtime affect me?

FAQ
115

Just when you thought you were beginning to understand how the Eclipse kernel worked, those pesky Eclipse developers replaced it all for Eclipse 3.0. The kernel is now built on another Java component framework, the Open Services Gateway initiative (OSGi). The reasons for this convergence between Eclipse and OSGi are manifold. The two frameworks had many similarities to begin with, and each framework had many features that the other lacked.

By bringing the two together, Eclipse gained the infrastructure for many new features, especially dynamic addition and removal of plug-ins and a more robust security model. Eclipse in turn has a powerful declarative model—extensions and extension points—that OSGi lacked, in addition to more advanced support for multiple versions, fragments, a commercial-quality open source implementation, and great tooling support. Rather than creating a derivative OSGi++, the Eclipse community is contributing a number of important Eclipse features back into the OSGi specification, paving the way for better interoperability between the two frameworks. All in all, it's what the marketing types like to call a win-win situation.

Now, to the question of how plug-ins are affected: The new runtime is 100 percent backward compatible with the runtime that existed in all versions before Eclipse 3.0. Plug-ins written prior to 3.0 will continue to run without requiring any modification. When you port a plug-in to 3.0, you can still make use of the old runtime API by explicitly importing the backward-compatibility layer, which is found in a separate plug-in. Although the `boot` and `runtime` plug-ins were imported automatically prior to Eclipse 3.0, the runtime must now be imported explicitly. The new runtime compatibility plug-in contains the deprecated portions of the API from the `boot` and `runtime` plug-ins and also exports the new runtime plug-in. In short, all you now have to import is the new runtime compatibility plug-in, and you will get access to both the new runtime API and the old. The following example from a `plugin.xml` file imports both the old and new runtimes:

```
<requires>
    <import plugin="org.eclipse.core.runtime.compatibility"/>
</requires>
```

Apart from that one change, you can continue using runtime facilities as you did prior to Eclipse 3.0. Over time, more elements of the old runtime will likely become deprecated, and plug-ins will begin to use the equivalent OSGi APIs instead. However, for release 3.0, the focus is on getting the technology in place with minimal disruption to the rest of the platform. For now, the fact that Eclipse is running on OSGi is an implementation detail that will not significantly affect you.

 FAQ 116 *What is a dynamic plug-in?*
The OSGi Web site (http://www.osgi.org)

**FAQ
116**

What is a dynamic plug-in?

Prior to Eclipse 3.0 the platform had to be restarted in order for added, removed, or changed plug-ins to be recognized. This was largely owing to the fact that the plug-in registry was computed statically at start-up, and no infrastructure was available for changing the registry on the fly. In Eclipse 3.0, plug-ins can be added or removed dynamically, without restarting. Dynamicity, however, does not come for free. Roughly speaking, plug-ins fall into four categories of dynamicity.

1. *Nondynamic* plug-ins do not support dynamicity at all. Plug-ins written prior to Eclipse 3.0 are commonly in this category. Although they can still often be dynamically added or removed, there may be unknown side effects. Some of these plug-ins' classes may still be referenced, preventing the plug-ins from being completely unloaded. A nondynamic plug-in with extension points will typically not be able to handle extensions that are added or removed after the plug-in has started.

2. *Dynamic-aware* plug-ins support other plug-ins being dynamic but do not necessarily support dynamic addition or removal of themselves. The generic workbench plug-in falls into this category. It supports other plug-ins that supply views, editors, or other workbench extensions being added or removed, but it cannot be dynamically added or removed itself. It is generally most important for plug-ins near the bottom of a dependency chain to be dynamic aware.

3. *Dynamic-enabled* plug-ins support dynamic addition or removal of themselves, but do not necessarily support addition or removal of plug-ins they interact with. A well-behaved plug-in written prior to Eclipse 3.0 should already be dynamically enabled. Dynamic enablement involves following good programming practices. If your plug-in registers for services, adds itself as a listener, or allocates operating system resources, it should always clean up after itself in its inherited `Plugin.shutdown` method. A plug-in that does this consistently is already dynamic enabled. It is most important for plug-ins near the top of a dependency chain to be dynamic enabled.

4. *Fully dynamic* plug-ins are both dynamic aware and dynamic enabled. A system in which all plug-ins are fully dynamic is very powerful, as any individual plug-in can be added, removed, or upgraded in place without taking the system down. In fact, such a system would never have any reason to shut down as it could heal itself of any damage or bug by doing a live update of the faulty plug-in. OSGi, the Java component architecture that is used to implement the Eclipse kernel, is designed around this goal of full dynamicity.

The dynamicity of a plug-in depends on the dynamic capabilities of the plug-ins it interacts with. Even if a plug-in is fully dynamic, it may not be possible to cleanly remove it if a plug-in that interacts with it is not dynamic aware. As long as someone maintains a reference to a class defined in a plug-in, that plug-in cannot be completely removed from memory. When a request is made to dynamically add or remove a plug-in, the platform will always make a best effort to do so, regardless of the dynamic capabilities of that plug-in. However, there may be unexpected errors or side effects if all plug-ins in the system that reference it are not well-behaved, dynamic citizens.

 FAQ 117 *How do I make my plug-in dynamic enabled?*
FAQ 118 *How do I make my plug-in dynamic aware?*

**FAQ
117**

How do I make my plug-in dynamic enabled?

Most of the effort required to make a plug-in dynamic enabled can be summed up as doing what you should be doing anyway as part of good programming practice. Most importantly, to be dynamic enabled, your plug-in has to properly clean up after itself in the `Plugin shutdown` method. You need to keep in mind the following checklist for your plug-in's `shutdown` method.

- If you have added listeners to notification services in other plug-ins, you need to remove them. This generally excludes any listeners on SWT controls created by your plug-in. When those controls are disposed of, your listeners are garbage collected anyway.

- If you have allocated SWT resources, such as images, fonts, or colors, they need to be disposed of.

- Any open file handles, sockets, or pipes must be closed.

- Any metadata stored by other plug-ins that may contain references to your classes needs to be removed. For example, session properties stored on resources in the workspace need to be removed.

- Other services that require explicit uninstall need to be cleaned up. For example, the runtime plug-in's adapter manager requires you to unregister any adapter factories that you have manually registered.

- If your plug-in has forked background threads or jobs, they must be canceled and joined to make sure that they finish before your plug-in shuts down.

Prior to Eclipse 3.0, the consequences of failing to clean up properly were not as apparent as plug-ins were shut down only when the VM was about to exit. In a potentially dynamic world, the consequence of not being tidy is that your plug-in cannot be dynamic enabled.

 FAQ 116 *What is a dynamic plug-in?*
FAQ 118 *How do I make my plug-in dynamic aware?*

How do I make my plug-in dynamic aware?

FAQ
118

Dynamic awareness requires extra steps that were not required prior to the introduction of dynamic plug-ins. Dynamic awareness requires that you remove all references to classes defined in other plug-ins when those plug-ins are removed from the system. In particular, if your plug-in defines extension points that load classes from other plug-ins—executable extensions—you need to discard those references when other plug-ins are dynamically removed. The extension registry allows you to add a listener that notifies you when extensions are being added or removed from the system. If your plug-in maintains its own cache of extensions that are installed on your extension point, your listener should update this cache for each added or removed extension.

The following is an example of a simple class that maintains its own cache of the set of extensions installed for a given extension point. This example is a bit contrived as simply caching the extension objects has no value. Typically, your plug-in will process the extensions to extract useful information and possibly load one or more classes associated with that extension. The basic structure of this cache example is as follows:

```
public class ExtCache implements IRegistryChangeListener {
    private static final String PID = "my.plugin";
    private static final String PT_ID =
        PID + "." + "extension.point";
    private final HashSet extensions = new HashSet();
    ...
}
```

The `extensions` field stores the set of installed extensions for a particular extension point.

The cache has a `startup` method that loads the initial set of extensions and then adds an extension registry listener in order to be notified of future changes:

```
public void startup() {
    IExtensionRegistry reg = Platform.getExtensionRegistry();
    IExtensionPoint pt = reg.getExtensionPoint(PT_ID);
    IExtension[] ext = pt.getExtensions();
    for (int i = 0; i < ext.length; i++)
        extensions.add(ext[i]);
    reg.addRegistryChangeListener(this);
}
```

The class implements the `IRegistryChangeListener` interface, which has a single method that is called whenever the registry changes:

```
public void registryChanged(IRegistryChangeEvent event) {
    IExtensionDelta[] deltas =
                        event.getExtensionDeltas(PID, PT_ID);
    for (int i = 0; i < deltas.length; i++) {
        if (deltas[i].getKind() == IExtensionDelta.ADDED)
            extensions.add(deltas[i].getExtension());
        else
            extensions.remove(deltas[i].getExtension());
    }
}
```

This class is now dynamic aware but is not yet dynamic enabled; that is, the class does not yet support itself being dynamically removed. The final step is to implement a `shutdown` method that clears all values from the cache and removes the listener from the extension registry:

```
public void shutdown() {
    extensions.clear();
    IExtensionRegistry reg = Platform.getExtensionRegistry();
    reg.removeRegistryChangeListener(this);
}
```

This `shutdown` method must be called from the `shutdown` method of the plug-in that defines the cache. For the complete source code of this example, see the `ExtCache` class in the FAQ Examples plug-in.

Note that not only extensions points acquire and maintain references to classes defined in other plug-ins. You need to be especially aware of static fields and caches that contain references to objects whose class is defined in other plug-ins.

If you hold onto classes defined in other plug-ins through different mechanisms, you also need to discard those references when those other plug-ins are removed.

☞ **FAQ 116** *What is a dynamic plug-in?*
   FAQ 117 *How do I make my plug-in dynamic enabled?*

Chapter 6. Runtime Facilities

In chapter 5, we already discussed most of the basic functionality of the `org.eclipse.core.runtime` plug-in. This chapter covers the remaining facilities of Eclipse Platform runtime: APIs for logging, tracing, storing preferences, and other such core functionality. These various services, although not strictly needed by all plug-ins, are common enough that they merit being located directly alongside the Eclipse kernel. In Eclipse 3.0, this plug-in was expanded to add infrastructure for running and managing background operations. This chapter answers some of the questions that may arise when you start to use this new concurrency infrastructure.

How do I use progress monitors?

FAQ
119

A progress monitor is a callback interface that allows a long-running task to report progress and respond to cancellation. Typically, a UI component will create a monitor instance and pass it to a low-level component that does not know or care about the UI. Thus, an `IProgressMonitor` is an abstraction that allows for decoupling of UI and non-UI components.

Each monitor instance has a strictly defined lifecycle. The first method that must be called is `beginTask`, which specifies a description of the operation and the number of units of work that it will take. This work value doesn't need to be very precise; your goal here is to give the user a rough estimate of how long it will take. If you have no way of estimating the amount of work, you can pass a work value of `IProgressMonitor.UNKNOWN`, which will result in a continuously animated progress monitor that does not give any useful information to the user.

After `beginTask`, you should call `subTask` and `worked` periodically as the task progresses. The sum of the values passed to the `worked` method must equal the total work passed to `beginTask`. The `subTask` messages can be sent as often as you like, as they provide more details about what part of the task is currently executing. Again, you don't need to be precise here. Simply give the user a rough idea of what is going on.

Finally, you must call `done` on the monitor. One consequence of calling `done` is that any unused portion of the progress bar will be filled up. If your code is part of a larger operation, failing to call done will mean that the portion of the progress bar allotted to your part of the operation will not be filled. To ensure done gets called, you should place it in a `finally` block at the very end of your operation.

Here is a complete example of a long-running operation reporting progress:

```
try {
    monitor.beginTask("Performing decathlon: ", 10);
    monitor.subTask("hammer throw");
    //perform the hammer throw
    monitor.worked(1);
    //... repeat for remaining nine events
} finally {
    monitor.done();
}
```

The monitor can also be used to respond to cancellation requests. When the user requests cancellation, the method `isCanceled` will return `true`. Your long-running operation should check this value occasionally and abort if a cancellation has occurred. A common method of quickly aborting a long-running operation is to throw `OperationCanceledException`.

 FAQ 120 *How do I use a* `SubProgressMonitor`*?*
FAQ 172 *Why should I use the new progress service?*

How do I use a `SubProgressMonitor`?

When using progress monitors in Eclipse, an important rule is that all API methods expect a fresh, unused progress monitor. You cannot pass them a monitor that has had `beginTask` called on it or a monitor that has already recorded some units of work. The reasons for this are clear. API methods can be called from a variety of places and cannot predict how many units of work they represent in the context of a long-running operation. An API method that deletes a file might represent all the work for an operation or might be called as a small part of a much larger operation. Only the code at the top of the call chain has any way of guessing how long the file deletion will take in proportion to the rest of the task.

But if every API method you call expects a fresh monitor, how do you implement an operation that calls several such API methods? The solution is to use a

SubProgressMonitor, which acts as a bridge between caller and callee. This monitor knows how many work units the parent has allocated for a given work task and how many units of work the child task thinks it has. When the child task reports a unit of progress, the SubProgressMonitor scales that work in proportion to the number of parent work units available.

If you are lost at this point, it is probably best to look at a simple example. This fictional move method is implemented by calling a copy method, followed by a delete method. The move method estimates that the copying will take 80 percent of the total time, and that the deletion will take 20 percent of the time:

```
public void move(File a, File b, IProgressMonitor pm) {
    try {
        pm.beginTask("Moving", 10);
        copy(a, b, new SubProgressMonitor(pm, 8));
        delete(a, new SubProgressMonitor(pm, 2));
    } finally {
        m.done();
    }
}
```

The copy and delete methods, in turn, will call beginTask on the SubProgressMonitor that was allocated to it. The copy method might decide to report one unit of work for each 8KB chunk of the file. Regardless of the size of the file, the SubProgressMonitor knows that it can report only eight units of work to the parent monitor and so it will scale reported work units accordingly.

☞ **FAQ 119** *How do I use progress monitors?*

How do I use the platform logging facility?

The Eclipse runtime plug-in provides a simple set of APIs for logging exceptions, warnings, or other information useful in debugging or servicing a deployed Eclipse product. The intent of the log is to record information that can be used later to diagnose problems in the field. Because this information is not directed at users, you do not need to worry about translating messages or simplifying explanations into a form that users will understand. The idea is that when things go wrong in the field, your users can send you the log file to help you figure out what happened.

Each plug-in has its own log associated with it, but all logged information eventually makes its way into the platform log file (see the getLogFileLocation method on Platform). The log for a plug-in is accessed from the plug-in's class, using getLog inherited from Plugin. You can attach a listener to an individual log or to the platform log if you are interested in receiving notification of logged events. Use addLogListener on either Platform or the result of Plugin.getLog().

You can write any kind of IStatus object to the log file, including a MultiStatus if you have hierarchies of information to display. If you create your own subclass of the utility class Status, you can override the getMessage method to return extra information to be displayed in the log file. Many plug-ins add convenience methods to their plug-in class for writing messages and errors to the log:

```
import org.eclipse.core.runtime.Status;
...
public void log(String msg) {
    log(msg, null);
}
public void log(String msg, Exception e) {
    getLog().log(new Status(Status.INFO, myPluginID,
                                    Status.OK, msg, e));
}
```

During development, you can browse and manipulate the platform log file using the PDE Error Log view (**Window > Show View > Other > PDE Runtime > Error Log**). You can also have the log file mirrored in the Java console by starting Eclipse with the -consoleLog command-line argument.

```
eclipse -vm c:\jre\bin\java.exe -consoleLog
```

We explicitly pass the VM because on Windows you have to use java.exe instead of javaw.exe if you want the Java console window to appear.

FAQ 27 *Where can I find that elusive* .log *file?*

How do I use the platform debug tracing facility?

During development, it is common practice to print debugging messages to standard output. One common idiom for doing this is

```
private static final boolean DEBUG = true;
...
if (DEBUG)
    System.out.println("So far so good");
```

The advantage of this approach is that you can flip the DEBUG field to false when it comes time to deploy your code. The Java compiler will then remove the entire if block from the class file as flow analysis reveals that it is unreachable. The downside of this approach is that all the hard work that went into writing useful debug statements is lost in the deployed product. If your user calls up with a problem, you will have to send a new version of your libraries with the debug switches turned on before you can get useful feedback. Eclipse provides a tracing facility that is turned off by default but can be turned on in the field with a few simple steps.

To instrument your code, use the methods Plugin.isDebugging and Platform.getDebugOption to add conditions to your trace statements:

```
private static final String DEBUG_ONE =
    "org.eclipse.faq.examples/debug/option1";
...
String debugOption = Platform.getDebugOption(DEBUG_ONE);
if (ExamplesPlugin.getDefault().isDebugging() &&
            "true".equalsIgnoreCase(debugOption))
    System.out.println("Debug statement one.");
```

This approach will also allow you to turn on tracing dynamically using the method Plugin.setDebugging. This can be very useful while debugging if you want to limit the amount of trace output that is seen. You simply start with tracing off and then turn it on when your program reaches a state at which tracing is useful.

If you do not need dynamic trace enablement or if you are concerned about code clutter or performance, another tracing style yields cleaner and faster source:

```
private static final boolean DEBUG_TWO =
    ExamplesPlugin.getDefault().isDebugging() &&
        "true".equalsIgnoreCase(Platform.getDebugOption(
        "org.eclipse.faq.examples/debug/option2"));
...
if (DEBUG_TWO)
    System.out.println("Debug statement two.");
```

This tracing style is not quite as good as the standard approach outlined at the beginning of this FAQ. Because the debug flag cannot be computed statically, the compiler will not be able to completely optimize out the tracing code. You will still be left with the extra code bulk, but the performance will be good enough for all but the most extreme applications.

To turn tracing on, you need to create a trace-options file that contains a list of the debug options that you want to turn on. By default, the platform looks for a file called .options in the Eclipse install directory. This should be a text file in the Java properties file format, with one key=value pair per line. To turn on the trace options in the preceding two examples, you need an options file that looks like this:

```
org.eclipse.faq.examples/debug=true
org.eclipse.faq.examples/debug/option1=true
org.eclipse.faq.examples/debug/option2=true
```

The first line sets the value of the flag returned by Plugin.isDebugging, and the next two lines define the debug option strings returned by the getDebugOption method on Platform.

Hint: If you use tracing in your plug-in, you should keep in your plug-in install directory a .options file that contains a listing of all the possible trace options for your plug-in. This advertises your tracing facilities to prospective users and developers; in addition, the Run-time Workbench launch configuration will detect this file and use it to populate the Tracing Options page (Figure 6.1). If you browse through the plug-in directories of the Eclipse SDK, you will see that several plug-ins use this technique to document their trace options; for example, see org.eclipse.core.resources or org.eclipse.jdt.core.

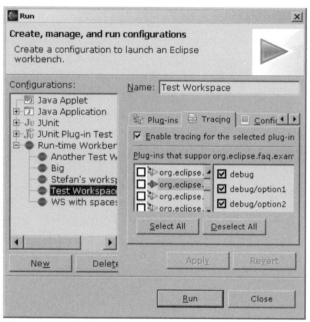

Figure 6.1 Tracing Options page

Finally, you need to enable the tracing mechanism by starting Eclipse with the
-debug command-line argument. You can, optionally, specify the location of the
debug options file as either a URL or a file-system path after the -debug
argument.

How do I load and save plug-in preferences?

FAQ
123

Each plug-in has a local workspace preference store for saving arbitrary primitive
data types and strings. Preferences displayed in the Workbench Preferences
dialog are typically stored in these local plug-in preference stores. The **Import**
and **Export** buttons in the Workbench Preferences page also operate on these
plug-in preference stores.

Retrieving values from plug-in preferences is fairly straightforward:

```
Plugin plugin = ExamplesPlugin.getDefault();
Preferences prefs = plugin.getPluginPreferences();
int value = prefs.getInt("some.key");
```

When preferences are changed, the preference store must be explicitly saved to disk:

```
prefs.setValue("some.key", 5);
plugin.savePluginPreferences();
```

The plug-in preference store can also store default values for any preference in that plug-in. If a value has not been explicitly set for a given key, the default value is returned. If the key has no default value set, a default default value is used: zero for numeric preferences, `false` for Boolean preferences, and the empty string for string preferences. If the default default is not appropriate for your preference keys, you should establish a default value for each key by overriding the `initializeDefaultPluginPreferences` method in your `Plugin` subclass:

```
protected void initializeDefaultPluginPreferences() {
    prefs = plugin.getPluginPreferences();
    prefs.setDefault("some,key", 1);
}
```

Although you can change default values at any time, it is generally advised to keep them consistent so that users know what to expect when they revert preferences to their default values. Programmatically reverting a preference to its default value is accomplished with the `setToDefault` method.

 FAQ 124 *How do I use the preference service?*

FAQ
124

How do I use the preference service?

In addition to the plug-in preferences for the local workspace obtained via `Plugin.getPluginPreferences`, a preference service new in Eclipse 3.0 can be used to store preferences in different places. This facility is similar to the Java 1.4 preferences API. Each preference object is a node in a global preference tree. The root of this preference tree is accessed by using the `getRootNode` method on `IPreferenceService`. The children of the root node represent different scopes. Each scope subtree chooses how and where it is persisted: whether on disk, in a database, or not at all. Below the root of each scope are typically one or more levels of contexts before preferences are found. The number and format of these contexts depend on the given scope. For example, the instance and default scopes use a plug-in ID as a qualifier. The project scope uses two qualifiers: the project name and the plug-in ID. Thus, the fully qualified path of a preference node for the FAQ Examples plug-in in the workspace project `My Project` would be

```
/project/My Project/org.eclipse.faq.examples
```

Below the level of scopes and scope contexts, the preference tree can have further children for storing hierarchies of information. This is analogous to the `org.eclipse.ui.IMemento` facility used for persisting user-interface states. With the new preference mechanism, it is very easy to create hierarchies of preference nodes for storing hierarchical preference data.

Lookups in this global preference tree can be done in a number of ways. If you know exactly which scope and context you are looking for, you can start at the root node and navigate downward using the `node` methods. Each scope typically also provides a public class for obtaining preferences within that scope. For example, you can create an instance of `ProjectScope` on an `IProject` to obtain preferences stored in that project. Finally, the preference service has methods for doing preference lookups that search through all scopes. This can be used when you allow users to specify what scope their preferences are stored at and you want more local scopes to override values in more global scopes. For example, JDT compiler preferences can be specified at the project scope if you want to override preferences for a given project. They can also be stored at the instance scope to specify preferences that apply to all projects in a workspace.

☞ **FAQ 125** *What is a preference scope?*

What is a preference scope?

FAQ
125

The preference service uses the notion of *preference scopes* to describe the various areas where preferences can be saved. The platform includes the following four preference scopes:

1. *Configuration scope.* Preferences stored in this scope are shared by all workspaces that are launched using a particular configuration of Eclipse plug-ins. On a single-user installation, this serves to capture preferences that are common to all workspaces launched by that user. On a multi-user installation, these preferences are shared by all users of the configuration.

2. *Instance scope*. Preferences in this scope are specific to a single Eclipse workspace. The old API method `getPluginPreferences` on `Plugin` stores its preferences at this scope.

3. *Default scope*. This scope is not stored on disk at all but can be used to store default values for all your keys. When values are not found in other scopes, the default scope is consulted last to provide reasonable default values.

4. *Project scope*. This scope stores values that are specific to a single project in your workspace, such as code formatter and compiler settings. Note that this scope is provided by the `org.eclipse.core.resources` plug-in, which is not included in the Eclipse Rich Client Platform. This scope will not exist in applications that don't explicitly include the `resources` plug-in.

Plug-ins can also define their own preference scopes, using the `org.eclipse.core.runtime.preference` extension point. If you define your own scope, you can control how and where your preferences are loaded and stored. However, for most clients, the four built in scopes will be sufficient.

FAQ 111 *What is a configuration?*
FAQ 124 *How do I use the preference service?*

How do I use `IAdaptable` and `IAdapterFactory`?

Adapters in Eclipse are generic facilities for mapping objects of one type to objects of another type. This mechanism is used throughout the Eclipse Platform to associate behavior with objects across plug-in boundaries. Suppose that a plug-in defines an object of type *X*, another plug-in wants to create views for displaying *X* instances, and another wants to extend *X* to add some extra features. Extra state or behavior could be added to *X* through subclassing, but that allows for only one dimension of extensibility. In a single-inheritance language, clients would not be able to combine the characteristics of several customized subclasses of *X* into one object.

Adapters allow you to transform an object of type *X* into any one of a number of classes that can provide additional state or behavior. The key players are

- `IAdapterFactory`, a facility for transforming objects of one type to objects of another type.

- `IAdaptable`, an object that declares that it can be adapted. This object is typically the input of the adaptation process.

- Adapters, the output of the adaptation process. No concrete type or interface is associated with this output; it can be any object.

- `IAdapterManager`, the central place where adaptation requests are made and adapter factories are registered.

- `PlatformObject`, a convenience superclass that provides the standard implementation of the `IAdaptable` interface.

Adapter factories can be registered either programmatically, via the `registerAdapters` method on `IAdapterManager`, or declaratively, via the `adapters` extension point. The only advantage of programmatic registration is that it allows you to withdraw or replace a factory at runtime, whereas the declaratively registered factory cannot be removed or changed at runtime.

Adaptation typically takes place when someone requires an input of a certain type but may obtain an input of a different type, often owing to the presence of an unknown plug-in. For example, `WorkbenchLabelProvider` is a generic JFace label provider for presenting a model object in a tree or table. The label provider doesn't really care what kind of model object is being displayed; it simply needs to know what label and icon to display for that object. When provided with an input object, `WorkbenchLabelProvider` adapts the input to `IWorkbenchAdapter`, an interface that knows how to compute its label and icon. Thus, the adapter mechanism insulates the client—in this case, the label provider—from needing to know the type of the input object.

As another example, the `DeleteResourceAction` action deletes a selection of resources after asking the user for confirmation. Again, the action doesn't really care what concrete types are in the selection, as long as it can obtain `IResource` objects corresponding to that selection. The action achieves this by adapting the selected objects to `IResource`, using the adapter mechanism. This allows another plug-in to reuse these actions in a view that does not contain actual `IResource` objects but instead contains a different object that can be adapted to `IResource`.

In all these cases, the code to perform the adaptation is similar. Here is a simplified version of the `DeleteResourceAction` code that obtains the selected resource for a given input:

```
Object input = ...;
IResource resource = null;
if (input instanceof IResource) {
    resource = (IResource)input;
} else if (input instanceof IAdaptable) {
    IAdaptable a = (IAdaptable)input;
    resource = (IResource)a.getAdapter(IResource.class);
}
```

Note that it is not strictly necessary for the object being adapted to implement `IAdaptable`. For an object that does not implement this interface, you can request an adapter by directly calling the adapter manager:

```
IAdapterManager manager = Platform.getAdapterManager();
... = manager.getAdapter(object, IResource.class);
```

For an excellent design story on why Eclipse uses adapters, see Chapter 31 of *Contributing to Eclipse* by Erich Gamma and Kent Beck.

 FAQ 177 *How can I use* `IWorkbenchAdapter` *to display my model elements?*

FAQ
127

Does the platform have support for concurrency?

In Eclipse 3.0, infrastructure was added to support running application code concurrently. This support is useful when your plug-in has to perform some CPU-intensive work and you want to allow the user to continue working while it goes on. For example, a Web browser or mail client typically fetches content from a server in the background, allowing the user to browse existing content while waiting.

The basic unit of concurrent activity in Eclipse is provided by the `Job` class. Jobs are a cross between the interface `java.lang.Runnable` and the class `java.lang.Thread`. Jobs are similar to runnables because they encapsulate behavior inside a `run` method and are similar to threads because they are not executed in the calling thread.

This example illustrates how a job is used:

```
Job myJob = new Job("Sample Job") {
    public IStatus run(IProgressMonitor monitor) {
        System.out.println("This is running in a job");
    }
};
myJob.schedule();
```

When `schedule` is called, the job is added to a queue of jobs waiting to be run. Worker threads then remove them from the queue and invoke their `run` method. This system has a number of advantages over creating and starting a Java thread:

- *Less overhead.* Creating a new thread every time you want to run something can be expensive. The job infrastructure uses a thread pool that reuses the same threads for many jobs.

- *Support for progress and cancellation.* Jobs are provided with a progress monitor object, allowing them to respond to cancellation requests and to report how much work they have done. The UI can listen to these progress messages and display feedback as the job executes.

- *Support for priorities and mutual exclusion.* Jobs can be configured with varying priorities and with scheduling rules that describe when jobs can be run concurrently with other jobs.

- *Advanced scheduling features.* You can schedule a job to run at any time in the future and to reschedule itself after completing.

Note that the same job instance can be rerun as many times as you like, but you cannot schedule a job that is already sleeping or waiting to run. Jobs are often written as singletons, both to avoid the possibility of the same job being scheduled multiple times and to avoid the overhead of creating a new object every time it is run.

FAQ 185 *How do I show progress for things happening in the background?*
FAQ 186 *How do I switch from using a Progress dialog to the Progress view?*
FAQ 218 *Actions, commands, operations, jobs: What does it all mean?*

How do I prevent two jobs from running at the same time?

The platform job mechanism uses a pool of threads, allowing it to run several jobs at the same time. If you have many jobs that you want to run in the background, you may want to prevent more than one from running at once. For example, if the jobs are accessing an exclusive resource, such as a file or a socket, you won't want them to run simultaneously. This is accomplished by using job-scheduling rules. A scheduling rule contains logic for determining whether it conflicts with another rule. If two rules conflict, two jobs using those rules will not be run at the same time. The following scheduling rule will act as a mutex, not allowing two jobs with the same rule instance to run concurrently:

```
public class MutexRule implements ISchedulingRule {
    public boolean isConflicting(ISchedulingRule rule) {
        return rule == this;
    }
    public boolean contains(ISchedulingRule rule) {
        return rule == this;
    }
}
```

The rule is then used as follows:

```
Job job1 = new SampleJob();
Job job2 = new SampleJob();
MutexRule rule = new MutexRule();
job1.setRule(rule);
job2.setRule(rule);
job1.schedule();
job2.schedule();
```

When this example is executed, `job1` will start running immediately, and `job2` will be blocked until `job1` finishes. Once `job1` is finished, `job2` will be run automatically.

You can create your own scheduling rules, which means that you have complete control of the logic for the `isConflicting` relation. For example, the `resources` plug-in has scheduling rules for files such that two files conflict if one is a parent of the other. This allows a job to have exclusive access to a complete file-system subtree.

The contains relation on scheduling rules is used for a more advanced feature of scheduling rules. Multiple rules can be "owned" by a thread at a given time only if the subsequent rules are all contained within the initial rule. For example, in a file system, a thread that owns the scheduling rule for c:\a\b can acquire a rule for the subdirectory c:\a\b\c. A thread acquires multiple rules by using the IJobManager methods beginRule and endRule. Use extreme caution when using these methods; if you begin a rule without ending it, you will lock that rule forever.

☞ **FAQ 127** *Does the platform have support for concurrency?*

What is the purpose of job families?

Several methods on IJobManager (find, cancel, join, sleep, and wakeUp) require a job family object as parameter. A job family can be any object and simply acts as an identifier to group and locate job instances. Job families have no effect on how jobs are scheduled or executed. If you define your job to belong to a family, you can use it to distinguish among various groups or classifications of jobs for your own purposes.

A concrete example will help to explain how families can be used. The Java search mechanism uses background jobs to build indexes of source files and JARs in each project of the workspace. If a project is deleted, the search facility wants to discard all indexing jobs on files in that project as they are no longer needed. The search facility accomplishes this by using project names as a family identifier. A simplified version of the index job implementation is as follows:

```
class IndexJob extends Job {
    String projectName;
    ...
    public boolean belongsTo(Object family) {
        return projectName.equals(family);
    }
}
```

When a project is deleted, all index jobs on that project can be cancelled using the following code:

```
IProject project = ...;
Platform.getJobManager().cancel(project.getName());
```

The `belongsTo` method is the place where a job specifies what families, if any, it is associated with. The advantage of placing this logic on the job instance itself—rather than having jobs publish a family identifier and delegate the matching logic to the job manager—is that it allows a job to specify that it belongs to several families. A job can even dynamically change what families it belongs to, based on internal state. If you have no use for job families, don't override the `belongsTo` method. By default, jobs will not belong to any families.

FAQ 127 *Does the platform have support for concurrency?*
FAQ 128 *How do I prevent two jobs from running at the same time?*

FAQ 130

How do I find out whether a particular job is running?

If you have a reference to a job instance, you can use the method `Job.getState` to find out whether it is running. Note that owing to the asynchronous nature of jobs, the result may be invalid by the time the method returns. For example, a job may be running at the time the method is called but may finish running between the time you invoke `getState` and the time you check its return value. For this reason, you should generally avoid relying too much on the result of this method.

The job infrastructure makes things easier for you by generally being very tolerant of methods called at the wrong time. For example, if you call `wakeUp` on a job that is not sleeping or `cancel` on a job that is already finished, the request is silently ignored. Thus, you can generally forgo the state check and simply try the method you want to call. For example, you do not need to do this:

```
if (job.getState() == Job.NONE)
    job.schedule();
```

Instead, you can invoke `job.schedule()` immediately. If the job is already scheduled or sleeping, the schedule request will be ignored. If the job is currently running, it will be rescheduled as soon as it completes

If you need to be certain of when a job enters a particular state, register a job change listener on the job. When using a listener, you can be sure that you will never miss a state change. Although the job may have changed state again by the time your listener is called, you are guaranteed that a given job listener will not receive multiple events concurrently or out of order.

If you do not have a job reference, you can search for it by using the method `IJobManager.find`. This method will find only job instances that are running, waiting, or sleeping. To give a concrete example, the Eclipse IDE uses this method when the user launches an application. The method searches for the autobuild job and, if it is running, waits for autobuild to complete before launching the application. Here is a snippet that illustrates this behavior; the actual code is more complex because it first consults a preference setting and might decide to prompt the user:

```
IJobManager jobMan = Platform.getJobManager();
Job[] build = jobMan.find(ResourcesPlugin.FAMILY_AUTO_BUILD);
if (build.length == 1)
    build[0].join();
```

Again, it is safe to call `join` here without checking whether the job is still running. The `join` method will return immediately in this case.

☞ **FAQ 127** *Does the platform have support for concurrency?*
FAQ 129 *What is the purpose of job families?*
FAQ 131 *How can I track the lifecycle of jobs?*

How can I track the lifecycle of jobs?

FAQ
131

It is quite simple to find out when jobs, including those owned by others, are scheduled, run, awoken, and finished. As with many other facilities in the Eclipse Platform, a simple listener suffices:

```
IJobManager manager = Platform.getJobManager();
manager.addJobChangeListener(new JobChangeAdapter() {
    public void scheduled(IJobChangeEvent event) {
        Job job = event.getJob();
        System.out.println("Job scheduled: "+job.getName());
    }
});
```

By subclassing `JobChangeAdapter`, rather than directly implementing `IJobChangeListener`, you can pick and choose which job change events you want to listen to. Note that the `done` event is sent regardless of whether the job was cancelled or failed to complete, and the result status in the job change event will tell you how it ended.

FAQ 127 *Does the platform have support for concurrency?*
FAQ 130 *How do I find out whether a particular job is running?*

FAQ
132

How do I create a repeating background task?

It is common to have background work that repeats after a certain interval. For example, an optional background job refreshes the workspace with repository contents. The workspace itself saves a snapshot of its state on disk every few minutes, using a background job. Setting up a repeating job is not much more difficult than setting up a simple job. The following job reschedules itself to run once every minute:

```
public class RepeatingJob extends Job {
   private boolean running = true;
   public RepeatingJob() {
      super("Repeating Job");
   }
   protected IStatus run(IProgressMonitor monitor) {
      schedule(60000);
      return Status.OK_STATUS;
   }
   public boolean shouldSchedule() {
      return running;
   }
   public void stop() {
      running = false;
   }
}
```

The same `schedule` method that is used to get the job running in the first place is also used to reschedule the job while it is running. Calling `schedule` while a job is running will flag the job to be scheduled again as soon as the run method exits. It does not mean that the same job instance can be running in two threads at the same time, as the job is added back to the waiting queue only after it finishes running. Repeating jobs always need some rescheduling condition to prevent them from running forever. In this example, a simple flag is used to check if the job needs to be rescheduled. Before adding a job to the waiting queue, the framework calls the `shouldSchedule` method on the job. This allows a job to indicate whether it should be added to the waiting job queue. If the call to `shouldSchedule` returns `false`, the job is discarded. This makes it a convenient place for determining whether a repeating job should continue.

Chapter 7. Standard Widget Toolkit (SWT)

One of the great success stories of the Eclipse Platform has been the overwhelming groundswell of support for its windowing toolkit, SWT. This toolkit offers a fast, thin, mostly native alternative to the most common Java UI toolkits, Swing and Abstract Windowing Toolkit (AWT). Religious debates abound over the relative merits of Swing versus SWT, and we take great pains to avoid these debates here. Suffice it to say that SWT generates massive interest and manages to garner as much, if not more, interest as the Eclipse Platform built on top of it.

The popularity of SWT has forced us to take a slightly different approach with this chapter. The SWT newsgroup was created in July 2003 and since then has generated an average of 136 messages *every day*. In this book, we could not even scratch the surface of the information available there. Although we could present the illusion of completeness by answering a couple dozen popular technical questions, we would not be doing the topic justice. Instead, we focus on answering a few of the higher-level questions and providing as many forward pointers as we can to further information on SWT available elsewhere. A benefit of SWT's popularity is the wealth of Web sites, discussion forums, books, and other forms of documentation out there. Thus, although we won't be able to answer all SWT questions, we hope at least to steer you to the resources that can. However, a handful of questions are asked so often that we can't resist answering them here.

What is SWT?

FAQ
133

Standard Widget Toolkit (SWT) is the UI toolkit used by the Eclipse Platform and most other Eclipse projects. Its stated goal, according to the SWT home page, is to provide "efficient, portable access to the user-interface features of the operating systems on which it is implemented." Its goal is not to provide a rich user-interface design framework but rather the thinnest possible user-interface API that can be implemented uniformly on the largest possible set of platforms while still providing sufficient functionality to build rich graphical user interface (GUI) applications.

SWT is implemented by creating thin native wrappers for the underlying operating system's user-interface APIs. The bulk of SWT's source is Java code, which defers as much work as possible to the appropriate operating system native. Thus, when you create a tree widget in SWT, it calls through to the operating system to create a native tree widget. The result is that SWT applications tend to look and behave exactly like native applications on the system they are running on. No Java emulation is done at all, except if no native API will satisfy the needs of the SWT API. Thus, if a platform does not provide a tree widget, SWT will implement an emulated tree widget in Java.

SWT does not make use of AWT or any other Java tool kit to implement its functionality. SWT also makes minimal use of Java class libraries, thus allowing it to be run with older JDKs or restricted class libraries on handheld computers. Implementations of SWT are currently available on the following platforms:

- Win32
- Linux Motif and GTK
- AIX Motif
- HPUX Motif
- MacOS Carbon
- Photon
- Pocket PC

**FAQ
134**

Why does Eclipse use SWT?

IBM's first-generation Java development environment, VisualAge for Java, was written in Smalltalk, using an in-house implementation of the language and an in-house virtual machine and widget toolkit. The purpose of the Smalltalk widget toolkit, called Common Widgets (CW), was to provide a thin set of common APIs for building Smalltalk GUIs that run on a broad variety of platforms, implemented using the native widgets available on each platform.

When the decision was made in 1998 to use Java as the implementation language for the next generation of tools, the brand new Swing toolkit was initially evaluated as a GUI toolkit. However, the design philosophy of Swing was based on a strategy of implementing widgets in Java rather than leveraging the native widgets provided by each platform. Based on their experience with Smalltalk, the Eclipse development team believed that native look, feel, and performance were critical to building desktop tools that would appeal to demanding developers. As a result, the team applied the technology they had built for Smalltalk to build SWT—a platform-independent widget API for Java implemented using native widgets.

As this Java tooling framework evolved into what is now called Eclipse, new reasons emerged for choosing SWT as the widget set. Eclipse was designed from the start as an integration platform; a fundamental goal was to provide a platform that integrated seamlessly with other user applications. SWT, with its native widgets, was a natural choice. SWT applications look and respond like native apps, and have tight integration with such operating system features as the clipboard, drag-and-drop, and ActiveX controls on Windows. To this day, many people getting their first glimpse of an Eclipse-based product don't believe that it is written in Java. It is difficult to differentiate from, and smoothly integrates with, other native applications on each of its target operating systems. The question then becomes, Why *shouldn't* Eclipse use SWT?

A major downside of SWT in the past was that it was not very compatible with Swing-based applications. This was a strike against Eclipse's primary goal as a tool-integration platform as companies with existing Swing-based applications were faced with the extra overhead of porting to SWT if they wanted to integrate cleanly with Eclipse. This was exacerbated by the fact that, as a new technology, few skilled SWT developers were in the market, and companies were reluctant to bet their tooling strategy on such an unknown quantity. As SWT has gained popularity, building a large community of developers and improved training and support, this has become less of an issue. In Eclipse 3.0, the final hurdle is coming down. There is now support for interoperability between SWT and Swing, as will be discussed in **FAQ 144**.

 FAQ 144 *How do I embed AWT and Swing inside SWT?*

Is SWT platform-specific?

**FAQ
135**

If you are asking about the implementation of SWT, the answer is yes. In fact, the implementation of SWT is the only part of Eclipse that is platform specific. Several plug-ins have platform-specific add-ons, but they are largely optional. Ninety-nine percent of the task of porting Eclipse to a new platform consists of porting SWT to the new platform.

The SWT APIs, on the other hand, are largely platform independent. To be more specific, all classes in the SWT packages not marked *internal* are guaranteed to be binary compatible across all platforms supported by SWT. Thus, if you write a Java application on SWT, you can compile it into JARs on one platform to run on all platforms supported by SWT without linkage errors. The exceptions to this binary-compatibility rule are packages whose names end with the windowing system name. For example, the package `org.eclipse.swt.ole.win32` is implemented only on Win32 platforms. Thus, most applications built on SWT obey the general Java credo of "write once, run anywhere."

Yet another angle on the platform-specific question is to ask whether the behavior of SWT is platform specific. You may have noticed the careful wording of the binary-compatibility promise, which guarantees only that you will have no *linkage* errors when changing to another platform. SWT does not promise consistent behavior across platforms. On each platform, SWT instead strives for behavior that is consistent with other applications on that platform. Thus, an SWT application on Windows should behave like other Windows apps, and the same SWT application on Motif should behave like other Motif apps. As most Java developers know, the goals of cross-platform consistency and platform integration are not always compatible. SWT attempts to meet both goals, but where these aims are mutually exclusive, it will opt for platform integration over cross-platform consistency.

Thus, although you don't have to worry about recompiling your application for every platform you want to support, it is a good idea to test your application on several platforms. On some platforms, subtle bugs emerge that do not appear on others owing to the vagaries of the platform's native widgets. In rare cases, this cross-platform brittleness needs to be worked around by tweaking your application code. The only reliable way to manage these subtle differences is to test early and test often on all platforms you are interested in supporting.

FAQ 136

Is SWT better than Swing?

This is equivalent to asking whether a hammer is better than a screwdriver. The answer, of course, depends on whether you are holding a nail or a screw.

SWT and Swing are different tools that were built with different goals in mind. The purpose of SWT is to provide a common API for accessing native widgets across a spectrum of platforms. The primary design goals are high performance, native look and feel, and deep platform integration. Swing, on the other hand, is designed to allow for a highly customizable look and feel that is common across all platforms.

The answer to which is better for your application depends on which of these trade-offs you and your customers prefer. Do you want an application that looks the same on all platforms or one that looks and behaves like other applications on each of the platforms it is running on?

Of course, a hammer wielded with sufficient force can probably drive a screw into a wall, and the butt of a screwdriver can be used in a pinch to knock in a nail. However, a good carpenter keeps both hammers and screwdrivers in her tool box and will use the tool that is appropriate for the job at hand.

☞ **FAQ 144** *How do I embed AWT and Swing inside SWT?*

Can I use SWT outside Eclipse for my own project?

FAQ
137

This can be interpreted as either a legal question or a technical question. You can find an official answer to the legal question on the SWT FAQ hosted on the SWT development team home page at eclipse.org. The answer to the technical question is an unqualified yes! However, because SWT has a native component, the technical details are a bit more involved than they are for simple Java libraries.

Each platform you want your project to run on will need its own native libraries. Luckily, this is easier than it used to be because the download section of eclipse.org now includes SWT drops. Download the appropriate SWT drop for the platform you are interested in running on, and set up the VM's classpath and library path accordingly. Here is a command line that was used to launch the BrowserSnippet stand-alone program:

```
java -cp swt.jar;. -Djava.library.path=. BrowserSnippet
```

This command line assumes that java is on your execution path and that both swt.jar and the SWT dynamic link library are located in the current working directory.

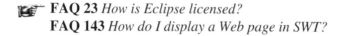

FAQ 23 *How is Eclipse licensed?*
FAQ 143 *How do I display a Web page in SWT?*

**FAQ
138**

Are there any visual composition editors available for SWT?

Several free and commercial products provide visual composition editors, or GUI builders, for SWT. These tools are especially appealing to people who are not yet skilled in all the intricacies of the SWT layout mechanisms and do not yet know what kinds of widgets are available to choose from.

After doing an informal poll, we discovered that none of the respondents in the Eclipse development team uses a visual builder to implement Eclipse. The UI for Eclipse is written manually in SWT, using an additional UI framework called JFace to take care of some of the repetitive aspects of writing UIs. Furthermore, when defining a new dialog, the developers often use the "Monkey see, monkey do" rule: They first find one that is close to the intended result; then, the new UI is cloned from the inspiration source and modified until it fits the needs of the new application.

With the growing popularity of SWT, more and more developers want to prototype and develop user interfaces with SWT. Visual builders help less experienced developers by eliminating most of the guesswork from the UI design labor. Widgets can be selected from a panel, and attributes can be chosen and assigned values from a limited set of options. The most successful builders offer fully synchronized views of the UI being developed and the generated source code to implement the UI.

Visual builders have been a long time coming for SWT, but a number of free and commercial GUI builders are finally available. The following is a brief listing of the free plug-ins we know about:

- *The Eclipse Visual Editor Project.* The goal of this Eclipse project is to build a framework for creating Eclipse-based GUI builders. This project follows the general Eclipse philosophy of creating a platform- and language-independent framework, with language- and platform-specific layers on top. This project aims to provide Java-based reference implementations of SWT and Swing GUI builders. The project has not yet produced a stable release, but pre-1.0 versions are available.

- *V4ALL Assisi GUI–Builder*. This SourceForge GUI builder project targets both SWT and Swing. So far, it is the work of a single developer, and there does not appear to be much activity on it.

- *JellySWT (jakarta.apache.org/commons/sandbox/jelly/jellyswt.html)*. Jelly is a scripting engine that uses XML as its scripting language. The goal of JellySWT is to allow you to describe a UI by using Jelly script and then have it generate the Java code automatically. The idea is that it takes care of the tedious layout code for you. This isn't really a visual composition editor, but it is a GUI builder of sorts.

The following are known commercial plug-ins:

- *SWT designer (swt-designer.com)*. This commercial plug-in to Eclipse, which targets only SWT, is fairly new as a commercial product but is based on an open source project that has been around for a while and has a strong following.

- *SWT GUI Builder (www.swtguibuilder.com)*. This commercial plug-in provides a visual editor for SWT only. The company also sells a product called Swing2SWT that ports Swing applications to SWT.

- *Jigloo GUI Builder (cloudgarden.com/jigloo)*. This fairly new GUI builder for both SWT and Swing is a commercial product, but a free version is licensed for noncommercial use only.

As with most listings of Eclipse plug-ins, this list will probably be outdated by the time this book goes to print. Check the plug-in listings in **FAQ 9** for a more up-to-date list.

 FAQ 9 *What open source projects are based on Eclipse?*

FAQ
139

Why do I have to dispose of colors, fonts, and images?

This question was asked so often that the SWT team wrote an article to explain why. The eclipse.org article "Managing Operating System Resources," by Carolyn McLeod and Steve Northover, can be found in the articles section at eclipse.org. The article describes SWT's philosophy on resource management and defends its reasons for not relying on the Java garbage collector for disposing of unused resources. The philosophy, in short, is this: If you create it, you dispose of it. The capsule summary of the reasoning is that the specification for Java finalization is too weak to reliably support management of operating system resources. This is also why database connections, sockets, file handles, and other heavyweight resources are not handled by the Java garbage collector. If you are still not convinced, read the article.

 FAQ 154 *How do I use image and font registries?*

Why do I get an invalid thread access exception?

On most operating systems, drawing to the screen is an operation that needs to be synchronized with other draw requests to prevent chaos. A simple OS solution for this resource-contention problem is to allow drawing operations to occur only in a special thread. Rather than drawing at will, an application sends in a request to the OS for a redraw, and the OS will, at a time it deems appropriate, call back the application. An SWT application behaves in the same way.

When the end user of your application activates a menu or clicks a button, the OS will notify SWT, which in turn will call anyone listening to that button, until eventually the call chain ends with you. All these calls are made in the same event loop thread. Normally, a UI does not act on its own but reacts to stimuli from others. In general, GUI applications are passive.

Therefore, when an application decides that it needs to live a life on its own, one option is for it to create another Java thread. A typical sample is the following:

```
new Thread(new Runnable() {
    public void run() {
        while (true) {
            try { Thread.sleep(1000); } catch (Exception e) { }
            Display.getDefault().asyncExec(new Runnable() {
                public void run() {
                    ... do any work that updates the screen ...
                }
            }
        }
    }
}).start();
```

This starts a timer that goes off every second and does some work. Because the work will be done in an unsafe thread, we need to request that SWT performs the task in a safe manner. We do this by requesting that the default SWT display runs our runnable when it can using `asyncExec`. In practice, this request is served as soon as possible. Execution is performed asynchronously. In other words, the request is placed in a queue with all other `asyncExec` requests and dealt with in a first-come first-served manner.

The call to `Display.asyncExec` returns immediately, before the drawing takes place. If you need to be guaranteed that the changes to the display took place before continuing, use `Display.syncExec`, which will suspend execution of the calling thread until the operation has finished.

Just about any SWT method that accesses or changes a widget must be called in the UI thread. If you are unsure, check the method javadoc. Any method that must be called in the UI thread will declare that it throws `SWTException` with value `ERROR_THREAD_INVALID_ACCESS`.

Avoid long-running processes in the UI thread as they will make the UI unresponsive. Do work that does not require UI access in a separate thread, and use the `asyncExec` call only for UI updates.

☞ **FAQ 127** *Does the platform have support for concurrency?*
FAQ 187 *Can I make a job run in the UI thread?*

How do I get a `Display` instance?

FAQ
141

Most users deploy Eclipse as one top-level window and manage their code in perspectives, explorers, editors, and views. However, SWT has been designed to optionally control a multitude of displays wherever this is allowed by the local operating system. The implication is that when creating something like a dialog window, SWT needs to be told *what* display to use for creating the dialog's frame. Ideally, your application should keep its own references to the display where it is needed, but if for some reason you don't have an instance, you have two ways to find one. The first way is by calling `Display.getCurrent`. A display is forever tied to the thread that created it, and a thread can have only one active display; a display is active until it is disposed of.

If you call `Display.getCurrent`, it returns the display that was created in that thread, if any. Here is an example:

```
public static Display getDisplay() {
    Display display = Display.getCurrent();
    //may be null if outside the UI thread
    if (display == null)
        display = Display.getDefault();
    return display;
}
```

A calling thread that does not have an active display will return `null`. Therefore, this method is useful only when you are absolutely certain that you are in the thread that created the display. This brings us to the second way you can obtain a display instance: `Display.getDefault()`. It will return the first display that was created. If your application has only one display, this is an acceptable way of obtaining the display.

FAQ 140 *Why do I get an invalid thread access exception?*

FAQ 142

How do I prompt the user to select a file or a directory?

SWT provides native dialogs for asking the user to select a file (`FileDialog`) or a directory (`DirectoryDialog`). Both dialogs allow you to specify an initial directory (`setFilterPath`), and `FileDialog` also allows you to specify an initial selection (`setFileName`). Neither of these settings will restrict the user's ultimate choice as the dialogs allow the user to browse to another directory regardless of the filter path. `FileDialog` also allows you to specify permitted file extensions (`setFilterExtensions`), and the dialog will not let the user select a file whose extension does not match one of the filters. The following example usage of `FileDialog` asks the user to open an HTML file:

```
FileDialog dialog = new FileDialog(shell, SWT.OPEN);
dialog.setFilterExtensions(new String [] {"*.html"});
dialog.setFilterPath("c:\\temp");
String result = dialog.open();
```

By default, `FileDialog` allows the user to select only a single file, but with the `SWT.MULTI` style bit, it can be configured for selecting multiple files. In this case, you can obtain the result by using the `getFileNames` method. The returned file names will always be relative to the filter path, so be sure to prefix the filter path to the result to obtain the full path.

FAQ 308 *How do I prompt the user to select a resource?*

How do I display a Web page in SWT?

In Eclipse 3.0, SWT introduced a browser widget for displaying a native HTML renderer inside an SWT control. Prior to the introduction of this browser, it was necessary to invoke an external Web browser program for displaying rendered HTML. The browser can be instructed to render either a URL or a supplied string containing HTML content. The browser widget does not include the usual controls for navigation, bookmarks, and all the usual bells and whistles associated with a Web browser. As such, it can be used for highly controlled applications, such as displaying help text or even for showing decorated and interactive text inside a view or an editor.

The browser has API for programmatically manipulating the content, such as browsing forward or back in the navigation history, refreshing the content, or halting a rendering in process. You can install listeners on the browser to be notified when the location is changing or when the title changes or to receive progress notification as a page loads. It is fairly straightforward to implement basic Web browser functionality around this browser widget. For more details, take a look at `BrowserAction` in the `org.eclipse.faq.examples` plug-in. This action implements a fully functional Web browser in fewer than 60 lines of code!

For a richer example, look at the `org.eclipse.ui.examples.browser` project in the Eclipse repository (dev.eclipse.org). This project implements a Web browser as a stand-alone Eclipse RCP application. As a quick example, here is a stand-alone SWT snippet that opens a browser shell on this book's Web site.

A title listener is added to the browser in order to update the shell title with the name of the Web page being displayed:

```
Display display = new Display();
final Shell shell = new Shell(display, SWT.SHELL_TRIM);
shell.setLayout(new FillLayout());
Browser browser = new Browser(shell, SWT.NONE);
browser.addTitleListener(new TitleListener() {
    public void changed(TitleEvent event) {
        shell.setText(event.title);
    }
});
browser.setBounds(0,0,600,400);
shell.pack();
shell.open();
browser.setUrl("http://eclipsefaq.org");
while (!shell.isDisposed())
    if (!display.readAndDispatch())
        display.sleep();
```

Figure 7.1 shows the resulting browser inside a simple shell. The browser widget is not yet available on all platforms as not all platforms that SWT supports have an appropriate native control that can be exploited. For Eclipse 3.0, the browser will at least be available on Windows, Linux, QNX, and MacOS. For platforms that do not have a browser widget available, the Browser constructor will throw an SWT error, allowing you to catch the condition and fall back to an alternative, such as a user-specified external browser.

Figure 7.1   SWT browser widget

How do I embed AWT and Swing inside SWT?

In Eclipse 3.0, APIs have been introduced for integrating AWT and Swing with SWT. This support is "product-quality" on Windows and has only early access support on Linux under JDK 1.5. The main entry point for AWT integration is the class `SWT_AWT`. It provides a factory method, `new_Frame`, that creates an AWT `Frame` that is parented within an SWT `Composite`. From there, you can create whatever AWT components you want within that frame. The bridging layer created by `SWT_AWT` handles forwarding of SWT events to the corresponding AWT events within the frame.

 FAQ 136 *Is SWT better than Swing?*

Where can I find more information on SWT?

Books. Before 2004, comprehensive information on SWT was not available outside the SWT source code and javadoc itself. This situation changed in 2004 with the publication of *SWT: The Standard Widget Toolkit* in the Addison-Wesley Eclipse Series. This book was written by Steve Northover and Mike Wilson, two of the original architects and developers of SWT. When the acronym first appeared, it was jokingly referred to as Steve's Widget Toolkit. Nobody knows SWT better than these authors, and their book is the most authoritative guide to the subject. If you're doing extensive development using SWT, it's indispensable. Volume 2 of their book is forthcoming.

Several other Eclipse books include a chapter or more on SWT:

- Eric Clayberg and Dan Rubel, *Eclipse: Building Commercial-Quality Plug-ins* (Addison-Wesley, 2004), Chapter 4.

- Erich Gamma and Kent Beck, *Contributing to Eclipse* (Addison-Wesley, 2004), Chapter 34.

- Sherry Shavor, et al., *The Java Developer's Guide to Eclipse* (Addison-Wesley, 2004), Chapter 14.

- Rob Warner and Robert Harris, *The Definitive Guide to SWT and JFace*, (Apress, 2004), major part of book.

Web sites. The information hub for SWT is the SWT development team home page (http://eclipse.org/swt). The main page has a basic SWT overview, and the Development Resources page has loads more information, including a comprehensive library of stand-alone SWT programs—called snippets—illustrating many of the important concepts in SWT. This page also hosts the official SWT FAQ maintained by the SWT development team, as well as development plans, platform porting status, and much more.

Visit www.cs.umanitoba.ca/~eclipse, hosted by the computer science department of the University of Manitoba, for extensive tutorials on using SWT, from a simple introduction to advanced applications. This site has a lot of high-quality information that can help you write your first stand-alone SWT application.

The home page for the SWT and JFace portion of the Eclipse wiki (www.eclipse−wiki.info) has links to other resource pages, but some information is here, along with a collection of FAQs.

The site www.swtworkbench.com is hosted by a company that does consulting and develops commercial SWT products. Its community page has discussion forums, news, links, and more, with a particular emphasis on SWT.

Articles. The first place to look for articles is the articles page on eclipse.org. We won't bother listing all the articles here as the list would probably be stale by the time this book goes to print. Of particular note is the two-part article entitled "SWT: The Standard Widget Toolkit." These articles were written by the SWT development team to describe some of the design rationale behind the project. The CD included with this book has PDF versions of all the articles, captured in May, 2004.

IBM developerWorks (www.ibm.com/developerworks) also has some technical articles focusing on SWT: "Using JFace and SWT in stand-alone mode," and "How to Deploy an SWT application using Java Web Start."

Discussion forums. The main forum for discussion of SWT is the eclipse.platform.swt newsgroup. This is the place to go for all kinds of SWT questions for users of all levels, from novices taking their first steps with SWT to highly experienced SWT developers. The SWT develoment team regularly reads this newsgroup, so you can be sure of authoritative answers. Be sure to do a quick search (http://eclipse.org/search), before posting, to avoid asking a question that's been asked before.

The platform-swt-dev mailing list is for discussion among members of the SWT development team and other contributors to SWT. If you are fixing SWT bugs, porting SWT to another platform, or looking for solutions to advanced questions that have not been answered on the newsgroup, you are welcome to ask here. SWT users are welcome to subscribe and follow along with the discussion, but to avoid cluttering the developer list, please use the newsgroup for your questions.

Some other Java forums have been known to host discussion threads on SWT. Unfortunately, these forums can sometimes deteriorate into flame wars on Swing versus SWT. One notable example is www.javalobby.org, which has had several SWT discussion threads.

FAQ 13 *What Eclipse newsgroups are available?*
FAQ 15 *What Eclipse mailing lists are available?*
FAQ 16 *What articles on Eclipse have been written?*
FAQ 17 *What books have been written on Eclipse?*

Chapter 8. JFace

JFace is a Java application framework based on SWT. The goal of JFace is to provide a set of reusable components that make it easier to write a Java-based GUI application. Among the components JFace provides are such familiar GUI concepts as wizards, preference pages, actions, and dialogs. These components tend to be the bits and pieces that are integral to the basic widget set but are common enough that there is significant benefit to drawing them together into a reusable framework. Although its heritage is based on a long line of frameworks for writing IDEs, most of JFace is generally useful in a broad range of graphical desktop applications. JFace has a few connections to classes in the Eclipse runtime kernel, but it is fairly straightforward to extract JFace and SWT for use in stand-alone Java applications that are not based on the Eclipse runtime. JFace does not make use of such Eclipse-specific concepts as extensions and extension points.

What is a viewer?

FAQ 146

The purpose of a viewer is to simplify the interaction between an underlying model and the widgets used to present elements of that model. A viewer is not used as a high-level replacement for an SWT widget but as an adapter that sits beside an SWT widget and automates some of the more mundane widget-manipulation tasks, such as adding and removing items, sorting, filtering, and refreshing.

A viewer is created by first creating an SWT widget, constructing the viewer on that widget, and then setting its content provider, label provider, and input. This snippet is from the BooksView class in the FAQ Examples plug-in, which creates a table viewer to display a library of books:

```
int style = SWT.MULTI | SWT.H_SCROLL | SWT.V_SCROLL;
Table table = new Table(parent, style);
TableViewer viewer = new TableViewer(table);
viewer.setContentProvider(new BookshelfContentProvider());
viewer.setLabelProvider(new BookshelfLabelProvider());
viewer.setInput(createBookshelf());
```

In general, JFace viewers allow you to create a model-view-controller (MVC) architecture. The view is the underlying SWT widget, the model is specified by the framework user, and the JFace viewer and its associated components form the controller. The viewer input is a model element that seeds the population of the viewer.

The JDT Package Explorer uses a `TreeViewer` to display the contents of a workspace, represented as a `JavaModel`. The UI manifests itself as shown in Figure 8.1.

Figure 8.1   Package Explorer showing the workspace contents

The corresponding Spider diagram (Figure 8.2) shows the relationships among the Package Explorer, its viewer, its model, the underlying widget, and the label and content providers for the JDT Package Explorer.

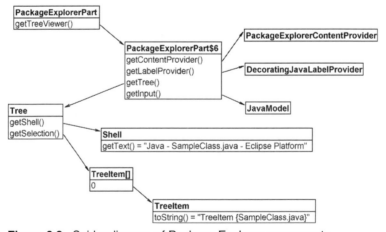

Figure 8.2   Spider diagram of Package Explorer components

☞ **FAQ 147** *What are content and label providers?*
FAQ 150 *How do I sort the contents of a viewer?*
FAQ 151 *How do I filter the contents of a viewer?*
FAQ 195 *What is a view?*
FAQ 196 *What is the difference between a view and a viewer?*

What are content and label providers?

**FAQ
147**

Minimally, all content viewers require you to supply a content provider and the label provider to interact with your model. The content provider is the viewer's gateway to the structure of the model elements that will be displayed in the viewer. When an input is provided to a viewer, the viewer asks the content provider what elements to show for that input. For more complex structures, such as trees, the viewer asks the content provider when it needs to know the children or parent of a given model element.

In addition to answering these questions from the viewer, the content provider must also notify the viewer whenever the model has been changed. The content provider does this by calling the various incremental update methods on the viewer subclasses. Although these methods look slightly different, depending on the kind of viewer, they generally follow a naming convention:

- `add`, for adding a single new element or batches of new elements.

- `remove`, for removing single elements or batches of elements.

- `update`, for updating the appearance of a single item, such as the label or icon. Optionally, this method takes a list of properties that are passed to the label provider, filters, and sorters to determine whether they are affected by the change.

- `refresh` for naive updating of an element and its children.

Although `refresh` is the easiest of these methods to use, it is also generally the least efficient. Because it is provided with no context information to figure out exactly what has changed, it simply rebuilds the view from scratch, starting with the provided element. This can in turn trigger costly sorting and filtering of the elements.

The label provider deals only with presentation of individual model elements. The viewer asks the label provider only what text and what icon, if any, are associated with each model element? The label provider is also responsible for disposing of any images it creates when the viewer is disposed of.

FAQ 146 *What is a viewer?*
FAQ 149 *Why should I use a viewer?*
FAQ 152 *How do I use properties to optimize a viewer?*

FAQ 148

What kinds of viewers does JFace provide?

JFace includes the following basic types of viewers:

- `TreeViewer` connects to an SWT `Tree` widget.

- `TableViewer` connects to an SWT `Table` widget.

- `ListViewer` connects to an SWT `List` widget. Note that because the native `List` widget cannot display icons, most applications use a `TableViewer` with a single column instead.

- `TableTreeViewer` connects to an SWT `TableTree` widget. A `TableTree` is a table whose first column can contain a tree, and each row of the table corresponds to a single item in the tree. The Properties view by default uses a `TableTree`.

- `TextViewer` connects to an SWT `StyledText` widget.

- `CheckboxTreeViewer` and `CheckboxTableViewer` are just like their namesakes, but have a check box next to each tree and table entry.

In addition to these basic viewer types, you are free to implement your own or to subclass an existing viewer to obtain specialized functionality. Viewers, however, are designed to be extremely customizable without the need to create a subclass.

As a historical footnote, an earlier version of JFace used viewer subclassing as the mechanism for customization. This led to a profusion of "monolithic" subclasses that were specialized for a particular purpose. The problem with subclassing is that it provides only one dimension of reuse. If you wanted to create a new viewer that filtered its contents like viewer *X* but displayed its contents like viewer *Y*, you were stuck with subclassing the viewer with the most contents in common and using copy and paste or other ad-hoc forms of reuse to get what you needed. With the current JFace viewer architecture, each pluggable component provides a new dimension of reuse. You can still subclass a viewer for very specialized situations, but you can generally get away with instantiating one of the standard viewers and installing the necessary pieces to get the behavior you want.

FAQ 146 *What is a viewer?*
FAQ 149 *Why should I use a viewer?*

Why should I use a viewer?

The main benefit of JFace viewers is that they allow you to work directly with your model elements instead of with low-level widgets. Instead of creating, disposing of, and modifying `TreeItem` instances in a `Tree` widget, you use the `TreeViewer` convenience methods, which deal directly with objects from your domain model. This makes your code cleaner and simpler, off-loading the complex work of finding and updating the widgets corresponding to your model elements when they change. These viewer methods have also been heavily tested and optimized over the years, which means that you will probably get a much more efficient, bug-free implementation than you would if you had written it yourself.

Another benefit of the viewer framework is that it is designed to encourage reuse. Viewers are customized by plugging in modular pieces rather than by subclassing. Each of these modular pieces addresses a specific concern, such as structure, appearance, and sorting. These pieces act as the unit of reuse: Any given piece can be reused in multiple viewers independently of the others. Thus, the piece that describes the appearance of your model elements—the label provider—can be reused in several viewers, independently of the piece that describes the relationship between elements—the content provider.

Aside from these main benefits, JFace viewers provide numerous other features that we don't have room to describe in detail.

Here is a quick overview of some of the main benefits of JFace viewers.

- `TreeViewer` populates lazily, avoiding the work of creating and updating items that are not visible.

- They support simple, model-based drag-and-drop.

- They have methods for querying or changing the selection and for adding selection listeners.

- They support pluggable sorters and content filters.

- Cell editors allow the user to modify table values in place.

- Decorators are available for adding annotations to the text and icons of viewer items.

In an earlier version of JFace, predating open source, viewers largely encapsulated the underlying widget toolkit, allowing you to create an application with few direct dependencies on the underlying widgets. Porting the application to another toolkit would thus mainly consist of porting JFace. This saved a great deal of effort when early prototypes built on JFace switched from a Swing-based implementation to an SWT-based implementation. But it was decided that this encapsulation required far too much duplication of SWT-level functionality and didn't always allow the native look and feel to shine through. Viewers were then simplified to their current form as adapters on the side of an SWT widget, enhancing but not hiding its function.

 FAQ 146 *What is a viewer?*
FAQ 148 *What kinds of viewers does JFace provide?*

FAQ
150

How do I sort the contents of a viewer?

Structured viewers are sorted by plugging in an instance of `ViewerSorter`, using the `StructuredViewer.setSorter` method. For simple sorting based on label text, use the generic `ViewerSorter` class itself, optionally supplying a `java.text.Collator` instance to define how strings are compared. For more complex comparisons, you'll need to subclass `ViewerSorter`. You can override the `category` method to divide the elements up into an ordered set of categories, leaving the text collator to sort the elements within each category. For complete customization of sorting, override the `compare` method, which acts much like the standard `java.util.Comparator` interface.

☞ **FAQ 146** *What is a viewer?*
FAQ 152 *How do I use properties to optimize a viewer?*

How do I filter the contents of a viewer?

**FAQ
151**

You do this with a `ViewerFilter`. `ViewerFilters` are added to a structured viewer by using the `addFilter` method. When a filter is added, it defines a subset of the original elements to be shown. Writing your own filter is trivial: Subclass `ViewerFilter` and override the method `select`. This method returns `true` if the element should be shown and `false` if it should be hidden. If more than one filter is added, the viewer will show only their intersection; that is, all filters must return `true` in their `select` method for the element to be shown.

One final tidbit of useful information: `StructuredViewer` has a convenience method, `resetFilters`, for removing all of a viewer's filters. This is more efficient than removing filters one at a time as each time a filter is added or removed, the entire viewer needs to be refreshed.

☞ **FAQ 146** *What is a viewer?*
FAQ 150 *How do I sort the contents of a viewer?*
FAQ 152 *How do I use properties to optimize a viewer?*

How do I use properties to optimize a viewer?

**FAQ
152**

The word *property* is one of those unfortunate programming terms that is overused because it can mean just about anything. The downside of using such a semantically weak term is that in different contexts it can mean very different things. The Eclipse Project certainly does not escape this foible: At the time of this writing, 154 classes and 1,105 methods contain the word *property* in the Eclipse SDK code base.

In the context of JFace viewers, *property* means any aspect that has relevance to how the domain objects being displayed are presented. Concretely, this means that whenever a property changes, the visual presentation of the viewer has to be updated in some way.

The interface `IBasicPropertyConstants` defines some simple properties—parent, children, text, and image—but the set of possible properties is open ended. Let's say, for example, that you have a tree viewer that is showing a person's ancestral tree. The label of each tree item may contain different information, such as the person's name and year of birth. The viewer may have several filters for showing subsets of the family tree, such as gender or hair color. You could define a set of domain-specific properties for that viewer to enumerate all these values:

```
public interface IAncestralConstants {
    public static final String BIRTH_YEAR = "birth-year";
    public static final String NAME = "name";
    public static final String GENDER = "gender";
    public static final String HAIR_COLOR= "hair-color";
}
```

Note that a property doesn't necessarily represent something that is directly visible but rather something that affects the presentation in some way.

The label provider, filters, and sorters associated with the viewer define which properties affect them. In this case, the label provider cares only about the name and birth year, so it would override the `isLabelProperty` method on `IBaseLabelProvider` as follows:

```
public boolean isLabelProperty(Object el, String prop) {
    return IAncestralConstants.NAME.equals(prop) ||
        IAncestralConstants.BIRTH_YEAR.equals(prop);
}
```

Similarly, a sorter that sorts entries by name would override the method `ViewerSorter.isSorterProperty` to return `true` only for the NAME property. A filter that defines a subset based on hair color would override `ViewerFilter.isFilterProperty` to return `true` only for the HAIR_COLOR property.

Still not seeing the point of all this? Well, here's the interesting bit. When changes are made to the domain objects, the viewer's `update` method, defined on `StructuredViewer`, can be passed a set of properties to help it optimize the update:

```
viewer.update(person, new String[] {NAME});
viewer.update(person, new String[] {GENDER, HAIR_COLOR});
```

The viewer update algorithm will ask the label provider and any installed sorter and filters whether they are affected by the property being changed. This information can allow the `update` method to make some very significant optimizations. If the sorter and filters are not affected by the change, the update is very fast. If any sorter or filter is affected by the change, significant work has to be done to update the view.

You can ignore this whole mechanism by passing `null` as the properties to the `update` method, but it means that a complete refresh will happen on every update. Resist the temptation to do this, especially if your viewer will ever have sorters or filters attached to it. For a viewer that contains a large number of values, the speedup from using properties can be significant.

☞ **FAQ 146** *What is a viewer?*

What is a label decorator?

**FAQ
153**

A `DecoratingLabelProvider` can be used when an element's text and image need to be annotated to show different states or properties. This is accomplished by bringing together a standard label provider with an optional decorator. The standard label provider is first asked to generate the text and image for the input element, and then the decorator, if installed, is allowed to augment or replace the original text and image with new values. JFace provides a helper class, `CompositeImageDescriptor`, to help you combine an image with one or more overlays. Because multiple overlays in a particular position will obscure one another, you must be careful to avoid overlapping decorators when creating a decorating label provider.

Figure 8.3 shows how the JDT's Package Explorer uses a decorating label provider to decorate resources with a decorator to indicate either a warning or an error.

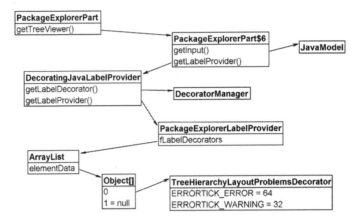

Figure 8.3 Spider diagram of the parts of a decorating label provider

Lightweight label decorators were introduced in Eclipse 2.1. These decorators abstract away the details of performing the image overlay. An implementation of `ILightWeightLabelDecorator` is provided with an `IDecoration` object, which it calls in order to add the decorations. The following simple example decorates a viewer containing `java.io.File` objects to indicate whether they are read-only:

```
ImageDescriptor readOnlyOverlay = ...;
public void decorate(Object element, IDecoration decoration) {
    if (!(element instanceof java.io.File))
        return;
    boolean readOnly = !((java.io.File) element).canWrite();
    if (!readOnly)
        return;
    decoration.addOverlay(readOnlyOverlay);
    decoration.addSuffix(" (read only)");
}
```

A decorating label provider is installed on a viewer in the same way as any other label provider:

```
ILabelProvider lp = ... the basic label provider
ILabelDecorator decorator = ... the decoration
viewer.setLabelProvider(
    new DecoratingLabelProvider(lp, decorator));
```

FAQ 146 *What is a viewer?*
FAQ 147 *What are content and label providers?*
FAQ 174 *How do I create a label decorator declaratively?*
FAQ 175 *How do I add label decorations to my viewer?*

How do I use image and font registries?

With SWT, you are responsible for managing the lifecycle of such operating
system resources as fonts, colors, and images. Most of the time, you can simply
tie the lifecycle of these resources to the lifecycle of the widget using them. They
can be allocated when a shell is opened, for example, and disposed of when the
shell is disposed of.

Sometimes, a resource is used very frequently or must be shared among several
widgets for unknown lengths of time. In these situations, the resources can be
stored in a permanent registry. JFace provides three such registries:
`FontRegistry`, `ImageRegistry`, and `ColorRegistry`. You can instantiate one of
these registries yourself or use the global ones accessible from the
`JFaceResources` class. The advantage to using a private instance is that you
don't have to worry about your keys overlapping with the keys of another
component. Here is an example of creating and accessing images in a private
image registry:

```
static final String IMAGE_ID = "my.image";
...
//declaring the image
ImageRegistry registry = new ImageRegistry();
ImageDescriptor desc = ImageDescriptor.createFromURL(...);
registry.put(IMAGE_ID, desc);
...
//using the image
Button button = new Button(...);
Image image = registry.get(IMAGE_ID);
button.setImage(image);
```

These registries create resources lazily as they are accessed, thus avoiding the
expense of creating resources that may never be used. The resources are disposed
of automatically when the display is disposed of.

A `FontRegistry` can also be loaded from a Java properties file, allowing you to
specify different fonts, depending on the operating system, windowing system, or
locale. See the javadoc for `FontRegistry` for more information on the format
and naming conventions for these property files. Finally, the JFace font registry
allows you to replace the font for a given key. This allows you to centralize the
handling of user font changes around the font registry. When the user changes the
font, you put the new value into the font registry. The registry

then sends out notifications to registered listeners, allowing them to update their presentation with the new font.

Keep in mind that it is not practical to store all your resources in a permanent registry. Windowing systems generally limit the number of resource handles that can be in use. A large application with many resources can cause the windowing system to run out of resource handles, causing failures in your application or even in other applications.

☞ **FAQ 139** *Why do I have to dispose of colors, fonts, and images?*

FAQ 155

What is a wizard?

A wizard is a series of pages that guide a user through a complex task. **Back** and **Next** buttons allow the user to move forward and backward through the pages. Typically, each page collects a piece of information; when the user clicks the **Finish** button, the information is used to perform a task. At any time before clicking **Finish**, the user can cancel the task, which should undo any side effects of the steps completed so far. Figure 8.4 shows a simple wizard that is included in the FAQ Examples plug-in.

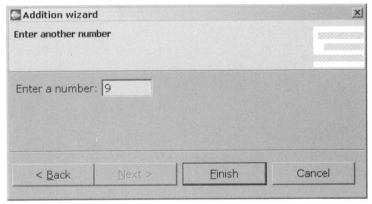

Figure 8.4 Sample wizard

A wizard is typically presented in a dialog, but this is not required. The abstraction called IWizardContainer represents the context in which a wizard runs. A wizard container is guaranteed to have a title, a message area, and a progress monitor. A wizard must implement IWizard, and each page within the wizard must implement IWizardPage.

☞ **FAQ 156** *How do I specify the order of pages in a wizard?*
FAQ 159 *How do I make my wizard appear in the UI?*

How do I specify the order of pages in a wizard?

In its simplest and most common form, a wizard is made up of a static, ordered list of pages. A wizard adds pages to the list by using the `Wizard.addPage` method, and the **Next** and **Back** buttons simply cycle through this ordered list. For a wizard with a static set of pages, you can simply override the `addPages` method and add all of your pages at once. This snippet is from `AddingWizard` in the FAQ Examples plug-in:

```
public class AddingWizard extends Wizard {
   private AddingWizardPage page1, page2;
   ...
   public void addPages() {
      page1 = new AddingWizardPage("Page1",
         "Please enter the first number");
      addPage(page1);
      page2 = new AddingWizardPage("Page2",
         "Enter another number");
      addPage(page2);
   }
}
```

If you want to change the behavior of the wizard, depending on the values that are entered, you can dynamically create new pages or change the page order after the wizard is opened. Pages must still be added to the wizard by using the `addPage` method, but the progression of pages through the wizard can change, depending on the user's input. This ordering is changed by overriding the wizard methods `getNextPage` and `getPreviousPage`, which are called when the user clicks on **Next** or **Back** button.

Even with dynamic wizards, you must create at least one page before the wizard is opened. If only one page is added at the beginning, but more pages will be added later on, you will need to call `Wizard.setForcePreviousAndNextButtons(true)` before the wizard is opened. Otherwise, the **Next** and **Back** buttons will appear only if more than one page is in the page list.

FAQ 155 *What is a wizard?*
FAQ 156 *How do I specify the order of pages in a wizard?*

FAQ
157

How can I reuse wizard pages in more than one wizard?

The wizard framework is designed to allow for very loose coupling between a wizard page and its containing wizard. Just as a wizard interacts with an abstraction of its container via `IWizardContainer`, a wizard page can interact with the wizard it is part of, using the generic `IWizard` interface. This allows the page to act as a reusable piece that can be incorporated into different concrete wizards.

Of course, it is up to the page implementer to ensure that tighter coupling does not creep in. Some wizard page implementations pass a reference to a concrete wizard in the page constructor, thus making it difficult or impossible to reuse the page in a different wizard. To avoid this, try to keep each wizard page as generic as possible. A page is really only a mechanism for gathering information from the user. The page should simply expose accessors for the information it collects, allowing the concrete wizard to pull together all the information and use it for that wizard's ultimate goal.

 FAQ 158 *Can I reuse wizards from other plug-ins?*

FAQ
158

Can I reuse wizards from other plug-ins?

Yes, as long as the wizards expose them as API. Most of the time, plug-ins will make their wizard pages API but will not make the wizard itself API. The reason is that most of the interesting functionality is in the pages anyway, and other plug-ins wanting to reuse a wizard will generally want to insert some of their own pages as well.

Almost all the wizard pages you see in the Eclipse SDK are available as API, so you can use them in your own wizard. The pages from the import and export wizards, along with the wizards for creating simple files, folders, and projects, are found in the `org.eclipse.ui.ide` plug-in in the `org.eclipse.ui.dialogs`

package. The import and export pages are abstract, but they allow subclasses to
insert the controls for the source or destination of the import, and the abstract
page takes care of the rest. The `org.eclipse.jdt.ui` plug-in exposes wizard
pages for creating Java projects, packages, and types in the
`org.eclipse.jdt.ui.wizards` package.

☞ **FAQ 157** *How can I reuse wizard pages in more than one wizard?*

How do I make my wizard appear in the UI?

FAQ 159

To make a wizard appear, you need an implementation of the wizard interface
called `IWizardContainer`. The container is responsible for all the presentation
outside the pages themselves, including a title area, button bar, and progress
indicator. You can implement this interface yourself if you want to embed a
wizard into a custom control. JFace provides a default wizard container that is a
simple modal dialog: `WizardDialog`. The following code snippet opens a wizard
in a wizard dialog:

```
Shell shell = window.getShell();
AddingWizard wizard = new AddingWizard();
WizardDialog dialog = new WizardDialog(shell, wizard);
int result = dialog.open();
```

☞ **FAQ 155** *What is a wizard?*
FAQ 181 *How do I add my wizard to the New, Import, or Export menu
categories?*

How do I run a lengthy process in a wizard?

FAQ 160

The `IWizardContainer` passed to your wizard extends `IRunnableContext`. This
means that you can pass it an `IRunnableWithProgress` and that it will give
progress feedback to the user while it runs. Keep in mind that as with all
long-running operations, the container will generally fork a different thread to
run your operation. If you want to manipulate any widgets from the operation,
you'll have to use `Display.asyncExec`.

The FAQ Examples plug-in includes a sample wizard, called AddingWizard, that
computes the sum of two integers, using the wizard container's progress monitor:

```
getContainer().run(true, true, new IRunnableWithProgress() {
    public void run(IProgressMonitor monitor) {
        int sum = n1 + n2;
        monitor.beginTask("Computing sum: ", sum);
        for (int i = 0; i < sum; i++) {
            monitor.subTask(Integer.toString(i));
            //sleep to simulate long running operation
            Thread.sleep(100);
            monitor.worked(1);
        }
        monitor.done();
    }
});
```

Your wizard can specify whether it needs a progress bar or a simple busy cursor.
For operations that may take more than a second, you should use a progress bar.
This is done by implementing needsProgressMonitor method on IWizard to
return true.

 FAQ 119 *How do I use progress monitors?*
FAQ 140 *Why do I get an invalid thread access exception?*

FAQ
161

How do I launch the preference page that belongs to my plug-in?

Sometimes, you want to allow the user to edit preferences for your plug-in
quickly, without manually opening the Preference dialog via **Window >
Preferences** and locating the page for your plug-in. You can do this by launching
the Preference dialog yourself with a customized PreferenceManager, a class
responsible for building the tree of preference nodes available on the left-hand
side of the Preference dialog.

For each preference page you want to display, create a PreferenceNode instance
that contains a reference to your page and some unique page ID. Pages are then
added to a preference manager. If you want to create a hierarchy of pages, use the
PreferenceManager method addTo, where the path is a period-delimited series
of page IDs above the page being added. Finally, create an instance of
PreferenceDialog, passing in the preference manager you have created. Here is

sample code for opening the Preference dialog on a single preference page called
`MyPreferencePage`:

```
IPreferencePage page = new MyPreferencePage();
PreferenceManager mgr = new PreferenceManager();
IPreferenceNode node = new PreferenceNode("1", page);
mgr.addToRoot(node);
PreferenceDialog dialog = new PreferenceDialog(shell, mgr);
dialog.create();
dialog.setMessage(page.getTitle());
dialog.open();
```

☞ **FAQ 178** *How do I create my own preference page?*

How do I ask a simple yes or no question?

The `MessageDialog` class provides a couple of convenience methods for asking
questions with Boolean answers. The `openQuestion` method will present a
dialog with Yes and No buttons and will return the result. The `openConfirm`
method is similar but uses Ok and Cancel as the button labels. If you want to use
different button labels or have more buttons, such as Yes/No/Always/Never, you
can construct a customized dialog yourself:

```
MessageDialog dialog = new MessageDialog(
    null, "Title", null, "Question",
    MessageDialog.QUESTION,
    new String[] {"Yes", "No", "Always", "Never"},
    0);, // yes is the default
int result = dialog.open();
```

The return value from the `open` method will be the index of the button in the
label array. If the user cancels or closes the dialog, a result of one is returned by
convention. This means that you should try to make your second button match
the behavior that makes sense for your circumstances. If you want completely
different behavior for dialog cancellation, you will need to subclass
`MessageDialog` and override the `cancelPressed` method.

The `MessageDialogWithToggle` class—introduced in Eclipse 3.0—is an
extension of `MessageDialog` that adds the capability of remembering the user's
selection to avoid having to prompt them again. This can be used for introductory
warning messages that advanced users want to be able to turn off.

MessageDialogWithToggle has similar static convenience methods as MessageDialog for common questions, but you can use the constructor to provide a customized set of buttons if necessary.

FAQ
163

How do I inform the user of a problem?

Warnings and errors can be reported to the user by using an ErrorDialog. Here is a very simple example of an Error dialog displaying a warning message:

```
IStatus warning = new Status(IStatus.WARNING,
    ExamplesPlugin.ID, 1, "You have been warned.", null);
ErrorDialog.openError(window.getShell(),
    "This is your final warning", null, warning);
```

The null parameter to the status constructor is for supplying an exception object. The exception object is not used by the Error dialog, so we'll leave it blank in this case. If you're creating a status object for another purpose, such as logging, you'll want to supply the exception, if there is one. The openError method has parameters for a title and a message, but both of these parameters are optional. If you don't supply a title, the method will use the generic **Problems Occurred** message. If you don't supply a message, the method will take the message from the supplied status object.

 FAQ 121 *How do I use the platform logging facility?*
FAQ 164 *How do I create a dialog with a details area?*

FAQ
164

How do I create a dialog with a details area?

Many dialogs in Eclipse have a **Details** button that shows or hides an extra area with more information. This functionality is provided by the JFace ErrorDialog. The naming of this class is a bit unfortunate as it doesn't fully express all the things it can be used for. A better name might have been StatusDialog as it is used to display any IStatus object, which can represent information, warnings, or errors. The dialog looks at the severity of the supplied status and uses an appropriate icon: an exclamation mark for errors, a yield sign for warnings, and an *i* character for information.

If you want to provide more information in the details area, you need to supply a
`MultiStatus` object. The dialog will obtain the message string from the
`MultiStatus` parent, and one line in the details area will be for the message from
each child status. The following example uses an error dialog to display some
information—the date—with more details provided in the details area:

```
Date date = new Date();
SimpleDateFormat format = new SimpleDateFormat();
String[] patterns = new String[] {
    "EEEE", "yyyy", "MMMM", "h 'o''clock'"};
String[] prefixes = new String[] {
    "Today is ", "The year is ", "It is ", "It is "};
String[] msg = new String[patterns.length];
for (int i = 0; i < msg.length; i++) {
    format.applyPattern(patterns[i]);
    msg[i] = prefixes[i] + format.format(date);
}
final String PID = ExamplesPlugin.ID;
MultiStatus info = new MultiStatus(PID, 1, msg[0], null);
info.add(new Status(IStatus.INFO, PID, 1, msg[1], null));
info.add(new Status(IStatus.INFO, PID, 1, msg[2], null));
info.add(new Status(IStatus.INFO, PID, 1, msg[3], null));
ErrorDialog.openError(window.getShell(), "Time", null, info);
```

FAQ 163 *How do I inform the user of a problem?*

How do I set the title of a custom dialog?

If you have created your own subclass of the JFace `Dialog` class, you can set the
dialog title by overriding the `configureShell` method:

```
protected void configureShell(Shell shell) {
    super.configureShell(shell);
    shell.setText("My Dialog");
}
```

The `configureShell` method can also be used to set the dialog menu bar image
(`Shell.setImage`), the font (`Shell.setFont`), the cursor (`Shell.setCursor`),
and other shell attributes.

How do I save settings for a dialog or wizard?

The IDialogSettings mechanism can be used to store any hierarchical collection of strings and numbers. It is used in Eclipse to persist preferences and history for most views, dialogs, and wizards. For example, dialogs will often store the last few values entered in each entry field and allow the user to select from these previous values, using a combo box. Views will use dialog settings to store filtering, sorting, and layout preferences. In all these cases, the basic steps involved are the same.

First, you need to find or create an instance of IDialogSettings. If your plug-in is a subclass of AbstractUIPlugin, your plug-in already has a global setting object. Simply call the method getDialogSettings on your plug-in to obtain an instance. If you're not using AbstractUIPlugin, you can create an instance of DialogSettings yourself.

Once you have a settings instance, you simply store the data values you want to keep on the settings object. If you're using a global settings object, you can add subsections, using addNewSection. Typically, each dialog, wizard page, and view will have its own settings section within the global settings instance.

Finally, the settings must be saved to disk at some point. If you're using the AbstractUIPlugin settings instance, it is saved automatically when the plug-in is shut down. If you created the settings yourself, you have to save the settings manually when you're finished changing them by calling the save method. Note that each plug-in has a state location allotted to it, and you can find out the location by calling getStateLocation on your plug-in instance. The following example loads a settings file from disk, changes some values, and then saves it again:

```
IPath path = ExamplesPlugin.getDefault().getStateLocation();
String filename = path.append("settings.txt").toOSString();
DialogSettings settings = new DialogSettings("Top");
settings.load(filename);
settings.put("Name", "Joe");
settings.put("Age", 35);
settings.save(filename);
```

FAQ 204 *How does a view persist its state between sessions?*

Chapter 9. Generic Workbench

This chapter covers FAQs relating to the generic workbench and its APIs. *Workbench* is the term used for the generic Eclipse UI. Originally the UI was called the *desktop*, but because Eclipse was a platform primarily for tools rather than for stationery, *workbench* was deemed more suitable. In Eclipse 3.0, tools are no longer the sole focus, so the term *Rich Client Platform*, is starting to creep in as the term for the generic, non-tool-specific UI. After all, people don't want to play mine sweeper or send e-mails to Mom from such a prosaically named application as a workbench. A rich client, on the other hand, is always welcome at the dinner table.

Many of the important workbench concepts, such as editors, views, and actions, generate enough questions that they deserve their own chapters. This chapter focuses on general questions about integrating your plug-in with the various extension hooks the workbench provides.

Pages, parts, sites, windows: What is all this stuff?

FAQ 167

Denizens of the Eclipse newsgroups, clearly expressing frustration with the overwhelming sea of terms, have been known to ask, "What is the Eclipsian word for X?," or "What is that thingy called in Eclipse Speak?." In an effort to assuage the suffering of new users, the following is a mile-high view of the pieces of the Eclipse UI.

The term used to represent the entire UI is *workbench*. The workbench itself has no physical manifestation, but the workbench object is used to access most of the general APIs and services available in the generic UI. The workbench is displayed in one or more *workbench windows*. These basic top-level windows make up an Eclipse application. Note that dialogs, wizards, and other transient pop-ups are not called workbench windows.

At the top of each window is the *title bar*, typically a native widget with a title and controls for resizing and closing. Next comes the *menu bar*, and after that is the *cool bar*. The cool bar is a fancy term for a bar of buttons that can be dragged around and reorganized across multiple lines. On the left, right, or bottom, depending on user preference, is the *fast view bar*, where *fast views*—iconified views—are stored. At the bottom is the *status line*, where various bits of information are shown; the far-right corner of the status line is called the *progress indicator*.

The main body of a workbench window is represented by the *workbench page*, which in turn is made up of *workbench parts*, which come in two varieties: *views* and *editors*. The initial size and orientation of the parts in the page are determined by a *perspective*.

Parts interact with the rest of the window via their *site*. The site is not a visible entity but simply an API mechanism to separate the methods that operate on the view from the methods that operate on controls and services outside the view. This allows the workbench implementers to add new features to the sites without breaking all the plug-ins that implement the parts. Figure 9.1 Spider graph shows how a view (`ContentOutline`) and an editor (`WelcomeEditor`) each has its own site, which is hosted by a page, inside a workbench window, owned by the workbench.

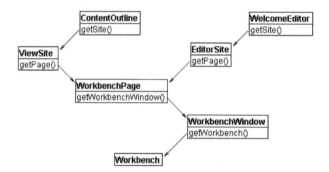

Figure 9.1   Spider diagram of site parts

In addition, sites bring together that functionality that different parts of the workbench had in common but could not be expressed well in a single inheritance hierarchy.

FAQ 193 *What is the difference between a perspective and a workbench page?*
FAQ 195 *What is a view?*
FAQ 206 *What is the difference between a view and an editor?*

How do I find out what object is selected?

The ISelectionService tracks all selection changes within the views and
editors of a workbench window or page. By adding a listener to this service, you
will be notified whenever the selection changes. Selections in views are typically
returned as IStructuredSelection instances, and selections in editors typically
implement ITextSelection. You should avoid any expensive computation from
within a selection listener, because this event fires quite frequently as the user is
moving around in the UI and typing in editors. A more efficient approach is to
avoid adding a listener, and simply asking the selection service for the current
selection when you need it.

You can also ask for the selection in a particular view by passing the view ID as
a parameter to the getSelection method:

```
IWorkbenchPage page = ...;
//the current selection in the entire page
ISelection selection = page.getSelection();
//the current selection in the navigator view
selection = page.getSelection(IPageLayout.ID_RES_NAV);
//add a listener
ISelectionListener sl = new ISelectionListener() {
   public void selectionChanged(IWorkbenchPart part,
      ISelection sel) {
      System.out.println("Selection is: " + sel);
   }
};
page.addSelectionListener(sl);
//add a listener to selection changes only
//in the navigator view
page.addSelectionListener(sl,
   IPageLayout.ID_RES_NAV);
```

IWorkbenchPage implements ISelectionService directly. You can also access
a selection service to track selection within a workbench window by using
IWorkbenchWindow.getSelectionService.

 FAQ 169 *How do I find out what view or editor is selected?*
FAQ 170 *How do I find the active workbench page?*
FAQ 203 *How do I make a view respond to selection changes in another view?*
FAQ 305 *How do I access the active project?*

How do I find out what view or editor is selected?

To find out what view or editor is selected, use the IPartService. As with ISelectionService, you can add a listener to this service to track the active part or simply query it whenever you need to know. Note, saying that the part is *active* does not imply that it has *focus*. If a dialog opens on top of the workbench window, the active part does not change, even though the active part loses focus. The part service will also notify you when parts are closed, hidden, brought to the top of a stack, and during other lifecycle events.

Two types of listeners can be added to the part service: IPartListener and the poorly named IPartListener2. You should always use this second one as it can handle part-change events on parts that have not yet been created because they are hidden in a stack behind another part. This listener will also tell you when a part is made visible or hidden or when an editor's input is changed:

```
IWorkbenchPage page = ...;
//the active part
IWorkbenchPart active = page.getActivePart();
//adding a listener
IPartListener2 pl = new IPartListener2() {
   public void partActivated(IWorkbenchPartReference ref)
      System.out.println("Active: "+ref.getTitle());
   }
   ... other listener methods ...
};
page.addPartListener(pl);
```

IWorkbenchPage implements IPartService directly. You can also access a activation service by using IWorkbenchWindow.getPartService.

FAQ 168 *How do I find out what object is selected?*
FAQ 170 *How do I find the active workbench page?*
FAQ 189 *Why do the names of some interfaces end with the digit 2?*

How do I find the active workbench page?

Many workbench APIs are accessible only from `IWorkbenchWindow` or
`IWorkbenchPage`. This generally raises the question, How do I get a reference to
a window or a page? As it turns out, the answer isn't always straightforward
There appears to be an obvious API on `IWorkbench` for getting this:

```
IWorkbench wb = PlatformUI.getWorkbench();
IWorkbenchWindow = win = wb.getActiveWorkbenchWindow();
IWorkbenchPage page = win.getActiveWorkbenchPage();
```

However, if you read the fine print on these methods, you'll see that they will
return `null` if the active shell is not a window. This means that when a dialog or
other shell has focus, you might not be able to sue these APIs to access the active
window or page.

To avoid getting `null` windows and pages, you can get your hands on a window
or a page in another way. From within the implementation of any view or editor,
you can do the following:

```
IWorkbenchPage page = getSite().getPage();
```

From an action defined in a workbench action set, you can access the window
from the `init` method:

```
class MyAction implements IWorkbenchWindowActionDelegate {
   private IWorkbenchWindow window;
   ...
   public void init(IWorkbenchWindow win) {
      this.window = win;
   }
}
```

Similarly, actions contributed to the `popupMenus` extension point always have an
initialization method that sets the current part before the action's `run` method is
called. All wizard extension points also have an `IWorkbenchWizard init`
method that supplies the wizard with the current workbench window before the
wizard is launched. In short, if you look carefully, you can almost always get at
the current window or page, no matter where you are in the Eclipse UI.

FAQ
171

How do I show progress on the workbench status line?

The status line has two areas for showing progress. The status line manager has a progress monitor that can be used when you want to block the user from continuing to work during an operation. This progress bar is used as follows:

```
IActionBars bars = getViewSite().getActionBars();
IStatusLineManager statusLine = bars.getStatusLineManager();
IProgressMonitor pm = statusLine.getProgressMonitor();
pm.beginTask("Doing work", IProgressMonitor.UNKNOWN);
pm.worked(1);
.... the actual work is done here...
pm.done();
```

If the amount of work to be done can be estimated ahead of time, a more intelligent value can be passed to `beginTask`, and calls to `worked` can be used to provide better progress feedback than a continuous animation.

The far right-hand side of the status line is used to show progress for things happening in the background. In other words, when progress is shown here, the user can generally continue working while the operation runs.

 FAQ 119 *How do I use progress monitors?*
FAQ 172 *Why should I use the new progress service?*
FAQ 185 *How do I show progress for things happening in the background?*

FAQ
172

Why should I use the new progress service?

Eclipse 3.0 introduced a central new workbench *progress service*. This service combines the advantages of busy cursors and Progress dialogs by switching from one to the other, depending on the length of the long-running task. The service also handles a further wrinkle caused by the introduction of background jobs. It is now possible for a short-running task to become blocked by a longer-running job running in the background, owing to contention for various resources. When this happens, the progress service opens a richer Progress dialog with a details area showing all running background jobs. This allows the user to see what is happening and to cancel either the foreground or the background task, depending on which is more important.

The service is used much like the SWT `BusyIndicator`. Simply pass an `IRunnableWithProgress` instance to the `busyCursorWhile` method. The UI will prevent further user input and report progress feedback until the runnable completes. Note that the runnable executes in a non-UI thread, so you will have to use `asyncExec` or `syncExec` to execute any code within the runnable that requires access to UI widgets:

```
IWorkbench wb = PlatformUI.getWorkbench();
IProgressService ps = wb.getProgressService();
ps.busyCursorWhile(new IRunnableWithProgress() {
    public void run(IProgressMonitor pm) {
        ... do some long running task
    }
});
```

This progress service was introduced to unify a number of progress-reporting mechanisms in Eclipse 2.1. JFace provides a Progress Monitor dialog, SWT provides a busy indicator, and the workbench provides a progress indicator on the status line. Each of these mechanisms has its own advantages and disadvantages. The busy cursor is the least obtrusive and works well for tasks that typically take a second or less. The Progress dialog provides much more information and allows the user to cancel but is visually distracting, especially on short tasks as it pops up over the user's work. The status line progress monitor is a bit less obtrusive but doesn't give an obvious indication that the UI is not accepting further input, and the space for presenting progress indication is very constrained. The new progress service tries to achieve a balance by automatically adapting between a busy cursor and a dialog, depending on the situation.

FAQ 140 *Why do I get an invalid thread access exception?*
FAQ 186 *How do I switch from using a Progress dialog to the Progress view?*
FAQ 218 *Actions, commands, operations, jobs: What does it all mean?*
FAQ 306 *What are `IWorkspaceRunnable`, `IRunnableWithProgress`, and `WorkspaceModifyOperation`?*

**FAQ
173**

How do I write a message to the workbench status line?

When pressing Ctrl+j in a text editor, the editor enters incremental find mode and prints messages in the status bar in the lower left-hand corner.
This can be done from within any view as follows:

```
IActionBars bars = getViewSite().getActionBars();
bars.getStatusLineManager().setMessage("Hello");
```

Editors can access the status line via IEditorActionBarContributor, which is given a reference to an IActionBars instance in its init method. The contributor is accessed from an editor by using

```
IEditorPart.getEditorSite().getActionBarContributor();
```

Note that the status line is shared by all views and editors. When the active part changes, the status line updates to show the new active part's message.

Parts can also specify an error message on the status line, using the method setErrorMessage. The error message, if provided, always takes precedence over any non-error message that was previously shown. When the error message is cleared, the non-error message is put back on the status line.

**FAQ
174**

How do I create a label decorator declaratively?

The workbench provides the org.eclipse.ui.decorators extension point, for contributing label decorators. These decorators can either be entirely declarative, or they can contribute an implementation of the interface called ILightweightLabelDecorator to perform the decoration. The mechanics of implementing decorators are well described in the online Eclipse articles and in the platform documentation.

 FAQ 153 *What is a label decorator?*
FAQ 175 *How do I add label decorations to my viewer?*
eclipse.org article "Understanding Decorators in Eclipse"
Go to **Platform Plug-in Developer Guide > Programmer's Guide > Plugging into the workbench > Other workbench extensions**

How do I add label decorations to my viewer?

Suppose that your viewer contains model elements for which other plug-ins have defined label decorators. To make those decorations appear in your viewer, you need to install a decorating label provider. Assuming that you have already written your own basic label provider, simply do the following to add declarative decorations from other plug-ins:

```
ILabelProvider lp = ... your basic label provider
ILabelDecorator decorator = PlatformUI.getWorkbench().
      getDecoratorManager().getLabelDecorator();
viewer.setLabelProvider(
      new DecoratingLabelProvider(lp, decorator));
```

FAQ 153 *What is a label decorator?*
FAQ 174 *How do I create a label decorator declaratively?*

How do I make the workbench shutdown?

You can force the workbench to exit by calling the `close` method on `IWorkbench`. This is the same behavior as would occur if the end user had selected **File > Exit**. If you want the workbench to close and immediately restart—for example, if a new plug-in has been installed and you have a plug-in that does not support dynamic plug-ins—you can instead call the `restart` method.

Note that although API exists for exiting and restarting the workbench, this measure is fairly drastic and should not be employed lightly. As support for dynamically installed plug-ins increases, it will become increasingly unacceptable to restart the workbench to install new plug-ins. At the very least, before calling either of these methods, you should prompt the user as to whether he or she want to exit.

**FAQ
177**

How can I use `IWorkbenchAdapter` to display my model elements?

The `IAdaptable` mechanism in Eclipse can be used to add visual presentation to your model objects without introducing UI code in your model layer. This follows the layering principle followed in the Eclipse Platform, where core code has no dependency on UI code. To do this, your model objects must implement the `IAdaptable` interface. This is typically achieved by simply subclassing `PlatformObject`, but if that's not possible, you can implement the interface directly. See the javadoc of `PlatformObject` for more details.

In your UI layer, you need to register an adapter factory that can return an implementation of `IWorbenchAdapter` for your model objects. If your adapter doesn't need to maintain any state, it's a good idea to make it a singleton to avoid creating extra objects for each model element. See the class `WorkbenchAdapterFactory` in the `org.eclipse.ui.ide` plug-in for an example of an adapter factory that creates `IWorkbenchAdapter` instances for `IResource` objects.

Once you have defined and registered such a factory, you can simply use `WorkbenchContentProvider` and `WorkbenchLabelProvider` in any tree or table viewer that contains your model objects. These special providers delegate their implementations to the underlying model objects by asking their `IWorkbenchAdapter` to compute the label or children of the elements.

 FAQ 126 *How do I use* `IAdaptable` *and* `IAdapterFactory`?

**FAQ
178**

How do I create my own preference page?

JFace provides infrastructure for creating and presenting preference pages within a Preference dialog. Pages implement `IPreferencePage`, usually by subclassing the default implementation `PreferencePage` or `FieldEditorPreferencePage`. The `org.eclipse.ui.workbench` plug-in defines an extension point for contributing preference pages to the workbench preference dialog, typically available via **Window > Preferences**. Note that you can use the preference page infrastructure without even using the preferences extension point if you want to present preference pages outside the standard workbench Preference dialog.

FAQ 161 *How do I launch the preference page that belongs to my plug-in?*
eclipse.org article "Preferences in the Eclipse Workbench UI (Revised for 2.0)"
eclipse.org article "Simplifying Preference Pages with Field Editors"
eclipse.org article "Mutatis Mutandis—Using Preference Pages as Property Pages"
Go to **Platform Plug-in Developer Guide > Programmer's Guide > Preference pages**

How do I use property pages?

FAQ
179

The workbench provides two facilities for presenting the properties of an object: the Property dialog and the Properties view.

The Property dialog is invoked by selecting an object and pressing Alt+Enter or by selecting **File > Properties**. The workbench provides an action, `PropertyDialogAction`, that you can add to your own view's menu for opening the Property dialog. The Property dialog contains pages contributed by the `org.eclipse.ui.propertyPages` extension point. Plug-ins can contribute pages in this way for any type of domain object.

The Properties view, also known as the property sheet, is not populated using an extension point but is activated through API, by the PDE editors, or manually, through **Window > Show View**. This view, like the Outline view, asks the active workbench part to contribute its contents. When a part becomes active, the property sheet asks it to adapt to `IPropertySheetPage`, using the `IAdaptable` mechanism:

```
IWorkbenchPart.getAdapter(IPropertySheetPage.class);
```

If it wants a completely customized property page, the part can respond to this request and provide its own page. If the part does not provide a page, the property sheet presents a default page that solicits key/value pairs from the active part's selection. This again uses the `IAdaptable` mechanism to ask the selected element whether it wants to contribute properties. This time it asks the element for an implementation of `IPropertySource`. The property source is responsible for providing its keys and values, changing values, and restoring default values.

FAQ 126 *How do I use* `IAdaptable` *and* `IAdapterFactory`?
FAQ 293 *How do I store extra properties on a resource?*
eclipse.org article "Take control of your properties"
eclipse.org article "Simplifying Preference Pages with Field Editors"
eclipse.org article "Mutatis mutandis—Using Preference Pages as Property
Pages"
Go to **Platform Plug-in Developer Guide > Programmer's Guide > IDE UI
Concepts**

**FAQ
180**

How do I open a Property dialog?

The Property dialog appears when you select an object in a view and choose
Properties... from the context menu or **File** menu. If you want such an action for
your own view or editor, you can simply add an instance of
`org.eclipse.ui.dialogs.PropertyDialogAction` to your view's context
menu. This action will compute what property pages are applicable for the
current selection and then open a dialog on those property pages.

You can also open a Property dialog on a set of property pages of your own
choosing. This works exactly like the JFace Preference dialog: You supply the
dialog with a `PreferenceManager` instance that knows how to build the set of
pages to be shown. The only difference with the Property dialog is that you must
also supply it with the current selection:

```
ISelection sel = ... obtain the current selection
PropertyPage page = new MyPropertyPage();
PreferenceManager mgr = new PreferenceManager();
IPreferenceNode node = new PreferenceNode("1", page);
mgr.addToRoot(node);
PropertyDialog dialog = new PropertyDialog(shell, mgr, sel);
dialog.create();
dialog.setMessage(page.getTitle());
dialog.open();
```

 FAQ 161 *How do I launch the preference page that belongs to my plug-in?*
FAQ 168 *How do I find out what object is selected?*

How do I add my wizard to the New, Import, or Export menu categories?

Some special kinds of wizards have to be registered with the platform in your `plugin.xml` file. These wizards are found under the **File > New**, **File > Import**, and **File > Export** menu actions. These wizards are declared using the `org.eclipse.ui newWizards`, `importWizards`, and `exportWizards` extension points, respectively. Once you have declared your wizard with the appropriate extension point, the platform will take care of displaying it in the appropriate places. Following is an example declaration of a new wizard:

```
<extension
      point="org.eclipse.ui.newWizards">
   <wizard
         name="New Addition"
         class="org.eclipse.faq.examples.AddingWizard"
         id="org.eclipse.faq.examples.addingWizard">
   </wizard>
</extension>
```

This wizard will appear by default under **File > New > Other...**. To make the wizard appear under the new-project category, add the attribute `project="true"` to the extension declaration.

To add your own wizard category, use

```
<category
      id="org.eclipse.faq.examples.MyWizard"
      name="FAQ Wizards">
</category>
<category
      id="org.eclipse.faq.examples.WizardSubCategory"
      name="More Specific FAQ Wizards"
      parentCategory="org.eclipse.faq.examples.MyWizard">
</category>
```

FAQ 159 *How do I make my wizard appear in the UI?*

Can I activate my plug-in when the workbench starts?

You shouldn't. The principle of lazy plug-in activation is very important in a platform with an open-ended set of plug-ins. All plug-in writers like to think that their plug-in are important enough to contravene this rule, but when an Eclipse install can contain thousands of plug-ins, you have to keep the big picture in mind. Having said that, you can use a mechanism to activate your plug-in when the workbench starts. In special circumstances or for hobby plug-ins that aren't meant for wider use, you can use the `org.eclipse.ui.startup` extension point to activate your plug-in as soon as the workbench starts up.

The `startup` extension point allows you to specify a class that implements the `IStartup` interface. If you omit the `class` attribute from the extension, your `Plugin` subclass will be used and therefore must implement `IStartup`. This class will be loaded in a background thread after the workbench starts, and its `earlyStartup` method will be run. As always, however, your `Plugin` class will be loaded first, and its `startup` method will be called before any other classes are loaded. The `earlyStartup` method essentially lets you distinguish eager activation from normal plug-in activation.

Note that even when this extension point is used, the user can always veto the eager activation from the **Workbench > Startup** preference page. This illustrates the general Eclipse principle that the user is always the final arbiter when conflicting demands on the platform are made. This also means that you can't rely on eager activation in a production environment. You will always need a fallback strategy when the user decides that your plug-in isn't as important as you thought it was.

 FAQ 101 *When does a plug-in get started?*

How do I create an image registry for my plug-in?

If you're writing a plug-in with UI components, it should be a subclass of
`AbstractUIPlugin`. This superclass already provides you with an empty image
registry accessible by calling `getImageRegistry`. When the registry is first
accessed, the hook method `initializeImageRegistry` will be called. You
should override this method to populate your image registry with the image
descriptors you need. You don't have to use this registry if you don't need it, and
because it is created lazily on first access, there is no performance overhead if
you never use it. Here is an example of a plug-in that adds a `sample.gif` image
to its image registry:

```
public class ExamplesPlugin extends AbstractUIPlugin {
   public static final String PLUGIN_ID =
                             "org.eclipse.faq.examples";
   public static final String IMAGE_ID = "sample.image";
   ...
   protected void initializeImageRegistry(
                             ImageRegistry registry) {
      Bundle bundle = Platform.getBundle(PLUGIN_ID);
      IPath path = new Path("icons/sample.gif");
      URL url = Platform.find(bundle, path);
      ImageDescriptor desc =
                 ImageDescriptor.createFromURL(url);
      registry.put(IMAGE_ID, desc);
   }
}
```

☞ **FAQ 154** *How do I use image and font registries?*
FAQ 184 *How do I use images defined by other plug-ins?*

How do I use images defined by other plug-ins?

In general, you should not rely on images defined in other plug-ins as they could
be changed or removed at any time. The exception to this rule is an image that
has been declared by a plug-in as an API. The convention is to create an interface
called `ISharedImages` that defines IDs for all images that you want to declare as
API. Several plug-ins, including `org.eclipse.ui.workbench`,
`org.eclipse.jdt.ui`, and `org.eclipse.team.ui`, declare such an

ISharedImages class. Here is an example snippet that options the folder icon
from the workbench's shared image API:

```
IWorkbench workbench = PlatformUI.getWorkbench();
ISharedImages images = workbench.getSharedImages();
Image image = images.getImage(ISharedImages.IMG_OBJ_FOLDER);
```

If you want to share images from your plug-in as API, you should define your
own ISharedImages class with constants for all the images you want to make
public.

 FAQ 183 *How do I create an image registry for my plug-in?*

**FAQ
185**

How do I show progress for things happening in the background?

A Progress view was introduced in Eclipse 3.0 to provide feedback for activities
occurring in the background. This view also allows the user to cancel background
activity and to find out details when errors occur in the background. The progress
animation icon on the right-hand side of the status line is also associated with this
view. The icon is animated whenever anything is running in the background.
There is no API for reporting progress directly to any of these progress
indicators.

These indicators are used to show progress reported by Job objects. The only
way to report progress in these areas is to create and schedule a background job.
When a Job instance is executed, an IProgressMonitor instance is passed to the
run method. Any progress sent to this monitor, including task and subtask names
and units of work completed, will be shown in the Progress view. Use this
monitor just as you would use a monitor in a Progress dialog.

 FAQ 119 *How do I use progress monitors?*
FAQ 127 *Does the platform have support for concurrency?*

FAQ
186

How do I switch from using a Progress dialog to the Progress view?

If you have an existing plug-in that uses a `ProgressMonitorDialog`, you can easily switch to using the Progress view by rewriting your operation as a `org.eclipse.core.runtime.Job`. Assume that your original code looks like this:

```
IRunnableWithProgress op = new IRunnableWithProgress() {
   public void run(IProgressMonitor monitor) {
      runDecathlon(monitor);
   }
};
IWorkbench wb = PlatformUI.getWorkbench();
IWorkbenchWindow win = wb.getActiveWorkbenchWindow();
Shell shell = win != null ? win.getShell() : null;
new ProgressMonitorDialog(shell).run(true, true, op);
```

The equivalent code using `org.eclipse.core.runtime.Job` would look like this:

```
class DecathlonJob extends Job {
   public DecathlonJob() {
      super("Athens decathlon 2004");
   }
   public IStatus run(IProgressMonitor monitor) {
      runDecathlon(monitor);
      return Status.OK_STATUS;
   }
};
new DecathlonJob().schedule();
```

Both use an `IProgressMonitor` to report progress to the user. The major difference is that the `ProgressMonitorDialog` is a modal dialog and blocks access to the entire UI during the execution of `runDecathlon`. When a `Job` is used, it will run in the background, and the user can continue working on something else.

Although the changes required here appear to be simply cosmetic, keep in mind that there are subtle implications to running your operation in the background. Foremost, you must ensure that your operation code is thread safe in case two copies of the operation start running simultaneously. You also need to think about whether your background operation will be in contention with other ongoing processes for exclusive resources, such as Java object monitors. Contention between threads can block the user interface; worse, it can lead to deadlock. Read up on your concurrent programming before you venture down this path.

 FAQ 119 *How do I use progress monitors?*
FAQ 127 *Does the platform have support for concurrency?*
FAQ 218 *Actions, commands, operations, jobs: What does it all mean?*

FAQ 187

Can I make a job run in the UI thread?

If you create and schedule a simple job, its `run` method will be called outside the UI thread. If you want to schedule a job that accesses UI widgets, you should subclass `org.eclipse.ui.progress.UIJob` instead of the base `Job` class. The UI job's `runInUIThread` method will, as the name implies, always be invoked from the UI thread. Make sure that you don't schedule UI jobs that take a long time to run because anything that runs in the UI thread will make the UI unresponsive until it completes.

Although running a UI job is much like using the SWT's `Display` methods `asyncExec` and `timerExec`, UI jobs have a few distinct advantages.

- They can have scheduling rules to prevent them from running concurrently with jobs in other threads that may conflict with them.

- You can install a listener on the job to find out when it completes.

- You can specify a priority on the job so the platform can decide not to run it immediately if it is not as important.

 FAQ 127 *Does the platform have support for concurrency?*
FAQ 140 *Why do I get an invalid thread access exception?*

Are there any special Eclipse UI guidelines?

FAQ
188

A wealth of Eclipse UI guidelines exists. Mentioning any in this single FAQ would seem to do no justice to Nick Edgar, Kevin Haaland, Jin Li, and Kimberley Peter. Please refer to their online Eclipse article "Eclipse User Interface Guidelines." In their seminal work, they brush on such topics as icon sizes and color palettes, wizards, editors, dialogs, commands, views, perspectives, windows, properties, widgets, navigators, tasks, preferences, outlines, properties, bookmarks, text editors, the flat-look design, accelerators, best practices, and a checklist for developers.

In fact, the 100-page article is a great source of inspiration for any plug-in developer. Study it before you create any Eclipse plug-in with a visual representation to avoid mistakes made by others and to learn from the experts how to design high-quality UI designs.

 eclipse.org article "Eclipse User Interface Guidelines"

Why do the names of some interfaces end with the digit 2?

FAQ
189

Owing to evolution in the use of Eclipse, some interfaces had to be extended with additional functionality. However, because of the dynamic nature of Eclipse, with many products relying on existing plug-ins, changing the signature of an interface requires that all the downstream plug-ins be not only recompiled but also fixed to implement the new methods required by the interface change.

This evolutionary side effect posed a big dilemma: cause all plug-ins to break and require intrusive enhancements from customers or introduce a totally new interface containing only the new functionality? Eclipse has chosen the second option. When you press Ctrl+Shift+T to locate a type and enter I*2, you will be shown a list of 20 such interfaces.

Note that additional overhead can occur. For instance, in class
`org.eclipse.ui.internal.PluginAction`, special code needs to verify that
the target implements the interface:

```
public void runWithEvent(Event event) {
    ...
    if (delegate instanceof IActionDelegate2) {
        ((IActionDelegate2)delegate).runWithEvent(this, event);
        return;
    }
    // Keep for backward compatibility with R2.0
    if (delegate instanceof IActionDelegateWithEvent) {
        ((IActionDelegateWithEvent) delegate).
            runWithEvent(this, event);
        return;
    }
    ...
}
```

The code gets messy owing to an early decision to name the interface differently.
Although interfaces were added to Java to separate *types* from their
implementations, in the case of a successfully adopted platform such as Eclipse,
they are not resilient to evolution. Changing them breaks too much existing code.
If subclassing is used, the contract can easily be enhanced with a default
implementation in the base class. The subclasses would not have to be changed
or even recompiled.

Chapter 10. Perspectives and Views

This chapter answers questions about two central concepts in the Eclipse Platform UI. *Perspectives* define the set of actions and parts that appear in a workbench window and specify the initial size and position of views within that window. *Views* are the draggable parts that make up the bulk of a workbench window's contents. This chapter does not deal with any specific perspectives or views, but with questions that arise when you implement your own perspectives and views.

How do I create a new perspective?

FAQ 190

Use the `org.eclipse.ui.perspectives` extension point. This extension point allows you to define an initial layout of views relative to the editor area, in addition to specifying the contents of the window's menu and toolbars. Everything you can do from **Window > Customize Perspective** can be done programmatically with the `perspectives` extension point. The steps for creating your own perspective are well described in the *Platform Plug-in Developer Guide*.

☞ eclipse.org article "Using Perspectives in the Eclipse UI"
Go to **Platform Plug-in Developer Guide > Programmer's Guide > Plugging into the workbench > Perspectives**

How can I add my views and actions to an existing perspective?

FAQ 191

Use the `org.eclipse.ui.perspectiveExtensions` extension point. This extension point allows a third party to define the position of views in another plug-in's perspective. This extension point can also be used to add actions to the menus and toolbars. An interesting attribute of this extension point is that it is purely declarative. No Java code is associated with a perspective extension; it is purely XML markup. The mechanics of writing perspective extensions are well described in the *Platform Plug-in Developer Guide*.

eclipse.org article "Using Perspectives in the Eclipse UI"
Go to **Platform Plug-in Developer Guide > Programmer's Guide > Plugging into the workbench > Perspectives**

FAQ
192

How do I show a given perspective?

Two APIs show a perspective: `IWorkbench.showPerspective` and `IWorkbenchPage.setPerspective`. You should generally use the first of these two because it will honor the user's preference on whether perspectives should be opened in the same window or in a separate window. Here's a quick sample snippet that opens the perspective with ID `perspectiveID`:

```
IWorkbench workbench = PlatformUI.getWorkbench();
workbench.showPerspective(perspectiveID,
    workbench.getActiveWorkbenchWindow());
```

Usually, the method `getActiveWorkbenchWindow` comes with the caveat that you must check for a `null` return value. In this case, `null` is acceptable: The `showPerspective` method uses the window parameter as a hint about what window to show the perspective in. If a `null` window is passed, it will pick an appropriate existing window or open a new one.

FAQ
193

What is the difference between a perspective and a workbench page?

The workbench page is the main body of a workbench window: between the toolbar and the status line, the area that contains views and editors. In Eclipse 1.0, each workbench window could have multiple pages, but this is no longer the case. The workbench page can have one or more perspectives associated with it that define the layout of the views and editors in the page. Each workbench page has at most one instance of each kind of view and one editor per unique editor input. When the perspective is changed, the position and visibility of views and editors change, but the set of open views and editors does not change.

 FAQ 167 *Pages, parts, sites, windows: What is all this stuff?*

How do I create fixed views and perspectives?

New APIs in Eclipse 3.0 allow perspectives more control over how their views are presented. These APIs are useful in RCP applications that want different view-presentation models. The `IPageLayout` interface, provided when your perspective factory is creating its initial layout, has methods for customizing how views will be presented in that perspective. The `setFixed` method on `IPageLayout` indicates that a perspective should be *fixed*. In a fixed perspective, views and editors cannot be moved or zoomed by the user.

A *stand-alone view*, created with the method `addStandaloneView`, cannot be stacked together with other views and can optionally hide its title bar. A view with its title bar hidden cannot be closed, minimized, or moved. For further control over whether views can be closed or moved, you can obtain an `IViewLayout` instance for any view in the perspective. Following is an example of a fixed perspective that creates a stand-alone view above the editor area that cannot be moved or closed.

```
class RecipePerspective implements IPerspectiveFactory {
    public void createInitialLayout(IPageLayout page) {
        page.setEditorAreaVisible(true);
        page.setFixed(true);
        page.addStandaloneView(
            RecipePlugin.VIEW_CATEGORIES,
            false, IPageLayout.TOP, 0.2f,
            IPageLayout.ID_EDITOR_AREA);
        IViewLayout view = page.getViewLayout(
            RecipePlugin.VIEW_CATEGORIES);
        view.setCloseable(false);
        view.setMoveable(false);
    }
}
```

You can add fixed and stand-alone views to perspectives from other plug-ins using the `perspectiveExtensions` extension point. See the extension point documentation for more details.

☞ **FAQ 191** *How can I add my views and actions to an existing perspective?*
FAQ 199 *Why can't I control when, where, and how my view is presented?*

FAQ 195

What is a view?

Views are one of the two kinds of parts that make up a workbench window. At their most basic, views are simply a subclass of the SWT `Composite` class, containing arbitrary controls below a title bar. The title bar contains the view name, an area for toolbar buttons, and one or two drop-down menus. The drop-down menu on the upper left is simply the standard shell menu with actions for moving, resizing, and closing the view. The menu on the upper right and the button area are the view's *action bar* and may contain arbitrary actions defined by the implementer of that view.

A view interacts with the rest of the workbench via its *site*. Browse through the interfaces `IViewSite`, `IWorkbenchPartSite`, and `IWorkbenchSite` to see what site services are available to a view.

 FAQ 146 *What is a viewer?*
FAQ 167 *Pages, parts, sites, windows: What is all this stuff?*
FAQ 196 *What is the difference between a view and a viewer?*
FAQ 206 *What is the difference between a view and an editor?*

FAQ 196

What is the difference between a view and a viewer?

An unfortunate choice of terminology resulted in one of the basic building blocks of the Eclipse workbench having a remarkably similar name to a central construct in JFace. The apprentice Eclipse programmer often falls into the trap of using the terms *view* and *viewer* interchangeably and then becomes horribly confused by conflicting accounts of their usage. In reality, they are completely different and fundamentally unrelated constructs. As outlined earlier, JFace viewers are SWT widget adapters that, among other things, perform transformations between model objects and view objects. Views, on the other hand, are one of the two kinds of visible parts that make up a workbench window.

To confuse matters, a view often contains a viewer. The Navigator view, for example, contains a tree viewer. This is not always true, however. A view may contain no viewers, or it may contains several viewers. Viewers can also appear outside of views; for example, in dialogs or editors. In short, views and viewers have no fixed relationship. To put it mathematically, they are orthogonal concepts that often intersect.

FAQ 146 *What is a viewer?*
FAQ 195 *What is a view?*

How do I create my own view?

FAQ
197

The simplest way is to use the PDE wizard to create a view example and go from there. Select **File > New > Other... > Plug-in Development > Plug-in Project**, and choose a name and ID for your plug-in. Then, in the plug-in code generator wizard page, choose **Plug-in with a view**. Look at the generated `plugin.xml` file for the generated extension point code.

To add a view to an existing plug-in, edit your `plugin.xml` with the Manifest Editor, choose the **Extensions** tab, click **Add...**, select **Extension Templates**, and choose **Sample View**.

To see how other plug-ins use views, search on the `org.eclipse.ui.views` extension point in the Search dialog. Choose the **Plug-in Search** tab, and enter the name of the extension point.

How do I set the size or position of my view?

FAQ
198

The short answer is that you can't always control the size and position of your view. If you create your own perspective, you can specify the initial size and position of the view relative to other views. Once the perspective has been opened, the user is free to move the view elsewhere and change its size. At this point, you no longer have control over the view's size and position.

In a similar manner, you can influence the initial size and position of your view in other perspectives by using the `perspectiveExtensions` extension point. As with perspectives, this extension point allows you to specify the size and position of your view relative to other views that are known to be in that perspective. Note that you shouldn't generally make your view appear by default in perspectives provided by other plug-ins. If many plug-ins did this, the host perspective would quickly become cluttered and difficult to use. To ensure that your view does not appear by default, specify the attribute `visible="false"` in your extension declaration.

FAQ 190 *How do I create a new perspective?*
FAQ 191 *How can I add my views and actions to an existing perspective?*
FAQ 199 *Why can't I control when, where, and how my view is presented?*

Why can't I control when, where, and how my view is presented?

Plug-in writers implementing views are often frustrated by their lack of control over when and how their views are presented to the user. Common questions include the following:

- How do I control when users can open my view?

- How do I ensure that my two views are always open at the same time?

- How do I make a view appear in a floating shell or dialog?

- How can I ensure that my view is a certain size?

The answer to such questions is more philosophical than some plug-in writers would like.

As an integration platform, Eclipse must balance between customizability and conformity. The platform needs to be customizable in order to adapt to the unforeseeable needs of plug-ins being integrated into the platform. On the other hand, in order to provide a coherent user experience, components need to be presented consistently. The ultimate goal is for the user to perceive the end product as a coherent and self-consistent application rather than as a collection of isolated components that don't know anything about one another.

The platform seeks this balance with views by giving the view implementer limited control over how views are presented. The view writer has control over the body of the view but little or no control over where the view appears in the workbench page, what size it has, and when it is opened or closed. This approach prevents individual views from exerting too much control over the rest of the workbench window. Because the view implementer can never foresee exactly what configuration of views and editors the end user may want to have open, it cannot make reasonable choices about what happens beyond its borders. Only users are in a position to know exactly what kind of layout they want.

Giving limited power to individual views also gives the platform the flexibility to change its look and feel between releases without breaking API compatibility. For example, version 1.0 of the platform allowed views to float as separate shells outside the workbench window, but this capability was removed in version 2.0. The API designers expose only functionality that they are confident can be supported for the long term.

☞ **FAQ 194** *How do I create fixed views and perspectives?*

How will my view show up in the Show View menu?

FAQ 200

All views show up automatically under **Show View > Other...**. The `category` attribute in your view extension declaration defines what folder your view appears under in this dialog. And no, you cannot prevent your view from appearing in this dialog.

The active perspective defines the set of views that appear in the **Show View** submenu. If you define your own perspective or a perspective extension to another plug-in's perspective, you get to contribute entries to this list. The user is always allowed to customize the perspective to change the set of views that appear here.

☞ **FAQ 190** *How do I create a new perspective?*
FAQ 191 *How can I add my views and actions to an existing perspective?*

How do I make my view appear in the Show In menu?

The **Navigate > Show In** menu displays a list of views that the user can jump to from the active editor or view. This facility allows linking between views and editors that may not even know about each other. The active perspective gets to decide what views appear in this list, but you can contribute your views to this list by using the `perspectiveExtensions` extension point. Here is an extension definition that adds the bookshelf example Chapters view to the **Show In** menu of the Resource perspective:

```
<extension
    point="org.eclipse.ui.perspectiveExtensions">
    <perspectiveExtension targetID =
        "org.eclipse.ui.resourcePerspective">
    <showInPart id = "org.eclipse.faq.examples.ChaptersView"/>
    </perspectiveExtension>
</extension>
```

The Chapters view then implements the `show` method from the `IShowInTarget` interface. This method is called by the platform when the user selects the view in the **Show In** menu. The method has a parameter, `ShowInContext`, that is passed from the view that is the source of the **Show In** action. The method must return `true` if it accepts the context as a valid input for that view and `false` otherwise. Here is the example implementation from the Chapters view:

```
public boolean show(ShowInContext context) {
    if (viewer == null || context == null)
        return false;
    ISelection sel = context.getSelection();
    if (sel instanceof IStructuredSelection) {
        IStructuredSelection ss = (IStructuredSelection)sel;
        Object first = ss.getFirstElement();
        if (first instanceof Book) {
            viewer.setInput(first);
            return true;
        }
    }
    return false;
}
```

A view that wants to act as a source for the **Show In** menu must implement `IShowInSource`. This interface defines the method `getShowInContext`, which creates the context object to be passed to the target. In our bookshelf example, the Books view will act as a **Show In** source by implementing the `getShowInContext` method as follows:

```
public ShowInContext getShowInContext() {
    return new ShowInContext(null, viewer.getSelection());
}
```

The context instance may contain an input object and a selection. If your view needs to provide extra context information, you can create your own `ShowInContext` subclass that carries additional data. Of course, only views that know about that special subclass will be able to make use of the extra information, so you should also provide the basic context information if you can.

☞ **FAQ 191** *How can I add my views and actions to an existing perspective?*

How do I add actions to a view's menu and toolbar?

FAQ
202

Each view has a drop-down menu in two locations:

- *Under the icon on the view's tab item.* This menu contains layout and view-manipulation actions. You don't have any control over this menu; its actions are all added by the platform.

- *In the view's toolbar.* The drop-down menu on the right-hand side, a small downward-pointing triangle, is controlled by your view. This menu will exist only if you add actions to it.

Actions are added to the menu and toolbar by using the `IActionBars` interface. This interface is used to access the standard JFace menu and toolbar manager objects used for creating menus throughout Eclipse.

The following code, usually invoked from the view's `createPartControl` method, adds a single action to the view's menu and toolbar:

```
Action action = ...;
IActionBars actionBars = getViewSite().getActionBars();
IMenuManager dropDownMenu = actionBars.getMenuManager();
IToolBarManager toolBar = actionBars.getToolBarManager();
dropDownMenu.add(action);
toolBar.add(action);
```

 FAQ 232 *How do I build menus and toolbars programmatically?*

FAQ 203

How do I make a view respond to selection changes in another view?

Views can be made to respond to selection changes in other views with `org.eclipse.ui.ISelectionService`. A selection service allows views to work together without having to couple their views tightly. It also adds flexibility and extensibility to your design.

Say you have one view that shows a list of books and another view that displays the chapters within a book. When the user selects a book in the first view, you want to display the chapters of that book in the second view. Now say that another plug-in is installed that provides a graphical Book view and a Metrics view that displays various metrics about a selected book. If your original views were linked using explicit coupling, selection changes in your Books view would not activate the Metrics view. Conversely, selection changes in the graphical Books view would not correctly update your Chapters view. Using the selection service gives an opportunity for other plug-ins to connect to your view by listening to your selection changes or providing selections that your views can respond to.

Follow three simple steps to make use of an `ISelectionService` in your views. First, find an appropriate selection service. Two selection services are available to a view: window selection and page selection. The first is used for tracking selection changes in an entire workbench window, and the second is constrained to selection changes within a single page. Typically, you want to track selection changes only within the current page. Because only one page is visible at a time anyway, responding to selection changes in other pages is generally a waste of effort. The window-selection service is accessible via

`IWorkbenchWindow.getSelectionService`. The page-selection service extends the `ISelectionService` interface and is available from `IWorkbenchPage`.

Second, register the view-selection provider with the selection service. The view that wants to broadcast selection changes simply has to register itself with the `ISelectionService` by supplying an implementation of `org.eclipse.jface.viewers ISelectionProvider`. In most cases, your view will contain a JFace viewer, all of which implement `ISelectionProvider` directly. If your view does not contain a viewer, you will have to implement the `ISelectionProvider` interface directly. Here is a sample of a view's `createPartControl` method, which creates a viewer and then registers it with the page-selection service:

```
public void createPartControl(Composite parent) {
    int style = SWT.SINGLE | SWT.H_SCROLL | SWT.V_SCROLL;
    viewer = new TableViewer(parent, style);
    getSite().setSelectionProvider(viewer);
    ...
}
```

The final step is to register a selection listener with the selection service. The view that wants to respond to selection changes must register an implementation of `org.eclipse.ui ISelectionListener` with the selection service. The following example defines the Chapters view described earlier. This view responds to selection changes where the selection is a book and displays the chapters of that book. It is important for your selection listener to ignore selections that it does not understand. The selection service will be broadcasting all kinds of selection changes that are not relevant to your view, so you need to listen selectively.

```
public class ChaptersView extends ViewPart {
    private TableViewer viewer;
    ISelectionListener listener = new ISelectionListener() {
        public void selectionChanged(IWorkbenchPart part,
            ISelection sel) {
            if (!(sel instanceof IStructuredSelection))
                return;
            IStructuredSelection ss = (IStructuredSelection) sel;
            Object o = ss.getFirstElement();
            if (o instanceof Book)
                viewer.setInput(ss.size()==1 ? o : null);
        }
    };
    public void createPartControl(Composite parent) {
        ...
```

```
        getSite().getPage().addSelectionListener(listener);
    }
    public void dispose() {
        getSite().getPage().removeSelectionListener(listener);
    }
}
```

Again, note how this example completely ignores selections that don't contain books. If the selection contains a single book, the view will display its chapters. If the selection contains several books, it will display nothing. Also note in this example that the view is responsible for removing the selection listener when it closes. As a general rule with listeners, the code for adding a listener should never be very far from the code for removing the listener. If you forget to remove your listener when the view is closed, your selection listener will cause errors later on.

☞ **FAQ 168** *How do I find out what object is selected?*

**FAQ
204**

How does a view persist its state between sessions?

Storing view state is done in two commons ways, depending on whether you want to store settings between workbench sessions or across invocations of your view. The first of these facilities is found directly on `IViewPart`. When the workbench is shut down, the method `saveState` is called on all open views. The parameter to this method is an `IMemento`, a simple data structure that stores hierarchies of nodes containing numbers and strings.

Here is an example from the recipe application in the FAQ examples, where a view is persisting the current selection of a list viewer in a memento:

```
private static final String STORE_SELECTION =
    "ShoppingList.SELECTION";
public void saveState(IMemento memento) {
    super.saveState(memento);
    ISelection sel = viewer.getSelection();
    IStructuredSelection ss = (IStructuredSelection) sel;
    StringBuffer buf = new StringBuffer();
    for (Iterator it = ss.iterator(); it.hasNext();) {
        buf.append(it.next());
        buf.append(',');
    }
```

```
        memento.putString(STORE_SELECTION, buf.toString());
    }
```

When the workbench is reopened, the method `init(IViewSite, IMemento)` is
called the first time each view becomes visible. The `IMemento` will contain all the
information that was added to it when the workbench was shut down. Note that
`init` is called before the `createPartControl` method, so you will not be able to
restore widget state directly from the `init` method. You can store the `IMemento`
instance in a field and restore state later on when your widgets have been created.
Continuing this example, here is the code for restoring the viewer selection when
the view is reopened:

```
private IMemento memento;
...
public void init(IViewSite site, IMemento memento)
    throws PartInitException {
    super.init(site, memento);
    this.memento = memento;
}
public void createPartControl(Composite parent) {
    //create widgets ...
    if (memento == null) return;
    String value = memento.getString(STORE_SELECTION);
    if (value == null) return;
    IStructuredSelection ss = new StructuredSelection(
        value.split(","));
    viewer.setSelection(ss);
}
```

Note that the `IMemento` instance can be `null` if the view state was not saved from
a previous session; for example, when the view is first created.

Another mechanism for persisting view state is the JFace `IDialogSettings`
facility. The advantage of dialog settings over the view `save`/`init` mechanism is
that you can control when settings are persisted. The `saveState` method is called
only if your view is open when the workbench shuts down, so it is not useful for
storing view state when the view is closed by the user. Dialog settings, on the
other hand, can be changed and persisted whenever you want.

Views commonly use a combination of both dialog settings and a memento for
persisting view state. Important settings, such as filters, sorters, and other view
preferences, will be stored as dialog settings; more transient attributes, such as
selection and expansion state, will be stored in the memento only when the
workbench is being shut down.

FAQ 166 *How do I save settings for a dialog or wizard?*

FAQ
205

How do I open multiple instances of the same view?

Eclipse 3.0 lifts the restriction of allowing only a single instance of each view type. You can now open any number of copies of a given view. Each copy needs a secondary ID to disambiguate the view reference. Here is a snippet that opens two copies of the Books view from the FAQ Examples plug-in:

```
IWorkbenchPage page = ...;
String id = "org.eclipse.faq.examples.BooksView";
page.showView(id, "1", IWorkbenchPage.VIEW_VISIBLE);
page.showView(id, "2", IWorkbenchPage.VIEW_ACTIVATE);
```

The first parameter is the view ID from the extension definition in the plugin.xml file. The second parameter is an arbitrary string that is used to identify that particular copy of the view. Finally, the third parameter is used to specify whether the view should be created but not made visible (VIEW_CREATE), created and made visible but not made active (VIEW_VISIBLE), or created and made visible and active (VIEW_ACTIVATE).

Once multiple copies of a view exist, they can be located by using the method IWorkbenchPage.findViewReference, where the primary and secondary view IDs are passed as a parameter.

Chapter 11. Generic Editors

In Eclipse, editors are parts that have an associated input inside a workbench window and additional lifecycle methods, such as `save` and `revert`. This chapter answers questions about interacting with editors and about writing your own editors, whether they are text based or graphical. See Chapter 15 for a complete treatment of questions about writing your own text-based editors.

What is the difference between a view and an editor?

FAQ 206

When they first start to write plug-ins that contribute visual components, people are often confused about whether they should write a view or an editor. Superficially, the two appear to be very similar: Both are parts that make up a workbench page, both can contain arbitrary visual subcomponents, and both have various mechanisms for plugging in actions and menus. Let's start with some common misconceptions about the differences between views and editors.

- Editors display the contents of a file, and views contain groups of files or things other than files. Wrong. Both editors and views can have arbitrary contents from a file or multiple files or be from something that is not a file at all.

- Editors display text and views display tables or trees. Wrong again. There are no constraints about what goes into an editor or a view. For example, the plug-in Manifest Editor is form-based, whereas the Console view shows plain text.

What are the real differences between views and editors? Here are the main ones.

- There is generally only one instance of a given view per workbench page, but there can be several instances of the same type of editor.

- Editors can appear in only one region of the page, whereas views can be moved to any part of the page and minimized as fast views.

- Editors can be in a dirty state, meaning that their contents are unsaved and will be lost if the editor is closed without saving.

- Views have a local toolbar, whereas editors contribute buttons to the global toolbar.

- Editors can be associated with a file name or an extension, and this association can be changed by users.

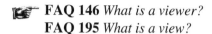 **FAQ 146** *What is a viewer?*
FAQ 195 *What is a view?*

**FAQ
207**

How do I open an editor programmatically?

Use the `openEditor` methods on `org.eclipse.ui.IWorkbenchPage` to open an editor on a given input. The `openEditor` methods require you to supply the ID of the editor to open. You can use the editor registry to find out what editor ID is appropriate for a given file name, using the `getDefaultEditor` method on `IEditorRegistry`. In Eclipse 3.0, the editor opening methods that were specific to `IFile` were moved to the `IDE` class.

```
IWorkbenchPage page = ...;
IFile file = ...;
IEditorDescriptor desc = PlatformUI.getWorkbench().
    getEditorRegistry().getDefaultEditor(file.getName());
page.openEditor(
    new FileEditorInput(file),
    desc.getId());
```

 FAQ 38 *Is Eclipse 3.0 going to break all of my old plug-ins?*
FAQ 170 *How do I find the active workbench page?*
FAQ 300 *How do I open an editor on a file in the workspace?*

**FAQ
208**

How do I open an external editor?

A special editor ID is used to indicate that a file should be opened using an external editor. When you ask it to open an editor with this ID, the platform delegates to the operating system to select and open an appropriate editor for the given input. This ID can be used to open an editor on `IFile` instances or on any other kind of input that implements `IPathEditorInput`. Here is an example snippet that opens an external editor on an `IFile` instance:

```
IWorkbenchPage page = ...;
IFile file = ...;
page.openEditor(
   new FileEditorInput(file),
   IEditorRegistry.SYSTEM_EXTERNAL_EDITOR_ID);
```

Note that this technique applies only to Eclipse 3.0 or greater. On older versions of Eclipse, a special convenience method, openSystemEditor on IWorkbenchPage, accomplished the same task. This method was removed from the workbench API as part of the Eclipse 3.0 rich client refactoring.

☞ **FAQ 170** *How do I find the active workbench page?*
FAQ 300 *How do I open an editor on a file in the workspace?*

How do I dynamically register an editor to handle a given extension?

FAQ
209

You can't. Editors, like most other extensions to the platform, must be specified declaratively in the plug-in manifest file. You cannot dynamically install a new editor except by dynamically installing a new plug-in containing the new editor.

The only thing you *can* currently do programmatically is specify the default editor to use for a given file name or extension. The editor must already be registered with the platform through a plug-in and must already declare that it supports files with that name or extension.

Here is an example snippet that sets the default editor for text files to be the built-in platform text editor:

```
IEditorRegistry registry =
        PlatformUI.getWorkbench().getEditorRegistry();
registry.setDefaultEditor("*.txt",
        "org.eclipse.ui.DefaultTextEditor");
```

☞ **FAQ 211** *How do I create my own editor?*

FAQ 210

How do I switch to `vi` or `emacs`-style key bindings?

Eclipse has a built-in key-binding configuration that emulates `emacs`-style key bindings. You can switch to this mode by using the **Keys** preference page. There is no equivalent configuration setting to emulate `vi`, largely because of its mode-oriented approach. On the Web, however, there is a plug-in that emulates `vi`-style key bindings in Eclipse.

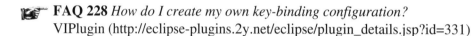 **FAQ 228** *How do I create my own key-binding configuration?*
VIPlugin (http://eclipse-plugins.2y.net/eclipse/plugin_details.jsp?id=331)

FAQ 211

How do I create my own editor?

All editors start by making a subclass of `EditorPart` from the `org.eclipse.ui.part` package. At this basic level, editors are very generic. They take an input object that implements `IEditorInput`, they know how to draw themselves by implementing the `createPartControl` method, and they may know how to respond to a request to save their contents. To create a bare-bones editor, you have to implement only a small handful of methods. Figure 11.1 shows a working editor that displays a simple label.

Figure 11.1 A minimal editor

Some required methods, declared abstract in `EditorPart`, have been omitted from this snippet, but the editor will work if their implementations are empty:

```
public class MinimalEditor extends EditorPart {
    private Label contents;
    public void createPartControl(Composite parent) {
        contents = new Label(parent, SWT.NONE);
        contents.setText("Minimal Editor");
    }
```

```
public void init(IEditorSite site, IEditorInput input) {
    setSite(site);
    setInput(input);
}
public void setFocus() {
    if (contents != null)
        contents.setFocus();
}
}
```

The plug-in manifest entry for defining this editor is as follows:

```
<editor
    name="Minimal Editor"
    extensions="min"
    icon="icons/sample.gif"
    class="org.eclipse.faq.examples.editor.MinimalEditor"
    id="org.eclipse.faq.examples.editor.MinimalEditor">
</editor>
```

The `extensions` attribute describes what file types this editor will automatically be associated with. In this case, the editor will be associated with files ending in `min`. An editor can instead be associated with a particular file name by replacing the `extensions` attribute with a `filenames` attribute. Either of these attributes can specify a comma-separated list for associating an editor with multiple file name extensions and/or file names. A user can always choose to associate an editor with a different file name or extension from the **Workbench > File Associations** preference page.

 FAQ 264 *How do I get started with creating a custom text editor?*
FAQ 335 *How do I write an editor for my own language?*

How do I enable the Save and Revert actions?

FAQ
212

An editor with unsaved changes is said to be *dirty*. If an editor is closed while dirty, changes made in the editor since the last save should be discarded. The framework asks an editor whether it is dirty by calling the `IEditorPart` method `isDirty`. When the dirty state of an editor changes, it lets the world know by firing a property change event, `IEditorPart.PROP_DIRTY`, on the property.

Here are the relevant minimal-editor example sections that control the dirty state:

```
public class MinimalEditor extends EditorPart {
   protected boolean dirty = false;
   ...
   public boolean isDirty() {
      return dirty;
   }
   protected void setDirty(boolean value) {
      dirty = value;
      firePropertyChange(PROP_DIRTY);
   }
}
```

The editor **Save** action should persist the current editor contents and then set the dirty state to `false`. Unlike most actions that are defined within an instance of `IAction`, the editor **Save** and **Save As...** actions are built directly into the editor part. These actions are always enabled when the editor is in a dirty state. The editor must support these actions by implementing the methods on `ISaveablePart`, which is extended by `IEditorPart`. Here are trivial implementations of these methods from the minimal-editor example:

```
public void doSave(IProgressMonitor monitor) {
   setDirty(false);
}
public void doSaveAs() {
   doSave(null);
}
public boolean isSaveAsAllowed() {
   return false;
}
```

Unlike the **Save** action, the **Revert** action is not built into the editor framework. The **Revert** action is one of the standard workbench global actions and is entirely optional for editors to implement. The global action is hooked in just like other global actions. The **Revert** action should be equivalent to closing an editor without saving, then reopening on the previously saved contents. Like the **Save** action, it should change the dirty state to `false` and fire a property change event on `IEditorPart.PROP_DIRTY` when it completes successfully.

☞ **FAQ 213** *How do I enable global actions such as **Cut**, **Paste**, and **Print** in my editor?*

How do I enable global actions such as Cut, Paste, and Print in my editor?

Your editor's `IEditorActionBarContributor`, defined in the editor definition in the `plugin.xml` file, is responsible for enabling global actions. Whenever your editor becomes the active part, the method `setActiveEditor` is called on the action bar contributor. This is where you can retarget the global actions for your editor. Keep in mind that each editor type has only one editor action bar contributor, so you need to update your actions to reflect the current editor. In this example, the global **Print** action is being retargeted to the active editor:

```
IAction print = ...;
public void setActiveEditor(IEditorPart part) {
   IActionBars bars= getActionBars();
   if (bars == null)
      return;
   print.setEditor(part);
   bars.setGlobalActionHandler(
      IWorkbenchActionConstants.PRINT, print);
   bars.updateActionBars();
}
```

☞ **FAQ 231** *How do I hook into global actions, such as **Copy** and **Delete**?*

How do I hook my editor to the Back and Forward buttons?

Each workbench page maintains a navigation history of interesting locations that have been visited in the page's editors. All editors, not only text editors, can contribute locations to this history, allowing the user to quickly jump between these locations by using the **Back** and **Forward** buttons on the toolbar. To enable this, your editor must implement `INavigationLocationProvider`. This interface is used to ask an editor to create an `INavigationLocation` object, which is a representation of the current editor state. When the user clicks the **Back** or **Forward** button, the previous or next location in the history restores its position using the `restoreLocation` method on `INavigationLocation`.

The contract that should be followed for an INavigationLocation is that when the user jumps in one direction, a subsequent jump in the opposite direction should take the user back to the starting point. To support this, your implementation of restoreLocation must add a history entry for the current location before restoring the old location.

You can imagine that this will quickly lead to duplication of entries if the user continues to jump backward and forward several times. This duplication is avoided by the mergeInto method on INavigationLocation. If the location to be merged is the same as or is overlapping the receiver location, the method should merge the two entries and return true. If the locations don't overlap, it simply returns false.

A navigation location can also choose to support persistence. When an editor closes, any locations associated with that editor are asked to store their state in an IMemento. When the user jumps back to a location in an editor that has been closed, the location will be given the editor's IEditorInput object and the IMemento that was stored. Using this information, the location instance must be able to restore its state and navigate to its location in the editor. Note that you can easily obtain the editor instance from the input object by using IWorkbenchPage.findEditor(IEditorInput).

Now we know how to create and restore editor locations, but how are entries added to the navigation history in the first place? Anyone can mark an interesting location in an open editor by calling the markLocation method on INavigationHistory. Code that causes the cursor or selection to jump to another location in an editor should call this method both before and after performing the jump. As mentioned, implementations of restoreLocation should also mark the current location before restoring an old one. Regardless of whether the specific editor has any support for navigation history, markLocation will work. If the editor doesn't implement INavigationLocationProvider, a history entry will be added, allowing the user to jump back to that editor but without returning to any particular location. The following snippet shows an action that is added to the sample HTML editor. When the action is invoked, it will add the current cursor position to the navigation history:

```
public class MarkLocationAction extends Action {
    private IEditorPart editor;
    public MarkLocationAction(IEditorPart editor) {
        super("Mark Location in History", null);
        this.editor = editor;
    }
    public void run() {
```

```
        IWorkbenchPage page = editor.getSite().getPage();
        page.getNavigationHistory().markLocation(editor);
    }
}
```

How do I create a form-based editor, such as the plug-in Manifest Editor?

The `org.eclipse.ui.forms` plug-in provides a framework for building form-based editors. The components in this plug-in have long been the framework for building the PDE and Install/Update editors and views but have been made into official API only in the Eclipse 3.0 release.

To give you a quick overview, a form-based editor is created by subclassing the abstract `FormEditor` class. This class allows you to add any number of tabbed pages, which can be either traditional editor components or form-based pages (`IFormPage`). Each form page creates the displays for a single `IForm`, and each form may contain multiple `FormParts` representing each section in the form.

There are various flavors of `IForm` subtypes, depending on whether you want multiple sections, scrolling, or different layout styles. An example of a form-based editor is the PDE plug-in Manifest Editor, implemented by the `ManifestEditor` class in the `org.eclipse.pde.ui` plug-in.

 FAQ 211 *How do I create my own editor?*

How do I create a graphical editor?

The Eclipse Platform and SDK do not have support for creating graphical editors. However, a subproject of the Eclipse Tools Project is dedicated to a framework for graphical editors: the Graphical Editor Framework (GEF). GEF provides viewers for displaying graphical information and a controller for managing the interaction between those viewers and your domain model.

GEF makes few assumptions about what your model looks like and imposes no restrictions on where its viewers can be displayed. This allows you to use GEF for displaying a wide variety of graphical information in dialogs, views, and editors within an Eclipse application.

 The GEF Web page (http://eclipse.org/gef)

**FAQ
217**

How do I make an editor that contains another editor?

In its most abstract sense, an editor is simply a container for arbitrary SWT controls. As such, an editor can contain views, editors, wizards, and any other visual control. In practice, many of these types of controls don't make sense in the context of an editor. However, an editor is commonly composed of several pages, some of which may also be used as stand-alone editors. The most common example is an editor that provides a rendered WYSIWYG (what you see is what you get) page and a source page that shows raw text. The PDE plug-in Manifest Editor, implemented by the `ManifestEditor` class in the PDE UI plug-in, is such an editor. The platform provides infrastructure for this common editor type in the `MultiPageEditorPart` class.

Creating a subclass of `MultiPageEditorPart` requires that you implement many of the same methods as you would for a standard editor. The main difference is that instead of implementing `createPartControl`, you must implement `createPages`. In this method, you must create the controls for each page within the editor. These pages can be either standard editor parts or arbitrary SWT controls. The nested editors don't need to know anything about their container; from their point of view they are simply standard editors.

Your subclass of `MultiPageEditorPart` isn't required to do much beyond creating the initial set of pages. The superclass will take care of implementing the presentation for displaying the pages and for allowing the user to switch pages. If necessary, you can programmatically add or remove pages at any time by calling `addPage` or `removePage`. You can also programmatically switch pages by using `setActivePage` and respond to page changes by overriding `pageChange`.

The simplest way to get going with a multi-page editor is to edit your `plugin.xml` with the Manifest Editor. Select the **Extensions** tab, click on **Add...**, select **org.eclipse.ui.editors** in the extension point list, and choose **Multi-page**

Editor from the list of available templates. This will add all the required pieces for a basic multi-page editor to your plug-in.

☞ **FAQ 215** *How do I create a form-based editor, such as the plug-in Manifest Editor?*

Chapter 12. Actions, Commands, and Activities

This chapter answers questions about creating menu bars, context menus, and tool bars and the actions that fill them. A variety of both declarative and programmatic methods are available for contributing actions to the Eclipse UI and for managing and filtering those actions once they have been defined. This chapter also discusses the various ways to execute the long-running tasks that can be triggered by menu and toolbar actions.

Actions, commands, operations, jobs: What does it all mean?

FAQ
218

Many terms are thrown around in Eclipse for units of functionality or behavior: runnables, actions, commands, operations, and jobs, among others. Here is a high- level view of the terms to help you keep things straight.

As a plug-in writer, you will be interested mostly in *actions*. When a toolbar button or a menu item is clicked or when a defined key sequence is invoked, the run method of some action is invoked. Actions generally do not care about how or when they are invoked, although they often require extra context information, such as the current selection or view. Actions that are contributed to the workbench declaratively in plugin.xml defer the actual work to an *action delegate*.

Commands are a meta-level glue that the platform uses to manage and organize actions. As a plug-in writer, you will never write code for a command directly, but you will use the org.eclipse.ui.commands extension point to define key bindings for your actions and to group your actions into configurations and contexts.

Operations aren't an official part of the workbench API, but the term tends to be used for a long-running unit of behavior. Any work that might take a second or more should really be inside an operation. The official designation for operations in the API is IRunnableWithProgress, but the term *operation* tends to be used in its place because it is easier to say and remember. Operations are executed within an IRunnableContext. The context manages the execution of the operation in a non-UI thread so that the UI stays alive and painting. The context provides progress feedback to the user and support for cancellation.

Jobs, introduced in Eclipse 3.0, are operations that run in the background. The user is typically prevented from doing anything while an operation is running but is free to continue working when a job is running. Operations and jobs belong together, but jobs needed to live at a lower level in the plug-in architecture to make them usable by non-UI components.

 FAQ 127 *Does the platform have support for concurrency?*
FAQ 306 *What are* `IWorkspaceRunnable`, `IRunnableWithProgress`, *and* `WorkspaceModifyOperation?`

FAQ 219

What is an action set?

An action set is a logical group of menus and actions that should appear together at the same time. For example, when you are debugging a Java program, you want all the debug actions, such as **Step** and **Resume**, to appear in the menus. Actions in an action set can appear either in the workbench window toolbar or in the main menus.

You can create your own action sets, thus contributing to the main menu and toolbar, using the `org.eclipse.ui.actionSets` extension point. Here is an action set definition from the FAQ Examples plug-in:

```
<extension
    point="org.eclipse.ui.actionSets">
  <actionSet
    label="Sample Action Set"
    visible="false"
    id="org.eclipse.faq.examples.actionSet">
    <menu>...</menu>
    <action>...</action>
    ...
  </actionSet>
</extension>
```

The action set declaration itself is followed by a series of menu and action attributes, which are discussed in more detail in the FAQs that follow this one. Action sets are an entirely declarative concept. They cannot be defined, customized, or manipulated programmatically.

☞ **FAQ 220** *How do I make my action set visible?*
FAQ 221 *How do I add actions to the global toolbar?*
Platform Plug-in Developer Guide, under **Reference > Extension Points Reference > org.eclipse.ui.actionSets**
eclipse.org article "Contributing Actions to the Eclipse Workbench"

How do I make my action set visible?

FAQ
220

Simply defining an action set does not guarantee that it will appear in the UI. This characteristic is very important, as an Eclipse product with thousands of plug-ins would quickly become overwhelmed with actions if their appearance in the UI was not carefully controlled. An action set can be made visible in a number of ways:

- Set the `visible` attribute to `true` in the action set declaration. This will add your action set unconditionally to all perspectives. You should *almost never* do this in a real application unless you are certain that your actions are needed all the time in all perspectives. Keep in mind the scalability problems with using this approach.

- Define a perspective or perspective extension. This will limit the appearance of your action set to a specified set of perspectives.

- Define an action set part association, using the extension point `org.eclipse.ui.actionSetPartAssociations`. This extension links an action set to one or more views and editors. The action set will appear only when one of those parts is visible.

- Finally, the user can always have the last say by customizing perspectives (**Window > Customize Perspective**). From here, the user can turn on or off any action sets for the current perspective. This will override all the other mechanisms for defining action set visibility.

☞ **FAQ 191** *How can I add my views and actions to an existing perspective?*

**FAQ
221**

How do I add actions to the global toolbar?

Actions are added to the workbench window's toolbar by using the
`org.eclipse.ui.actionSets` extension point. Here is a sample action element
that contributes an action to the workbench window toolbar:

```
<action
    class="org.eclipse.faq.examples.actions.ToolBarAction"
    toolbarPath="Normal/exampleGroup"
    icon="icons/sample.gif"
    tooltip="Sample toolbar action">
</action>
```

The `class` attribute is the fully qualified name of the action that will be run when
the toolbar button is clicked. This class must implement the interface
`IWorkbenchWindowActionDelegate`. The `toolbarPath` attribute has two
segments—the toolbar ID and the group ID—separated by a slash (`/`) character.
The toolbar ID is used to indicate which toolbar the action belongs to. This value
isn't currently used because the platform defines only one toolbar, but the
convention is to use the string `Normal` to represent the default toolbar. The group
ID is used to place similar actions together. All actions with the same group ID
will be placed in a fixed group in the toolbar. The string in the `tooltip` attribute
is shown when the user hovers over the toolbar button.

You can specify many more attributes on your action, including criteria for when
your action should be visible and when it should be enabled. However, the four
attributes shown earlier are the minimum set you need for a toolbar action. Some
of the other action attributes are discussed in other FAQs.

 FAQ 219 *What is an action set?*
Platform Plug-in Developer Guide, under **Reference > Extension Points
Reference > org.eclipse.ui.actionSets**, eclipse.org article "Contributing Actions
to the Eclipse Workbench"

How do I add menus to the main menu?

Menus and submenus are added to the main menu by using the
`org.eclipse.ui.actionSets` extension point. Here is an example of a top-level
menu defined by the FAQ Examples plug-in:

```
<menu
    label="FA&Q Examples"
    id="exampleMenu">
    <separator name="exampleGroup"/>
</menu>
```

Each menu contains one or more `separator` elements that define *groups* within
that menu. The menu ID, along with the separator name, is used by actions
contributing to that menu. If you want to create a submenu, you also need to
define a `path` attribute that specifies what menu and group your menu should
appear under. This `path` attribute has the same syntax as the `menubarPath`
attribute on action definitions. To add a submenu to the menu defined earlier, you
would add the following attribute:

```
path="exampleMenu/exampleGroup"
```

To add a submenu to the **File** menu after the **New** submenu, the path would be:

```
path="file/new.ext"
```

The syntax of menu paths is described in more detail in FAQ 223.

FAQ 219 *What is an action set?*
FAQ 223 *How do I add actions to the main menu?*
FAQ 225 *Where can I find a list of existing action group names?*

How do I add actions to the main menu?

As with menus and toolbar buttons, menu actions are added to the main menu by using the `org.eclipse.ui.actionSets` extension point. The FAQ Examples plug-in has many actions that are contributed to the menu in this way. Here is a sample action definition (a subelement of the `actionSets` element):

```
<action
    label="Open Error &Dialog"
    class=
        "org.eclipse.faq.examples.actions.OpenErrorDialogAction"
    menubarPath="exampleMenu/exampleGroup">
</action>
```

The `class` attribute specifies the fully qualified path of the `Action` class, which must implement `IWorkbenchWindowActionDelegate`. When the action is selected by the user, the action's `run` method will be invoked.

The `menubarPath` attribute specifies the location of the action within the menus. This path is one of the greatest sources of confusion—and one of the biggest FAQs—for new users of action sets, so it is worth explaining it here in detail. The path has two parts, both of which are required. Everything up to the last slash character (`/`) represents the path of the menu that the action will belong to. For top-level menus, this is a simple string.

The `IWorkbenchActionConstants` interface contains constants for the standard top-level menu names. For example, `file` is the path of the **File** menu, and `window` is the path of the **Window** menu. For menus defined in other plug-ins, consult the `plugin.xml` file to see the ID of their menus.

When contributing to a submenu, the menu path will be a slash-delimited string containing the IDs of each menu in the hierarchy. The FAQ Examples plug-in defines a top-level menu with ID `exampleMenu`, and a submenu below this with ID `exampleFile`. The `menubarPath` of an action contributed to this submenu would therefore start with `exampleMenu/exampleFile`.

The final part of the `menubarPath` attribute—after the last slash—is the group name. All menus are divided into groups as a means of organizing the actions within them. When contributing an action, you must specify the name of the group your action belongs to within that menu. Each action can belong to only one group in a single menu. Once again, the standard group names used in the top-level menus are defined in `IWorkbenchActionConstants`. Some examples of `menubarPath` attributes will help to illustrate how they are used. Here is the path for an action in the import/export group within the top-level **File** menu:

```
menubarPath="file/import.ext"
```

An action contributed to the group of **Show...** actions in the **Navigate** menu would have the following path:

```
menubarPath="navigate/show.ext"
```

Finally, an action contributed to the **Editor** submenu in the **FAQ Examples** menu would have this path:

```
menubarPath="exampleMenu/editorMenu/editorGroup"
```

Note that the group name is required even for menus that have only one group.

Menu actions have many more optional attributes, including those for specifying the action's visibility and enablement. Consult the extension point documentation for complete details.

FAQ 219 *What is an action set?*
FAQ 225 *Where can I find a list of existing action group names?*
eclipse.org article "Contributing Actions to the Eclipse Workbench"

Why are some actions activated without a target?

FAQ
224

Most of the time, an action is invoked on the *current selection* in the UI. One such example is the **Properties** menu action on a resource in the Navigator. This action is relevant only when a particular object has been selected. In other cases, the action is *global*, as is the action behind **Project > Build All**, which simply builds all projects in the workspace and is independent of the current selection.

The workbench does not distinguish between context-sensitive actions and global actions, and so it calls the `selectionChanged` method on all action delegates in case they want to update their enablement based on the selection. This is somewhat of a design mistake as many unnecessary selection change notifications are now sent out throughout the workbench. Furthermore, actions have to remember the current selection and store it in a field so it can be used if the `run` method is called. This is not a good design pattern.

Luckily, the workbench added an interface called `IActionDelegate2` in version 2.0 of the platform. When clients implement both `IActionDelegate` and `IActionDelegate2`, the workbench will not call the `run(IAction action)` method but will call the `runWithEvent` method instead.

This alternative solution allows clients to write more compact code with control flow localized to the execution of the action. A typical action would declare itself as follows:

```
class Handler extends ActionDelegate
                             implements IActionDelegate2 {
    public void runWithEvent(IAction action, Event event) {
        MessageDialog.openInformation(new Shell(),
            "Demo", "Handling: "+action+" on "+event);
    }
}
```

Interfaces like `IActionDelegate2` are an indication of how a platform like Eclipse struggles with the tension between adoption and innovation. Because too many client plug-ins already depended on the implementation of the old interface `IActionDelegate`, it could not be easily changed without breaking the existing Eclipse API. Instead, a parallel replacement was added, which is less elegant but comes back in multiple places in Eclipse. The existence of the `IActionDelegateWithEvent` interface shows how even naming mistakes have to persist for a while as some clients may rely on it.

FAQ
225

Where can I find a list of existing action group names?

Eclipse menus and toolbars are divided into groups to ensure that related actions appear together. These group names need to be clearly specified to allow plug-ins to contribute their actions to menus defined by other plug-ins. Group names can be specified either programmatically or declaratively in a `plugin.xml` file. For groups that are defined programmatically, the convention is to create an interface called `I*ActionConstants` containing constants for all the plug-in's group names. This serves to cement the group names as API, ensuring that they will stay consistent across releases of Eclipse. The base platform defines all its groups in `IWorkbenchActionConstants`, and the text infrastructure defines `ITextEditorActionConstants`. A similar pattern is used for other plug-ins, such as `IJavaEditorActionConstants` for the Java editor.

The other way to specify group names is in `plugin.xml`. Most plug-ins use this approach, making it fairly easy to track down the group names. Simply open the `plugin.xml` of the plug-in you want to contribute your action to and look for the definition of the `menu` element under an `actionSet` extension. These IDs are also treated as API, so they generally won't change from release to release.

FAQ 219 *What is an action set?*
FAQ 223 *How do I add actions to the main menu?*

What is the difference between a command and an action?

Commands and actions are two aspects of the same thing. You can think of commands as the declarative part—specified in the plug-in manifest—and actions as the programmatic part. Commands are used mainly to associate customizable key bindings with actions. If you look in the **Workbench > Keys** preference page, you will see a list of all commands known to the platform, including what context and configuration they belong to. Key bindings are hooked to commands, and then commands are hooked to actions. This extra level of indirection allows for added flexibility in the implementation. The user can change key bindings for a command without the associated actions knowing about it, and the action for a command can be dynamically changed for different circumstances without affecting the key bindings.

Note that although the Eclipse APIs contain both commands and actions, the UI very clearly uses only the term *command* when referring to them. The term *action* is avoided in the user interface. There's no point in confusing users with two names for the same thing!

How do I associate an action with a command?

Actions are associated with commands in various ways depending on how the actions are defined. For actions contributed via the `actionSets` extension point, the association with a command is done directly in the action definition. The `definitionId` attribute of the `action` element must match the ID of the command it is associated with:

```
<actionSet ...>
   <action
      definitionId="org.eclipse.faq.sampleCommand"
      ...>
   </action>
</actionSet>
<command
   id="org.eclipse.faq.sampleCommand"
   ...>
</command>
```

For actions created programmatically, associating the action with a command is a two-step process. As with declarative actions, the first step is to set the action's definition ID to match the ID of the command. The command must still be defined declaratively, using the `command` extension point. The definition ID is set by calling `Action.setDefinitionId`. The second step is to register the action with the platform, using the key-binding service. This service can be accessed from the `IWorkbenchPartSite`, which is accessible to both views and editors. Here is an example of these steps for an action in a view:

```
action.setActionDefinitionId("some.unique.id");
view.getSite().getKeyBindingService().registerAction(action);
```

☞ **FAQ 246** *How do I make key bindings work in an RCP application?*

How do I create my own key-binding configuration?

On the **Workbench > Keys** preference page, you can choose the active key-binding configuration. These configurations specify the keyboard shortcuts to use for the various tools, actions, and editor features in Eclipse. By default, the platform includes a standard configuration and an `emacs` configuration. There are no APIs for defining key-binding configurations programmatically, but you can create them in a plug-in by using the `org.eclipse.ui.commands` extension point. First, you need to define your configuration:

```
<keyConfiguration
    name="My Configuration"
    parent="org.eclipse.ui.defaultAcceleratorConfiguration"
    description="This is a simple configuration"
    id="org.eclipse.faq.sampleConfiguration">
</keyConfiguration>
```

By specifying a parent, you are saying that your configuration should inherit key bindings from the parent unless they are explicitly set in your configuration. When key bindings are defined, they will refer to the configuration they belong to. If you write your own configuration, you'll also need to define new key bindings for all the commands that you want to belong to your configuration.

☞ **FAQ 229** *How do I provide a keyboard shortcut for my action?*

How do I provide a keyboard shortcut for my action?

Keyboard shortcuts are created by defining a *key binding*, using the `org.eclipse.ui.commands` extension point. When you define a key binding, you generally specify four things:

1. The ID of the configuration to which it applies.

2. The context, or scope, for the key binding. For example, the text editor defines a context that can override bindings from the global context.

3. The ID of the command that you are creating a binding for. You can find command IDs by browsing the `plugin.xml` file of the plug-in that defines that action.

4. The accelerator sequence.

You can also define a key binding that applies only to a particular locale or platform. For example, you can define an accelerator that applies only to a German Linux GTK installation of Eclipse. See the `command` extension point documentation for more details on these advanced features.

The following is an example key-binding definition. This binding sets the accelerator for the Java **Sort Members** action, which by default has no key binding:

```
<keyBinding
    string="Ctrl+Shift+D"
    context="org.eclipse.ui.globalScope"
    command="org.eclipse.jdt.ui.edit.text.java.sort.members"
    configuration="org.eclipse.faq.sampleConfiguration">
</keyBinding>
```

The difference between a configuration and a context can be confusing at first. The configuration is explicitly set by the user; once it is set, it does not change. The context can be changed programmatically by any plug-in. For example, you can change the scope whenever your view or editor becomes active. Scopes can be queried and set by using the `IKeyBindingService`. This service can be accessed within a workbench part by using the method `getKeyBindingService` on `IWorkbenchPartSite`.

 FAQ 228 *How do I create my own key-binding configuration?*

FAQ
230

How can I change the name or tooltip of my action?

Actions contributed via XML have statically defined names, images, and tooltips. Often, you want to change these attributes dynamically, based on the current selection or some other state. Owing to the lazy-loading nature of the platform, you can't do this until your action has been run once. A common solution is to specify generic attributes in the XML and then make attributes more dynamic after the action has been run. For example, the action to enable or disable breakpoints is called **Toggle Breakpoint** when the platform is first started. After it has been run once, the action dynamically sets its name to be either **Enable Breakpoint** or **Disable Breakpoint**, depending on whether the selected breakpoint is enabled. Here is an example action that implements this behavior:

```
class ToggleAction
      implements IWorkbenchWindowActionDelegate {
   private boolean state = false;
   public void run(IAction action) {
      state = !state;
      String name = state ? "True Action" : "False Action";
      action.setText(name);
      action.setToolTipText(name);
   }
}
```

You can change many more action properties, including the action's image, accelerator key, and enablement. Look at the methods on `IAction` to see what other properties can be changed.

It is also common to update action properties when the selection changes. Although the preceding example uses a workbench window action delegate, which is not notified of selection changes by default, the action can register itself as a selection listener in the `init` method and then update its state during the `selectionChanged` callback.

 FAQ 168 *How do I find out what object is selected?*

How do I hook into global actions, such as Copy and Delete?

Certain standard toolbar and menu entries can be shared among several views and editors. These actions are called either *global* or *retargetable* actions and include such common tools as undo/redo, cut/copy/paste, print, find, delete, and more. Each view or editor is allowed to contribute a handler for these actions; when a new part becomes active, its handler takes control of that action.

A view typically registers its global action handlers in the `createPartControl` method:

```
IActionBars actionBars= getViewSite().getActionBars();
actionBars.setGlobalActionHandler(
    IWorkbenchActionFactory.COPY,
    copyAction);
```

You have to do this only once for each view that is created. The platform remembers your action handler and retargets the action each time the view becomes active. To unregister from a global action, simply invoke `setGlobalActionHandler` again and pass in a `null` value for the handler.

The `IWorkbenchActionConstants` interface in the `org.eclipse.ui` package contains a complete list of global actions. Look for constants in this interface with a comment saying "Global action." In Eclipse 3.0, you can also look at the `ActionFactory` and `IDEActionFactory` classes, which define factory objects for creating a variety of common actions.

 FAQ 213 *How do I enable global actions such as* **Cut**, **Paste**, *and* **Print** *in my editor?*

FAQ 232

How do I build menus and toolbars programmatically?

Menus and toolbars in JFace are based on two key interfaces: `IContributionItem` and `IContributionManager`. A contribution manager is simply an object that contains contribution items. The major types of contribution managers are menus, toolbars, and status lines. Contribution items represent any object that is logically contained within a menu or a toolbar, such as actions, submenus, and separators. These interfaces abstract away the differences between the contexts in which actions can appear. An action doesn't care whether it is invoked from a toolbar or a menu, and these interfaces help avoid unnecessary coupling between the items and the containers presenting them.

So, for each toolbar or menu, you need to create a contribution manager. For menus, including drop-down menus, context menus, and submenus, create an instance of `MenuManager`. For toolbars or cool bars, create an instance of `ToolBarManager` or `CoolBarManager`, respectively.

The following snippet creates a top-level menu and a submenu, each with one action:

```
IMenuManager mainMenu = ...;//get ref to main menu manager
MenuManager menu1 = new MenuManager("Menu &1", "1");
menu1.add(new Action("Action 1") {});
mainMenu.add(menu1);
MenuManager menu2 = new MenuManager("Menu &2", "2");
menu2.add(new Action("Action 2") {});
menu1.add(menu2);
```

FAQ 233 *How do I make menus with dynamic contents?*
FAQ 234 *What is the difference between a toolbar and a cool bar?*

How do I make menus with dynamic contents?

By default, menu managers in JFace are static; that is, contributions are added once when the view is created, and they remain unchanged each time the view is opened. Individual actions may enable or disable themselves, based on the current context, but the menu itself remains stable.

If you want the contents of your menus to change every time the menu is opened, you should make your menu manager dynamic. When the menu manager is created, make it dynamic by calling `setRemoveAllWhenShown`:

```
IMenuManager menu = new MenuManager("Name");
menu.setRemoveAllWhenShown(true);
```

By setting this flag, the menu manager will remove all actions and submenus from the menu every time the menu is about to be shown. Next, you need to install on the menu a listener that will add your actions:

```
IMenuListener listener = new IMenuListener() {
    public void menuAboutToShow(IMenuManager m) {
    if (daytime) {
      m.add(workAction);
      m.add(playAction);
    } else {
      m.add(sleepAction);
    }
};
menu.addMenuListener(listener);
```

This menu will now have different actions, depending on the value of the daytime variable.

It is possible to make a menu that is partially dynamic, with some actions added at creation time and some actions added or removed by a menu listener when the menu is opened. However, it is generally not worth the added complexity. Note that even for dynamically contributed actions, you should retain the same action instances and recontribute them each time the menu opens. Creating action instances from scratch every time the menu opens is not generally a good idea as actions often install themselves as listeners or perform other nontrival initialization.

FAQ
234

What is the difference between a toolbar and a cool bar?

A cool bar is a special kind of toolbar that allows the user to reposition its items dynamically. Cool bars will also add more rows as necessary when items are added or moved. You can lock cool bars programmatically by calling CoolBar.setLocked, preventing the user from making further layout changes. The only limitation of cool bars is that, unlike ordinary toolbars, they can be oriented only horizontally. Otherwise, they are created and used just like standard toolbars. In Eclipse 3.0, JFace introduced a CoolBarManager class for helping to manage contributions to a cool bar, just as ToolBarManager is used for regular toolbars.

 FAQ 232 *How do I build menus and toolbars programmatically?*

FAQ
235

Can other plug-ins add actions to my part's context menu?

They can, but only if you want them to. If you want other plug-ins to be able to add actions to your part's context menu, you need to do two things. First, you need to add a GroupMarker instance to your context menu with the special ID IWorkbenchActionConstants.MB_ADDITIONS. This placeholder tells the platform where actions contributed by other plug-ins should appear in the context menu.

Second, when it is created, you need to register with the platform your part's context menu by calling the `IViewSite` or `IEditorSite` method `registerContextMenu`. If it has more than one context menu, your part can contribute several menus by defining a unique ID for each one. By convention, a part that has only one context menu uses the part ID as the context menu ID. You should publish these context menu IDs in your plug-in's documentation so that other plug-in writers know what they are.

How do I add other plug-ins' actions to my menus?

Many plug-ins expose their actions as API, allowing you to instantiate them and add them to your menus. The trend in Eclipse 3.0 is to introduce factory methods for creating actions, allowing the actual action implementation to remain hidden. See `ActionFactory` and `IDEActionFactory` for examples of such action factories.

Views and editors can register their context menus with the platform to allow other plug-ins to add actions to them dynamically. However, most actions in the platform are not contributed dynamically. It would create a lot of clutter if everyone added actions to everyone else's views.

 FAQ 235 *Can other plug-ins add actions to my part's context menu?*

What is the purpose of activities?

The potential number of installed plug-ins in a given Eclipse instance is open ended. A user can buy or download a large Eclipse-based product and then start to add various extra plug-ins from the open source community or from plug-in vendors. As each of these plug-ins adds its views, actions, and other UI contributions, the user interface can become very cluttered. Some products have been known to have dozens of perspectives and wizards and hundreds of preference pages. Because the base platform doesn't know anything about these plug-ins or about the user's intentions, it is difficult to filter out unneeded contributions intelligently.

The platform uses a number of mechanisms to deal with this problem of user interface scalability. For example, the active perspective can, to a certain extent, customize the menus and toolbars available in that perspective. Furthermore, the user can customize each perspective, adding new capabilities from other plug-ins or removing menu and toolbar actions to reduce clutter. The problem with these approaches is that customization is suited mainly for advanced users who are intimately familiar with all the menus and know what the available commands are and which ones they need. The clutter problem, however, is most pressing for the novice user. People opening a product for the first time and inundated with rows of toolbar buttons and massive menus will have a difficult time finding what they are looking for. The fact that buried in one of those menus is an action that allows users to control what they see is of no use, as they won't know what they are showing or hiding.

The notion of an *activity* was introduced in Eclipse 3.0 to help address this cluttering problem. An activity roughly describes what the user is currently doing with an Eclipse-based product. This in turn maps to a set of features that need to be visible in the context of that activity. For example, a product might have "Java development" and "Web development" activities. When the user is doing Java development, only the menu actions, toolbar buttons, and views applicable to that activity are shown. As the user works, various activities can become active or inactive, depending on what the user is doing, and the user interface is filtered accordingly.

The key attribute of activities is that they enable progressive disclosure in the user interface. A user opening a product for the first time might begin with an introductory activity that has a very simple set of available features. As the user explores and begins working with different tools, new activities get enabled implicitly, ensuring that tools are available when needed, not before. Eventually, a power user may end up with all activities enabled and the user interface heavily cluttered again, which is okay because the power user won't be daunted by it.

You may notice that the term *activity* is not used in the Eclipse UI. Usability studies showed that the term was too vague and confusing for end-users, so the term *capability* is used instead. You will find that documentation and source code use the two terms interchangeably.

How do I add activities to my plug-in?

You don't. An important feature of activities is that they are not defined in the plug-ins alongside the functionality they describe. Because activities are designed to solve a scaling problem when large numbers of plug-ins are used together, attempting to define them at the plug-in level would be futile. For example, let's say that you create a small handful of plug-ins that implement development tools for the PHP programming language. If you are providing only basic editing and debugging functionality, chances are that your plug-ins alone do not present a UI scalability problem. However, if someone then takes your small handful of plug-ins and combines them with 500 more plug-ins from other sources, the UI starts to become cluttered and difficult to use. If you introduced a couple of activities in your plug-in to separate different types of PHP development and if the other 500 plug-ins also introduced activities, the activities themselves would become cluttered and unusable. The moral of the story is that activities need to be defined at the level where the scalability problem exists.

Typically activities will be defined by an administrator or product manager who is assembling an end-user application from a large pool of plug-ins. A power user who wants to coordinate a large set of plug-ins downloaded from the Web also may establish some activities. The administrator or power user defines activities entirely declaratively in a `plugin.xml` file in a plug-in. No Java code is involved! Let's dig into the actual mechanics of defining activities. Before you create any activities, you need to establish one or more activity *categories*. A category is simply a container for one or more activities. Here is a simple category defined in the FAQ Examples plug-in:

```
<category
    name="FAQ Category"
    id="org.eclipse.faq.faqCategory">
</category>
```

Note: All configuration elements in this FAQ must be contained in an extension to the `org.eclipse.ui.activities` extension point. The ID and name of the extension itself are not used.

Next, you need to define one or more activities and connect them to a category.

```
<activity
    name="FAQ Activity"
    id="org.eclipse.faq.faqActivity">
```

```
</activity>
<categoryActivityBinding
    activityId="org.eclipse.faq.faqActivity"
    categoryId="org.eclipse.faq.faqCategory">
</categoryActivityBinding>
```

Note that activities, categories, and bindings are all separate top-level elements. This allows you to define each of them in different plug-ins if desired.

After creating appropriate activities and categories, we get to the interesting part, connecting functionality to activities. An activity-pattern binding associates an activity with a regular expression that is used to match identifiers. The syntax of the regular expressions conforms to the usage defined in `java.util.regex.Pattern`. The identifiers describing functionality that can be filtered from the UI are of the form `<plugin-id>/<local-id>` or simply `<local-id>`.

When an activity is enabled, all functionality that matches the identifier patterns associated with that activity will be visible. If an identifier matches a disabled activity and does not match any enabled activity, the functionality associated with that ID will be invisible. Interpretation of exactly what `<local-id>` means is left up to the UI component that is doing the filtering, but typically it is the ID of an extension.

This all sounds very confusing, so let's look at a concrete example from the FAQ Examples plug-in:

```
<activityPatternBinding
    activityId="org.eclipse.faq.faqActivity"
    pattern="org.eclipse.faq*">
</activityPatternBinding>
```

This pattern binding says, when `faqActivity` is disabled, hide all functionality associated with any plug-in whose ID starts with `org.eclipse.faq`.

Let's try a slightly more complicated pattern:

```
<activityPatternBinding
    activityId="org.eclipse.faq.faqWizard"
    pattern="org.eclipse.faq.examples/[a-z[.]]*addingWizard">
</activityPatternBinding>
```

This pattern is much more selective. It will disable functionality only in the `org.eclipse.faq.examples` plug-in whose ID ends with the string `addingWizard`. This will disable only the `addingWizard` extension from the `org.eclipse.faq.examples` plug-in. By selecting your patterns carefully, you can define precisely which parts of the UI are filtered by a given activity.

To learn more about regular expressions in Java, see Jeffrey E. F. Friedl, *Mastering Regular Expressions* (O'Reilly, 1997).

How do activities get enabled?

FAQ
239

When a user starts a new workspace, all activities will typically be disabled. As the user explores the application and starts to use new features, more activities can become enabled as they are needed. This enablement typically happens automatically when the workbench determines that a user is starting to use features defined in a disabled activity. The workbench defines a number of *trigger points*, UI interactions that signal the introduction of a new activity. For example, the Eclipse IDE workbench considers creation of a project to be a trigger point. When a project is created, the workbench looks at the natures on that project and enables any activities that have pattern bindings matching any of the nature IDs.

You can define your own trigger points for any logical place where new plug-in functionality will be introduced. The trigger point itself doesn't need to know about any particular activities; it simply needs to define an identifier that represents the new functionality. The identifier should be in the form either `<plugin-id>/<local-id>` or simply `<local-id>`. Using that ID, you can enable any matching activities as follows:

```
String id = ...
IWorkbench wb = PlatformUI.getWorkbench();
IWorkbenchActivitySupport as = wb.getActivitySupport();
IActivityManager am = as.getActivityManager();
IIdentifier identifier = am.getIdentifier(id);
Set activities = new HashSet(am.getEnabledActivityIds());
if (activities.addAll(identifier.getActivityIds()))
    as.setEnabledActivityIds(activities);
```

The exact format of the ID used for your trigger point should be well documented so that activity writers will be able to write appropriate pattern bindings for activating their activities using your trigger points.

Activities can also be enabled or disabled explicitly by an end user. Again, this is something only the advanced user will do. The success of activities as a mechanism for scalability and progressive disclosure relies on carefully chosen trigger points in the user interface for seamlessly enabling activities.

What is the difference between perspectives and activities?

At first glance, perspectives and activities are very similar. Both modify the appearance of the workbench, adding and removing menus and toolbar buttons, depending on a course-grained user task. When trying to figure out how to carve up a large product into usable pieces, it is sometimes difficult to figure out when to use activities, perspectives, or both. Apart from the prosaic difference that perspectives were an Eclipse 1.0 invention and activities are new in Eclipse 3.0, a number of other subtle differences exist.

The most obvious difference between activities and perspectives is that activities are not intended to alter the layout of views and editors that are currently open. Activities change the menus and toolbars but don't make real estate changes that can cause the user to lose context. Perspectives have a dual role of dictating screen layout and altering the menus and toolbars. This connection is often not obvious to users, and they are often confused about why a certain menu or keyboard shortcut appears in one place but not another.

Second, activities are intended to be largely implicit. Whereas perspectives are explicitly visible and controlled entirely by the user, activities are not directly user controlled. Essentially, activities try to have some smarts about when they are needed and activate and deactivate accordingly, depending on what the user is doing. Although perspectives do this to a certain extent, such as switching to the Debug perspective automatically when an application is launched in debug mode, automatically changing the user interface layout is a general user interface no-no. Because activities are not tied to a particular screen layout, they can change automatically without causing the user to lose context.

Finally, perspectives are partially defined programmatically, whereas activities are defined entirely declaratively. The importance of this difference is that activities are not intended to be defined by programmers who are working on individual plug-ins. Because the designer of a single plug-in cannot envision the emergent behavior of a system built of hundreds of plug-ins—or at least not without violating the modular principles of the plug-in architecture—he or she has no way of knowing what set of activities might be appropriate. Activities are a form of meta-glue that regulate how plug-ins interact and so must be defined at a higher level. Typically, activities will be created by a system configurer or human-computer interaction (HCI) expert who has a better picture of the total functionality of the product.

Chapter 13. Building Your Own Application

Prior to the introduction of RCP, most of the Eclipse community was focused on developing plug-ins for a particular Eclipse application called the *workbench*. Eclipse, however, has always supported the ability to create your own stand-alone applications based on the Eclipse plug-in architecture. Eclipse applications can range from simple headless programs with no user interface to full-blown IDEs. In Eclipse 3.0, the platform began a shift toward giving greater power and flexibility to applications built on the Eclipse infrastructure. This chapter guides you through the process of building your own Eclipse application and explores some of the new Eclipse 3.0 APIs available only to applications.

What is an Eclipse application?

FAQ
241

Technically, an Eclipse application is a plug-in that creates an extension for the extension point `org.eclipse.core.runtime.applications`. However, the extension point is fairly special. Only one application gets to run in a given Eclipse instance. This application is specified either on the command line or by the primary feature. After the platform starts up, control of the VM's `main` thread is handed over to the application's `run` method. The application's entire lifecycle occurs within the scope of this method. When the `run` method returns, the platform shuts down.

The application is essentially the boss; it's the Eclipse analog of the C or Java `main` method. All other plug-ins in the configuration plug into the application. What goes into the `run` method is entirely up to you. It can be a graphical application, which will create a user interface and run some kind of event loop, or a completely headless application that runs without interacting with a user.

Because a running Eclipse instance has only one application in it, the philosophy of building applications is very different from the approach when building plug-ins. Essentially, the flexibility given to plug-ins must be mitigated by the fact that other plug-ins in the system may have competing requirements. The laws of plug-in behavior are designed to allow plug-ins to interact in ways that do not impinge on the behavior of other plug-ins. Such constraints are not as important for the application, which can have the final say when the needs of various plug-ins don't intersect. Whereas plug-ins are citizens of the Eclipse

Platform, the application is king. For example, because the application is always started first, the lazy-loading principle doesn't apply to it. The application can customize the menus and toolbars programmatically rather than using the various workbench extension points. The application can also determine whether views and editors have title bars and whether views can be closed or resized.

The Eclipse SDK is one particularly well-known example of an Eclipse application. To explore how it works, start by looking at the `IDEApplication` class in the `org.eclipse.ui.ide` plug-in.

**FAQ
242**

How do I create an application?

To create an application, you need a plug-in that adds an extension to the `org.eclipse.core.runtime.applications` extension point. An example application definition from a `plugin.xml` file is as follows:

```
<extension
    id="helloworld"
    point="org.eclipse.core.runtime.applications">
    <application>
        <run class="org.eclipse.faq.HelloWorld"/>
    </application>
</extension>
```

The `class` attribute of the `run` element must specify a class that implements `org.eclipse.core.boot.IPlatformRunnable`. Here is the source of a trivial application:

```
public class HelloWorld implements IPlatformRunnable {
    public Object run(Object args) throws Exception {
        System.out.println("Hello from Eclipse application");
        return EXIT_OK;
    }
}
```

To run the application, you need to specify the fully qualified ID of your application extension definition, using the `application` command-line argument when launching Eclipse:

```
eclipse -application org.eclipse.faq.helloworld.helloworld
```

The fully qualified extension ID is computed by prepending the plug-in ID to the simple extension ID from the `plugin.xml` file. In this example, the plug-in ID is `org.eclipse.faq.helloworld`, and the simple extension ID is `helloworld`.

What is the minimal Eclipse configuration?

FAQ
243

When you look at the collection of plug-ins in the Eclipse SDK, you're confronted with a daunting list. People wanting to create their own applications using Eclipse naturally ask how this list can be pared down so that only the essential plug-ins remain. If you take this exercise to its extreme, you'll be left with a tiny Eclipse kernel consisting of the following:

- `startup.jar`. This file contains a single class used to bootstrap the platform. Its sole purpose is to find and invoke the plug-in responsible for starting the platform.

- Boot or configurator. A plug-in is responsible for finding and loading the *plug-in configuration*, the set of plug-ins and fragments that are going to be used in a given application. If no configuration exists, the configurator creates one that includes all plug-ins in the `plugins` directory on disk. The `org.eclipse.core.boot` plug-in implemented this functionality in Eclipse 2.1. In Eclipse 3.0, this task can be delegated to any plug-in but by default is done by the `org.eclipse.update.configurator` plug-in.

- `org.eclipse.core.runtime`. The runtime plug-in is the heart of the running Eclipse Platform. When it starts, this plug-in parses the `plugin.xml` files for all plug-ins in the configuration and builds an in-memory registry. The runtime plug-in also contains a number of useful utility classes that are used by almost all plug-ins: `IPath`, `IStatus`, `IProgressMonitor`, and so on. The runtime plug-in is also responsible for finding and invoking the chosen Eclipse *application*. Think of the runtime plug-in as the `java.lang` and `java.util` of the Eclipse Platform.

- Runtime plug-ins. The runtime uses a few plug-ins as implementation details that vary according to the release you are using. Up to and including Eclipse 2.1, the runtime plug-in needed an XML parser to parse the `plugin.xml` files. This parser is contained in the `org.apache.xerces` plug-in. In Eclipse 3.0, the runtime is built on top

of a framework called OSGi, which is contained in three
`org.eclipse.osgi` plug-ins. You generally don't need to know
anything about these plug-ins as they are used "under the covers" to
implement the runtime's functionality.

And there you have the minimal Eclipse configuration. Starting with this set, you
can begin adding any plug-ins you need, such as SWT, JFace, and the platform
UI, or other plug-ins you need to build your application.

Here's a little trick for figuring out what prerequisite plug-ins are needed by a
given plug-in in the platform:

1. Open the **External Plug-ins and Fragments** import wizard.

2. In the list of plug-ins to import, select the one(s) you need for your
   application. For example, select `org.eclipse.ui` if you want generic UI
   features, or select `org.eclipse.jdt.ui` if you want the Java tools.

3. Select **Add Required Plug-ins**.

You now you have a list of all prerequisites, recursively, for the plug-in you
need. This trick is useful because the exact lists of prerequisites for a plug-in can
vary between releases of Eclipse. If you ask someone to tell you exactly what
plug-ins are needed for a particular kind of application, the answer is not likely to
be valid across multiple release of Eclipse.

This same technique can also be used when the time comes to deploy your
application. If you install your application plug-ins in the base development
environment, you can then use the plug-in import wizard to recursively compute
the required set of plug-ins for your application. This allows you to deploy your
application with a minimal footprint, as all unused plug-ins are removed.
However, it is possible that your end user may want to use functionality in
plug-ins that are not even referenced by your application plug-ins, so be careful
of what you chop out.

FAQ 111 *What is a configuration?*
FAQ 115 *How does OSGi and the new runtime affect me?*

How do I create a Rich Client application?

An Eclipse RCP application has full control over how the user interface is
created. The locus of control for an RCP application—the place where all
configuration starts—is the `WorkbenchAdvisor` class. Your subclass of
`WorkbenchAdvisor` controls the initial layout and appearance of the workbench
window, as well as what commands appear in the menus and toolbars. Here is an
example of a bare-bones RCP application:

```
public class MinimalRCPApp extends WorkbenchAdvisor
    implements IPlatformRunnable {
    public String getInitialWindowPerspectiveId() {
        return "org.eclipse.faq.minimalperspective";
    }
    public void preWindowOpen(
                    IWorkbenchWindowConfigurer wwc) {
        configurer.setShowMenuBar(false);
        configurer.setShowFastViewBars(false);
        configurer.setShowStatusLine(false);
        configurer.setShowCoolBar(false);
    }
    public Object run(Object args) throws Exception {
        Display d = PlatformUI.createDisplay();
        int ret = PlatformUI.createAndRunWorkbench(d, this);
        if (ret == PlatformUI.RETURN_RESTART)
            return EXIT_RESTART;
        return EXIT_OK;
    }
}
```

This application creates a blank workbench window with no toolbars, no menus,
no status line, and no views or editors (Figure 13.1). The application will run
until the user closes the workbench window.

Figure 13.1 Minimal RCP application

The application's `run` method is the one we've seen in previous application examples. You need to specify the name of the class with this method when declaring your application in the `plugin.xml` file. This example creates a workbench and runs the event loop by calling `createAndRunWorkbench`. The `preWindowOpen` method is your opportunity to customize the basic appearance of the window. Finally, the ID of the initial perspective to be displayed must be specified using the `getInitialWindowPerspectiveId` method.

That's all there is to it! The rest of an RCP application is developed just like any other plug-in. You need to create one or more perspectives and populate them with the views and editors that apply for your application. These are created by using the standard `org.eclipse.ui` extension points, all of which are available in a custom application.

A binary download of the RCP can be obtained for any Eclipse build from the eclipse.org downloads page. This download does not contain an application, but it can be set as the target platform for your own RCP application from the **Plug-in Development > Target Platform** preference page.

 FAQ 190 *How do I create a new perspective?*
FAQ 242 *How do I create an application?*

FAQ 245

How do I customize the menus in an RCP application?

Your RCP application must specify what menus and actions, if any, to include by default in the main workbench window menu bar. This is done by overriding the `WorkbenchAdvisor` `fillActionBars` method. Note that although other plug-ins are always free to create their own menus, it is common for plug-ins to assume the existence of some basic menus. You are responsible for creating the menus that you expect all plug-ins to your application to contribute to.

Here is a simple example of an advisor that creates two menus—**Window** and **Help**—and adds a single action to each:

```
public void fillActionBars(IWorkbenchWindow window,
    IActionBarConfigurer configurer, int flags) {
    if ((flags & FILL_MENU_BAR) == 0)
        return;
    IMenuManager mainMenu = configurer.getMenuManager();
```

```
        MenuManager windowMenu = new MenuManager("&Window",
            IWorkbenchActionConstants.M_WINDOW);
        mainMenu.add(windowMenu);
        windowMenu.add(ActionFactory.MAXIMIZE.create(window));
        MenuManager helpMenu = new MenuManager("&Help",
            IWorkbenchActionConstants.M_HELP);
        mainMenu.add(helpMenu);
        helpMenu.add(new AboutAction());
    }
```

Note how the menu IDs are taken from `IWorkbenchActionConstants`. It is important to use the standard menu IDs as plug-ins contributing to the `actionSets` extension point will be expecting these standard IDs. The action added to the **Window** menu is taken from the standard set of actions available from `org.eclipse.ui.actions.ActionFactory`. You will find many of the standard perspective, view, and editor manipulation actions here. The `AboutAction` in this snippet is a simple custom action that displays program information and credits, conventionally added by most applications at the bottom of the **Help** menu.

For simplicity, this snippet creates new actions each time `fillActionBars` is called. In a real application, you should create the actions only once and return the cached instances whenever this method is called. Because actions often add themselves as selection or part-change listeners, creating multiple action instances would introduce performance problems. The data cache provided by `IWorkbenchWindowConfigurer` is a common place to store action instances. Because each workbench window has its own configurer instance, this is an ideal place to store state specific to a given window. You can use a convenience method such as the following to lazily initialize and store your created actions:

```
    //configurer is provided by initialize method
    private IWorkbenchConfigurer configurer = ...;
    private static final String MENU_ACTIONS = &menu.actions&;
    private IAction[] getMenuActions(IWorkbenchWindow window) {
        IWorkbenchWindowConfigurer wwc =
            configurer.getWindowConfigurer(window);
        IAction[] actions = (IAction[]) wwc.getData(MENU_ACTIONS);
        if (actions == null) {
            IAction max = ActionFactory.MAXIMIZE.create(window);
            actions = new IAction[] {max};
            wwc.setData(MENU_ACTIONS, actions);
        }
        return actions;
    }
```

It is common practice to factor out action management code into a helper class and then store an instance of this helper class in the window configurer's cache.

 FAQ 232 *How do I build menus and toolbars programmatically?*

FAQ 246

How do I make key bindings work in an RCP application?

When actions are contributed via the `actionSets` extension point, key bindings are configured by associating the action with a declarative command. In this case, no code is required to hook the action to the key binding. However, if you programmatically create actions in an RCP application, you have to register actions yourself. This requires two steps. First, you need to specify the command ID for your action. If you are using built-in actions from an action factory, they usually have the command ID already set. If you create your own action, as a subclass of `Action`, you need to set the command ID yourself by calling the `setActionDefinitionId` method inherited from `Action`. Typically this is done from your action's constructor.

Now that your action is linked to a command, you need to register the action with the platform. You should do this the first time the platform calls your implementation of `WorkbenchAdvisor.fillActionBars`:

```
public void fillActionBars(IWorkbenchWindow window,
    IActionBarConfigurer configurer, int flags) {
    ...
    if (maximizeAction == null) {
       maximizeAction = ActionFactory.MAXIMIZE.create(window);
       configurer.registerGlobalAction(maximizeAction);
    }
    menu.add(maximizeAction);
}
```

The method `registerGlobalAction` will let the platform know that your action exists. When the key binding is invoked by the user, it will now be able locate and run your action.

 FAQ 226 *What is the difference between a command and an action?*
FAQ 227 *How do I associate an action with a command?*
FAQ 229 *How do I provide a keyboard shortcut for my action?*

Can I create an application that doesn't have views or editors?

When you create an RCP application using a workbench advisor, you are still constrained to using the standard Eclipse UI constructs of views, editors, and perspectives. If you have very different UI requirements but still want to use the plug-in infrastructure, you can always create an application built on only SWT and JFace. This has been possible since the first release of Eclipse as SWT and JFace have no other dependencies outside the base runtime plug-in. JFace provides a basic `ApplicationWindow` with optional menus, toolbar, and status line.

Configuration of a JFace application works through subclassing rather than plugging in an advisor. Your application needs to subclass the JFace class called `ApplicationWindow` and override the various methods that are used to customize the appearance and behavior of the window. The following is a simple JFace application window from the FAQ Examples plug-in. As with other applications, you begin by creating a class that implements `IPlatformRunnable`:

```
public class JFaceApp implements IPlatformRunnable {
    public Object run(Object args) throws Exception {
        Display display = new Display();
        JFaceAppWindow window = new JFaceAppWindow();
        window.open();
        Shell shell = window.getShell();
        while (!shell.isDisposed()) {
            if (!display.readAndDispatch())
                display.sleep();
        }
        return EXIT_OK;
    }
}
```

`JFaceAppWindow` is a subclass of the framework class `ApplicationWindow`. The subclass creates a simple window with a menu bar, a status line, and a single button inside the main window that is used to exit the application (Figure 16.2).

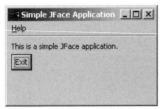

Figure 16.2   Simple JFace application

Complete source for the class can be found in the FAQ Examples plug-in, but here is the basic structure:

```
public class JFaceAppWindow extends ApplicationWindow {
    public JFaceAppWindow() {
        super(null);
        addMenuBar();
        addStatusLine();
    }
    protected void configureShell(Shell shell) {
        super.configureShell(shell);
        shell.setText("Simple JFace Application");
    }
    ...
}
```

The subclass also needs to override the `createContents` method to create the SWT widgets that will appear in the window's main content area. Override `createMenuManager` to populate the window's menus, `createToolBarManager` to populate the toolbar, and so on. If you browse through the `ApplicationWindow` class, you will see that many other hook methods allow your application to customize the appearance of the top-level window.

 FAQ 232 *How do I build menus and toolbars programmatically?*

How do I specify where application data is stored?

Plug-in metadata, as well as other data associated with an Eclipse application, is usually stored inside the *platform instance location*. This location is also known as the *instance data area* or the *workspace*. There are a number of ways that your application can specify this location:

- Pick a fixed location and specify it using the `-data` command-line argument on startup (for example, from your own native launcher or launch script).

- Pick a location and specify it programmatically when your application starts.

- Let the default location be used. By default, the data area will be under the current working directory on startup in a subdirectory called `workspace`. This typically corresponds to the `eclipse` base directory.

- Prompt the user to specify a location on startup. This should be done from your application's `run` method before you call `PlatformUI.createAndRunWorkbench` to open the workbench.

If you define a location programmatically (either by prompting the user or by other means), you must then set it as follows:

```
URL choice = ... pick a data location
Location loc = Platform.getInstanceLocation();
if (loc.setURL(choice, true))
    //success!
else
    //location is in use, or is invalid
```

If your end-user is allowed to manipulate the command line directly, there are other things you need to keep in mind. For example, the user may have already picked a location using `-data`. In this case, `Location.isSet()` will return `true`, but you are still responsible for locking the location using `Location.lock()` to prevent other instances of your application from trying to use the same location concurrently. To see all of the cases that need to be considered take a look at how the Eclipse IDE application does it. Look at `IDEApplication.checkInstanceLocation` to see all the subtleties of checking and prompting for an instance location.

FAQ 25 *How do I run Eclipse?*
FAQ 102 *Where do plug-ins store their state?*
FAQ 249 *Can I create an application that doesn't have a data location?*

Can I create an application that doesn't have a data location?

Yes, you can, if you are very careful. In Eclipse 3.0, the base Eclipse runtime was designed to be able to run without any data location at all. If you have a carefully crafted RCP application, you might be able to get away with not having a data location. To launch an Eclipse application with no data location at all, use the special -data @none command-line argument:

```
eclipse -data @none -application your.app.id
```

If you do this, an error will occur if any plug-in attempts to access the platform instance location, including the plug-in metadata location. In other words, this configuration makes sense only for a tightly controlled application in which you are absolutely certain that the instance location will never be used.

One advantage of this approach is that multiple instances of your application can run simultaneously without forcing the user to pick a different data location for each one. For most RCP applications, this type of configuration is too constrictive. A better approach for applications that don't need to store any interesting state is to pick a random location in a scratch directory, such as the directory provided by System.getProperty("java.io.tmpdir"). This will ensure that your application does not fail if a plug-in is installed that does want to access the instance location.

☞ **FAQ 248** *How do I specify where application data is stored?*

Chapter 14. Productizing an Eclipse Offering

In this chapter, we look at turning an Eclipse configuration into a product. When an Eclipse product is created, the anonymous collection of plug-ins takes on application-specific branding, complete with custom images, splash screen, and launcher. In creating your own product, you typically also need to write an installer and uninstaller and consider how your users will obtain and upgrade your product.

What is an Eclipse product?

FAQ
250

Strictly speaking, a product is an extension to the extension point called `org.eclipse.core.runtime.products`. The purpose of a product is to define application-specific branding on top of a configuration of Eclipse plug-ins. Minimally, a product defines the ID of the application it is associated with and provides a name, description, and unique ID of its own. A product also stores a table of additional properties, where the UI stores information such as the application window icon and the all-important blurb in the **Help > About...** dialog. It is quite possible to run Eclipse without a product, but if you want to customize the appearance of Eclipse for your particular application, you should define one.

Because more than one product can be installed at a given time, the main product is singled out in a special marker file called `.eclipseproduct` in the Eclipse install directory. This file denotes the name, ID, and version number of the main product that will be used. The product in turn is a plug-in in the `plugins` directory, which includes product branding elements, such as the splash screen and workbench window icons.

For more details, see the methods declared by the `IProduct` interface defined in the `org.eclipse.core.runtime` plug-in. `IProductConstants` in the `org.eclipse.ui.workbench` defines the keys of product properties that are of interest to Eclipse products having user interfaces.

FAQ 111 *What is a configuration?*
eclipse.org article *"Creating Product Branding"*

What is the difference between a product and an application?

At first glance, the notions of *product* and *application* in Eclipse seem similar. Both are contributed via an extension point, and both are used to bring order to the chaos of an otherwise random collection of executing Eclipse plug-ins. However, the two concepts have some important differences. First, whereas an application defines behavior—it has code associated with it—a product is purely declarative. That is, a product provides properties, such as icons and text, that are used to customize the appearance of a running application. A second distinction is that there is typically only one product, but that product may include several applications. For example, the Eclipse Platform is a single product but includes several applications, such as the workbench application and an application for running custom Ant build files. All applications under a given product have the same branding elements associated with them.

 FAQ 241 *What is an Eclipse application?*
FAQ 250 *What is an Eclipse product?*

How do I distribute my Eclipse offering?

That depends. If you just got started and are still testing your plug-ins or if you have few internal customers, you may be happy with simply building a plug-in and providing your users with a Zip file. Once you get more professional and have access to a Web site where people can access your plug-ins, an update site is recommended. To be in full control of how and where your offering is installed, you could use a more traditional form of product installation through a custom installer program.

 FAQ 92 *How do I create an update site (`site.xml`)?*
FAQ 253 *Can I use an installation program to distribute my Eclipse product?*

Can I use an installation program to distribute my Eclipse product?

FAQ
253

Most Eclipse-based commercial product offerings ship their own product plug-ins using a professional installation program, such as InstallShield, or using a free one, such as the Install Toolkit for Java (from IBM AlphaWorks). Such installation tools provide the flexibility of user-defined scripts that are run during installation to discover already installed Eclipse installations, to query the registry on Windows, and most important, to provide graceful uninstall capabilities.

For example, IBM's WebSphere Studio Device Developer is shipped as a set of plug-ins and embedded Java runtimes, together with the latest release of Eclipse, designed to install from a CD-ROM. The product can be installed stand-alone or added to an existing IBM product, such as WebSphere Studio Application Developer. Doing the installation with a product like InstallShield allows for this kind of flexibility during the installation.

Once the product has been installed, it is recommended that the Eclipse Update Manager be used to check for updates and that an update site be used for delivering new features or feature upgrades to users. This is the way users of WebSphere Studio Device Developer can add support for embedded platforms that were added recently or that are provided by third parties.

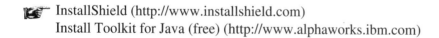 InstallShield (http://www.installshield.com)
Install Toolkit for Java (free) (http://www.alphaworks.ibm.com)

Can I install my product as an add-on to another product?

FAQ
254

Yes. A product that adds functionality to another installed product is called a *product extension*. A product extension is installed in a location separate from the main product, making it cleaner to install, uninstall, and upgrade both the product and any product extensions. The exact format of a product extension is well described in the *Platform Plug-in Developer Guide*, under **Programmer's Guide > Packaging and delivering Eclipse based products > Product extensions**.

FAQ 32 *Can I install plug-ins outside the main install directory?*
FAQ 250 *What is an Eclipse product?*
FAQ 253 *Can I use an installation program to distribute my Eclipse product?*

Where do I find suitable Eclipse logos and wordmarks?

The Eclipse Web site contains a list of suitable logos and wordmarks to download for varying use, such as either four-color-process offset printing, desktop publishing, Web sites, and embroidery applications. Users are advised to use the original artwork and not to redraw or redesign it for any purpose.

 Eclipse artwork (http://eclipse.org/artwork/main.html)

When do I need to write a plug-in install handler?

Writing a plug-in install handler is appropriate for most professional applications. Doing so is not only a comfort that most end users will expect but also allows you to perform custom installation, such as

- Moving data to other locations in the file system outside the install directory. This allows data to be shared by multiple applications or by multiple versions of your application.
- Reading or saving values in the Windows registry.
- Asking the user to confirm licensing terms.
- Searching for installed components, such as ActiveX or database drivers, that your application requires and installing them, if necessary.

When creating a feature using the PDE wizard, you get the option to specify an optional feature-specific install handler.

 FAQ 253 *Can I use an installation program to distribute my Eclipse product?*

How do I support multiple natural languages in my plug-in messages?

Almost all plug-ins in Eclipse use `java.util.ResourceBundle`, a `messages.properties` file, and look up messages by using a key. The `MessageFormat` class can be used to insert parameters into the translated message. Here is an example:

```
String translate(String key, String[] parms) {
    try {
        ResourceBundle bundle =
            ResourceBundle.getBundle("messages");
        String msg = bundle.getString(key);
        return MessageFormat.format(msg, parms);
    } catch (MissingResourceException e) {
        return key;
    }
}
```

Eclipse includes special support to replace constant strings in your plug-in source code by equivalent Java code that uses key-based lookup. Execute the context menu option **Source > Externalize Strings...** and follow the instructions. To save memory, we recommend choosing a short prefix for the generated keys.

If you reject translation of a given string, the externalization tool will place comments like `//$NON-NLS-1$` at the end of the line that contains the string. Otherwise, it will replace the string by the lookup code.

Caveat: In the current Eclipse distribution, the various plug-ins declare and ship around 30,000 property keys to support multiple languages. The bytes these keys occupy amount to roughly 8 percent of the uncompressed distribution size. But, more important, resource bundles are loaded whole, as in the preceding sample. This happens even when no string is ever loaded from it. Therefore, a large properties file can easily generate a lot of wasted space.

Conservative estimates have shown that a typical Eclipse launch uses upward of 1MB to store the keys in memory. This memory is used by the `ResourceBundle` implementation, which typically uses a hash table and by the classes that declare and pass a key to the resource bundle to translate the string. The keys are stored in the class files of the plug-in and saved somewhere in the JVM's data structures. In short, there is a big incentive to keep property keys short. For large offerings delivered on top of Eclipse, one should consider writing specialized `ResourceBundle` subclasses that use integer constants to lookup string bindings, for instance.

How do I replace the Eclipse workbench window icon with my own?

The Eclipse workbench icon is defined by the Eclipse product. This file is specified in the `about.ini` file in the product plug-in's install directory, using the key `windowImage` if only a single 16×16 icon is provided, or `windowImages` if the product has both 16×16 and 32×32 icons. Note that these `about.ini` constants are defined by the `IProductConstants` interface in `org.eclipse.ui.workbench`.

As a debugging aid, many Eclipse developers hack the icon for their runtime workbench to make it easy to distinguish from the development workbench. This saves you from accidentally deleting your work while you try to reproduce some bug in a test environment. Simply check out the `org.eclipse.platform` plug-in from the Eclipse repository, and replace `eclipse.gif` with any other icon. Now, every runtime workbench will have that custom icon in the upper left-hand corner.

 FAQ 79 *Where can I find the Eclipse plug-ins?*
FAQ 250 *What is an Eclipse product?*
eclipse.org article *"Creating Product Branding"*

How do I write my own `eclipse.exe` platform launcher?

Most of the time, it is not necessary to write your own customized native launcher. The default launcher supports a large number of command-line arguments, allowing you to customize the splash screen, plug-in configuration, JVM, and much more. In some cases, you may want to wrap the native launcher in another launcher to prime the set of command-line arguments passed to the default launcher.

If you do need to write your own native launcher, the obvious place to start is by looking at the source code for the Eclipse launcher. This source is found in the Eclipse CVS repository in the `platform-launcher` project.

☞ **FAQ 25** *How do I run Eclipse?*
FAQ 79 *Where can I find the Eclipse plug-ins?*

Who shows the Eclipse splash screen?

FAQ
260

The splash screen that appears during start-up is provided by the Eclipse product. On start-up, the platform looks for a file called `splash.bmp` in the product plug-in's install directory. The Eclipse launcher, such as `eclipse.exe` on Windows, specifies the name of the command to run for showing the splash screen using the `-showsplash` command-line argument. If you are not defining your own custom launcher, all you need to do is place the splash image in the product's install directory, and the launcher will find and open it.

☞ **FAQ 250** *What is an Eclipse product?*
eclipse.org article *"Creating Product Branding"*

How can I publish partial upgrades (patches) to my product?

FAQ
261

See the Eclipse Web site (http://eclipse.org) and click **Projects > The Eclipse Project > Platform > Update > Development Resources** for elaborate documentation on updating Eclipse-based products.

☞ **FAQ 91** *What is the Update Manager?*
FAQ 92 *How do I create an update site (`site.xml`)?*

Part III. The Eclipse IDE Platform

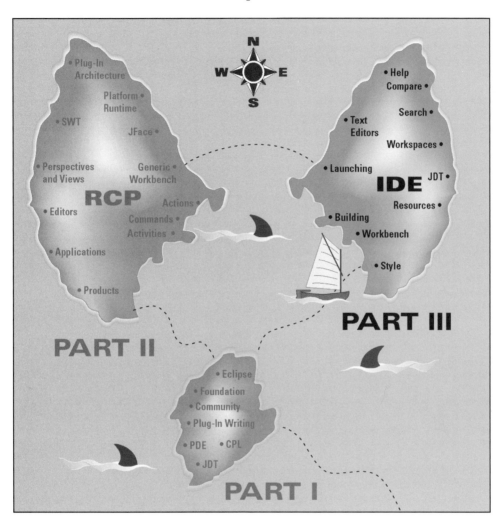

Chapter 15. Text Editors

The most important purpose of an IDE is to browse and edit code. Therefore, perhaps even more than any other IDE platform, the Eclipse editor framework has grown into a highly evolved, flexible, easy-to-use, and easy-to-extend environment for editing program source files. In this chapter, we look at what support exists for writing editors and how easy it is to plug them into the Eclipse IDE platform.

What support is there for creating custom text editors?

FAQ
262

Eclipse provides rich support for creating editors that operate on text, such as programming language editors or document editors. The framework has been designed in several layers of increasing coupling to the Eclipse Platform. Some of the lower-level components can easily be used outside Eclipse in stand-alone applications, and other parts can be used only within a running Eclipse Platform. Using this framework, you can quickly create a powerful editor with surprisingly little work.

The text infrastructure is so vast that it can be very difficult to figure out where to begin. Here is a little roadmap to the various plug-ins that provide facilities for text processing:

- `org.eclipse.text`. This plug-in is one of very few that have no connection to any other plug-ins. Because it has no dependence on the Eclipse Platform or even on SWT, this plug-in can easily be used in a stand-alone application. This plug-in provides a model for manipulating text and has no visual components, so it can be used by headless programs that process or manipulate text. Think of this plug-in as a rich version of `java.lang.StringBuffer` but with support for event change notification, partitions, search and replace, and other text-processing facilities.

- `org.eclipse.swt`. SWT is covered elsewhere in this book, but in the context of text editing, the class `StyledText` needs to be mentioned here. `StyledText` is the SWT user-interface object for displaying and editing text. Everything the user sees is rooted here: colors, fonts, selections, the caret (I-beam cursor), and more. You can add all kinds of listeners to this widget to follow what the user is doing. Some of the fancier features include word wrapping; bi-directional text, used by many non-Latin languages; and printing support.

- org.eclipse.jface.text. This plug-in is the marriage of the model provided by org.eclipse.text and the view provided by StyledText. True to the philosophy of JFace, the intent here is not to hide the SWT layer but to augment the visual presentation with a rich model and controllers. This plug-in is the heart of the text framework, and the list of features it provides is far too long to enumerate. To name just a few, it supports Content Assist, rule-based text scanners and partitioners, a vertical ruler, incremental reconciling, formatters, and hover displays. Many of these features are explored in more detail by other FAQs in this chapter.

- org.eclipse.ui.workbench.texteditor. This plug-in couples the text framework to the Eclipse Platform. You can't use the features provided here without being part of a running Eclipse workbench. In particular, this plug-in supports text editors that appear in the workbench editor area and features a large collection of Action subclasses for manipulating the contents of an editor, as well as support for annotations, incremental search, and more. If you're designing a text editor for use within the Eclipse Platform, you'll be subclassing the AbstractTextEditor class found in this plug-in. This abstract editor contains most of the functionality of the default text editor in Eclipse but without making any assumptions about where the content being edited is stored; it does not have to be in the workspace. This plug-in is appropriate for use in an RCP application that requires text editing support.

- org.eclipse.ui.editors. This plug-in provides the main concrete editor in the base Eclipse Platform: the default text editor. You generally don't need to use this plug-in when writing your own editor, as all the useful functionality has been abstracted out into the plug-ins we've already mentioned. This concrete editor is typically used on an IFileEditorInput on an IFile in the local workspace.

FAQ 263 *I'm still confused! How do all the editor pieces fit together?*
FAQ 264 *How do I get started with creating a custom text editor?*
FAQ 265 *How do I use the text document model?*

I'm still confused! How do all the editor pieces fit together?

Start browsing through the editor plug-ins, and a lot of names come out at you: IDocument, StyledText, ISourceViewer, ITextViewer, Text, ITextEditor, and many more. Furthermore, many of these pieces seem to overlap; they often provide similar functionality, and it's not easy to figure out which piece you should be looking at when implementing a feature.

It's not easy for the newcomer to grasp, but these overlapping pieces represent carefully designed layers of abstraction that allow for maximum reuse. Eclipse is designed to be extended by a large number of third parties with all kinds of different requirements. Instead of presenting a monolithic API that attempts to cater to all these needs, the editor framework gives you a loosely coupled toolkit that you can draw from, based on the needs of your particular application. A high-level overview helps when you're starting out.

The text-editing framework follows the same architectural principles as the rest of the Eclipse Platform. The four layers are the model (core), the view (SWT), the controller (JFace), and the presentation context (usually the workbench). The model and the view are self-contained pieces that know nothing about each other or the rest of the world. If you have a simple GUI application, you can get away with creating the view and manipulating it directly. Some tools operate directly on the model and don't care about the presentation. Often, the model, view, and controller are all used, but the same triad might appear in different contexts: in a workbench part, in a dialog, and so on. If your application demands it, you can replace any of these layers with a completely different implementation but reuse the rest.

Figure 15.1 show how these layers map onto the text-editing framework. The core is org.eclipse.jface.text.IDocument, with no dependency on any UI pieces. The view is org.eclipse.swt.custom.StyledText. Don't be fooled by org.eclipse.swt.widgets.Text; this is a (usually) native widget with very basic functionality. It's suitable for simple entry fields in dialogs but does not provide rich editing features. StyledText is the real widget for presenting text editors. The basic controller layer is provided by org.eclipse.jface.text.ITextViewer. This is extended by org.eclipse.jface.text.ISourceViewer to provide features particular to programming language editors. The context for presenting text editors in a workbench part is provided by org.eclipse.ui. texteditor.ITextEditor.

This is the text framework extension to the generic editor interface,
`org.eclipse.ui.IEditorPart`.

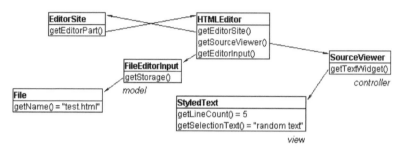

Figure 15.1   Model-view-controller collaboration in the Eclipse text-editing framework

 FAQ 262 *What support is there for creating custom text editors?*
FAQ 264 *How do I get started with creating a custom text editor?*

How do I get started with creating a custom text editor?

Follow the steps in **FAQ 211** to create a platform editor extension, but instead of
the basic `EditorPart`, subclass `AbstractTextEditor`. You don't need to
override `createPartControl` this time, because the abstract editor builds the
visual representation for you. In fact, you need to do nothing more; simply
subclassing `AbstractTextEditor` will give you a generic text editor
implementation right out of the box.

To customize your editor, you need to create your own subclass of
`SourceViewerConfiguration` defined in package
`org.eclipse.jface.text.source` when the editor is created. This class is the
locus of all editor customization. Just about every time you want to add a feature
to a text editor, you start by subclassing a method in the configuration. Browse
through the methods of this class to get an idea of the kinds of customization you
can add.

Another entry point for editor customization is the document provider. The
editor's document provider is a factory method for supplying the model object
(an `IDocument`) that represents the editor's contents. The document provider's
main function is to transform an `IEditorInput` into an appropriate `IDocument`.

By subclassing the generic document provider, you can create a customized document, such as a document that is divided into multiple partitions or a document that uses a different character encoding. This is also a good place for adding listeners to the document so you can be notified when it changes.

You'll also want to customize the actions available to your editor. The abstract text editor provides some actions, but if you want to add extra tools, you'll need actions for them. This is done by overriding the method createActions in your editor. Be sure to call super.createActions to allow the abstract editor to install the default set of text-editing actions, such as **Cut**, **Copy**, **Paste**, and **Undo**. The editor framework supplies more actions that are not automatically added to the abstract editor, but you can add them from your implementation of createActions. Look in the package org.eclipse.ui.texteditor for more available actions.

The FAQs in this chapter will use a running example of a simple HTML editor. We have used a simple text editor for writing HTML because it's the only editor that gives you complete control over the contents and won't insert all those funny tags that most editors insert to ensure that your pages won't be compatible with everyone's browser. Still, it's nice to have some syntax highlighting, Content Assist, and other time-saving features, so we wrote a simple HTML editor for Eclipse. The fact that this book is written in HTML gave us added incentive: another opportunity to eat our own dog food. As with all other examples in this book, complete source is available on the accompanying CD-ROM, and on this book's Web site (http://eclipsefaq.org).

Here is the skeleton of the HTMLEditor class, showing the customization entry points:

```
public class HTMLEditor extends AbstractTextEditor {
    public HTMLEditor() {
        //install the source configuration
        setSourceViewerConfiguration(new HTMLConfiguration());
        //install the document provider
        setDocumentProvider(new HTMLDocumentProvider());
    }
    protected void createActions() {
        super.createActions();
        //... add other editor actions here
    }
}
```

FAQ 262 *What support is there for creating custom text editors?*
Go to **Platform Plug-in Developer Guide > Programmer's Guide > Editors >
Configuring a source viewer**.

**FAQ
265**

How do I use the text document model?

The underlying model behind text editors is represented by the interface
IDocument and its default implementation, Document, both of which are declared
in the org.eclipse.jface.text package. You can use documents to
manipulate text inside and outside a text editor. Documents are created with a
simple constructor that optionally takes a string representing the initial input. The
document contents can be obtained and replaced by using get() and
set(String). The document model has a powerful search method and several
methods for querying or replacing portions of the document. The following
example uses a document to implement search and replace:

```
String searchAndReplace(String input, String search,
   String replace) throws BadLocationException {
   Document doc = new Document(input);
   int offset = 0;
   while (offset < doc.getLength()) {
      offset = doc.search(offset, search, true, true, true);
      if (offset < 0)
         break;
      doc.replace(offset, search.length(), replace);
      offset += replace.length();
   }
   return doc.get();
}
```

This example only scratches the surface of the capabilities of the IDocument
model. Documents also provide change notification, mapping between line
numbers and character offsets, partitions, and much more. Other FAQs in this
chapter dig into some of these concepts in more detail.

 FAQ 266 *What is a document partition?*
FAQ 270 *How do I insert text in the active text editor?*
Go to **Platform Plug-in Developer Guide > Programmer's Guide > Editors >
Documents and partitions**

What is a document partition?

Each document is divided into one or more nonoverlapping *partitions*. Many of the text-framework features can be configured to operate differently for each partition. Thus, an editor can have different syntax highlighting, formatting, or Content Assist for each partition. For example, the Java editor in Eclipse has different partitions for strings, characters, and comments.

If no partitions are explicitly defined, the single default partition is of type `IDocument.DEFAULT_CONTENT_TYPE`. If the explicitly defined partitions do not span the entire document, all remaining portions of the document implicitly belong to this default partition. In other words, every character in the document belongs to exactly one partition. Most editors define explicit partitions for small portions of the document that need custom behavior, and the bulk of the document remains in the default partition.

Documents are partitioned by connecting them to an instance of `org.eclipse.jface.text.IDocumentPartitioner`. In the case of editors, this is usually added by the document provider as soon as the document is created. You can implement the partitioner interface directly if you want complete control, but in most cases you can simply use the default implementation, `DefaultPartitioner`. This example from the HTML editor defines a partitioner and connects it to a document:

```
IDocumentPartitioner partitioner =
   new DefaultPartitioner(
      createScanner(),
      new String[] {
         HTMLConfiguration.HTML_TAG,
         HTMLConfiguration.HTML_COMMENT });
partitioner.connect(document);
document.setDocumentPartitioner(partitioner);
```

The default partitioner's constructor takes as arguments a scanner and an array of partition types for the document. The *partition scanner* is responsible for computing the partitions. It is given a *region* of the document and must produce a set of tokens describing each of the partitions in that region. When a document is created, the scanner is asked to create tokens for the entire document. When a document is changed, the scanner is asked to repartition only the region of the document that changed. Figure 15.2 shows the relationships among editor, document, partitioner, and scanner.

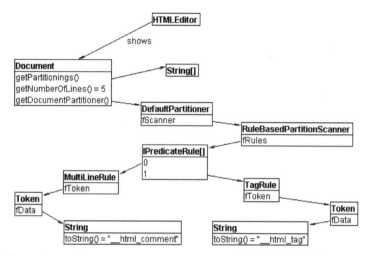

Figure 15.2   Partitioning a document using the Eclipse text-editing framework

The text framework provides a powerful rule-based scanner infrastructure for creating a scanner based on a set of predicate rules. You simply create an instance of the scanner and plug in the rules that define the regions in your document. Each rule is given a stream of characters and must return a token representing the characters if they match the rule. Browse through the type hierarchy of IPredicateRule to see what default rules are available. The following snippet shows the creation of the scanner for the HTML editor example:

```
IPartitionTokenScanner createScanner() {
    IToken cmt = new Token(HTMLConfiguration.HTML_COMMENT);
    IToken tag = new Token(HTMLConfiguration.HTML_TAG);
    IPredicateRule[] rules = new IPredicateRule[2];
    rules[0] = new MultiLineRule("", cmt);
    rules[1] = new TagRule(tag);
    RuleBasedPartitionScanner scanner =
      new RuleBasedPartitionScanner();
    scanner.setPredicateRules(rules);
    return sc;
}
```

FAQ 264 *How do I get started with creating a custom text editor?*
Go to **Platform Plug-in Developer Guide > Programmer's Guide > Editors > Documents and partitions**.

How do I add Content Assist to my editor?

As with most editor features, Content Assist is added to a text editor from your editor's `SourceViewerConfiguration`. In this case, you need to override the `getContentAssistant` method. Here is the implementation of this method in our HTML editor example:

```
public IContentAssistant
                getContentAssistant(ISourceViewer sv) {
    ContentAssistant ca = new ContentAssistant();
    IContentAssistProcessor pr =
                new TagCompletionProcessor();
    ca.setContentAssistProcessor(pr, HTML_TAG);
    ca.setContentAssistProcessor(pr,
                IDocument.DEFAULT_CONTENT_TYPE);
    ca.setInformationControlCreator(
                getInformationControlCreator(sv));
    return ca;
}
```

Although `IContentAssistant` is the top-level type that provides Content Assist, most of the work is done by an `IContentAssistProcessor`. Documents are divided into *partitions* to represent different logical segments of the text, such as comments, keywords, and identifiers. The `IContentAssistant`'s main role is to provide the appropriate processor for each partition of your document. In our HTML editor example, the document is divided into three partitions: comments, tags, and everything else, represented by the default content type.

In the preceding snippet, we have installed a single processor for tags and the default content type and no processor for comments. The final line before the return statement sets the information control creator for the content assistant. The information control creator is a factory for creating those information pop-ups that frequently appear in text editors, such as the Java editor. In the context of Content Assist, the information control creator is used to create the information pop-up that provides more details about a recommended completion.

After configuring the content assistant, the next step is to create one or more `IContentAssistProcessors`. When the user invokes Content Assist at a given position in the editor, the `computeCompletionProposals` method is called. This method's job is to figure out what completions, if any, are appropriate for that position. The method returns one or more `ICompletionProposal` instances, which is typically an instance of the generic class `CompletionProposal`.

A completion proposal encapsulates all the information that the text framework needs for presenting the completions to the user and for inserting a completion if the user selects one. Most of this information is self-explanatory, but a couple of items in the proposal need a bit more information: the context information and the additional proposal information.

Additional proposal info is displayed in a pop-up window when the user highlights a proposal but has not yet inserted it. As the name implies, the purpose of this information is to help the user decide whether the selected proposal is the desired completion. For our HTML tag processor, the additional information is a string describing the function of that tag. This information will be displayed only if your Content Assistant has installed an information control creator. See the earlier snippet of the `getContentAssistant` method to see how this is done.

Context information, if applicable, is displayed in a pop-up after the user has inserted a completion. The purpose here is to give the user extra information about what text needs to be entered after the completion has been inserted. This is best explained with an example from the Java editor. After the user has inserted a method using Content Assist in the Java editor, context information is used to provide information about the method parameters. As the user types in the method parameters, the context information shows the data type and parameter name for each parameter.

The final step in implementing Content Assist in your editor is to add an action that will allow the user to invoke Content Assist. The text framework provides an action for this purpose, but it is not installed in the abstract text editor because it isn't applicable to all flavors of text editors. The action is installed by overriding your editor's `createActions` method. The action class is `ContentAssistAction`. Here is a snippet from the `createActions` method in our example HTML editor:

```
Action action = new ContentAssistAction(resourceBundle,
    "ContentAssistProposal.", this);
String id =
    ITextEditorActionDefinitionIds.CONTENT_ASSIST_PROPOSALS
action.setActionDefinitionId(id);
setAction("ContentAssistProposal", action);
markAsStateDependentAction("ContentAssistProposal", true);
```

Line 1 creates the `Action` instance, supplying a resource bundle where the display strings should be taken from, along with a prefix for that action. The message bundle on disk would look something like this:

```
ContentAssistProposal.label=Content assist
ContentAssistProposal.tooltip=Content assist
ContentAssistProposal.description=Provides Content Assistance
```

Line 3 associates a well-known ID with the action that will tell the UI's command framework that this is the action for Content Assist. This allows the user to change the key binding for Content Assist generically and have it apply automatically to all editors that provide Content Assist.

Line 4 registers the action with the editor framework, using a unique ID. This ID can be used to identify the action when constructing menus and is used by the editor action bar contributor to reference actions defined by the editor. The final line in the snippet indicates that the action needs to be updated whenever the editor's state changes.

That's it! The Content Assist framework has a lot of hooks to allow you to customize the behavior and presentation of proposals and context information, but it would take far too much space to describe them here. See the sample HTML editor's implementation of Content Assist for a simple example to get you started. For a real-world example, we recommend browsing through the Java editor's Content Assist implementation. It can be found in the package `org.eclipse.jdt.internal.ui.text.java` in the `org.eclipse.jdt.ui` plug-in.

 FAQ 54 *How can Content Assist make me the fastest coder ever?*
FAQ 266 *What is a document partition?*
FAQ 336 *How do I add Content Assist to my language editor?*

How do I provide syntax coloring in an editor?

Syntax coloring in a JFace text editor is performed by a *presentation reconciler*, which divides the document into a set of tokens, each describing a section of the document that has a different foreground, background, or font style. Note that this sounds very similar to a partition token scanner, which divides the document into a series of partitions.

The tokens produced by the presentation reconciler are much more fine-grained than the ones produced by the partition scanner. For example, a Java file may be divided into partitions representing either javadoc or code. Within each partition, the presentation reconciler will produce separate tokens for each set of characters that have the same color and font. So, a Java keyword would be one token, and a string literal would be another. Each partition can have a different presentation reconciler installed, allowing for different rules to be used, depending on the type of content in the partition.

Once the initial presentation of a document is calculated, it needs to be incrementally maintained as the document is modified. The presentation reconciler uses two helper classes to accomplish this: a damager and a repairer. The damager takes as input a description of how the document changed and produces as output a description of the regions of the document whose presentation needs to be updated. For example, if a user deletes the ">" character representing the end of a tag in an HTML file, the region up to the next ">" character now needs to be colored as an HTML tag. The repairer's job is to update the presentation for all the damaged regions.

This all sounds very complicated, but the text framework will usually do most of this work for you. Typically you simply need to create a set of rules that describe the various tokens in your document. The framework has a default presentation reconciler that allows you to plug these rules into it, and the rest of the reconciling work is done for you. As an example, this is a scanner created by the sample HTML editor for scanning HTML tags:

```
ITokenScanner scanner = new RuleBasedScanner();
IToken string = createToken(colorString);
IRule[] rules = new IRule[3];
// Add rule for double quotes
rules[0] = new SingleLineRule("\"", "\"", string, '\\');
// Add a rule for single quotes
rules[1] = new SingleLineRule("'", "'", string, '\\');
// Add generic whitespace rule.
rules[2] = new WhitespaceRule(whitespaceDetector);
scanner.setRules(rules);
scanner.setDefaultReturnToken(createToken(colorTag));
```

This scanner creates unique tokens for string literals within a tag so it can color them differently. Outside of strings, the rest of the tag is divided into white-space-separated tokens, using a white-space rule.

The `createToken` method instantiates a `Token` object for a particular color:

```
private IToken createToken(Color color) {
    return new Token(new TextAttribute(color));
}
```

This scanner is finally fed to a standard presentation reconciler in the `SourceConfiguration` subclass. You need to specify a different damager/repairer for each partition of your document:

```
public IPresentationReconciler getPresentationReconciler(
  ISourceViewer sv) {
    PresentationReconciler rec = new PresentationReconciler();
    DefaultDamagerRepairer dr =
        new DefaultDamagerRepairer(getTagScanner());
    rec.setDamager(dr, HTML_TAG);
    rec.setRepairer(dr, HTML_TAG);
    ... same for other partitions ...
    return rec;
}
```

For more complex documents or for optimized reconciling, you can build your own custom damager and repairer instances by directly implementing `IPresentationDamager` and `IPresentationRepairer`, respectively. However, for most kinds of documents, a simple rule-based approach is sufficient.

 FAQ 266 *What is a document partition?*
Go to **Platform Plug-in Developer Guide > Programmer's Guide > Editors > Syntax coloring**.

How do I support formatting in my editor?

The JFace source viewer has infrastructure for supporting content formatters. A content formatter's job is primarily to adjust the whitespace between words in a document to match a configured style. A JFace formatter can be configured to operate on an entire document or on a region within a document. Typically, if a document contains several content types, a different formatting strategy will be used for each type. As usual, a formatter is installed from your subclass of `SourceViewerConfiguration`. To provide a configured formatter instance, override the method `getContentFormatter`. Most of the time, you can create an instance of the standard formatting class, `MultiPassContentFormatter`. This class requires that you specify a single *master* formatting strategy and optionally a *slave* formatting strategy for each partition in your document.

The following snippet from the Java source configuration installs a master strategy (`JavaFormattingStrategy`) that is used to format Java code and a slave formatting strategy for formatting comments:

```
MultiPassContentFormatter formatter=
    new MultiPassContentFormatter(
    getConfiguredDocumentPartitioning(viewer),
    IDocument.DEFAULT_CONTENT_TYPE);
formatter.setMasterStrategy(
    new JavaFormattingStrategy());
formatter.setSlaveStrategy(
    new CommentFormattingStrategy(...),
    IJavaPartitions.JAVA_DOC);
```

The work of formatting the characters in the document is performed by the formatting-strategy classes that are installed on the formatter. JFace doesn't provide much common infrastructure for doing this formatting as it is based largely on the syntax of the language you are formatting.

Finally, you will need to create an action that invokes the formatter. No generic formatting action is defined by the text infrastructure, but it is quite easy to create one of your own. The action's `run` method can simply call the following on the source viewer to invoke the formatter:

```
sourceViewer.doOperation(ISourceViewer.FORMAT);
```

FAQ 264 *How do I get started with creating a custom text editor?*

FAQ 270

How do I insert text in the active text editor?

Text editors have no public API to insert text. Furthermore, they do not expose their `StyledText` widget used to edit the underlying document. Therefore, inserting text in the currently active editor is not trivial. One could start with the SWT shell, search the widget containment hierarchy, and eventually locate the widget to enter text into. Fortunately, an easier way is available.

Text editors obtain a document model by using a *document provider*. This provider functions as synchronizer for multiple editors, notifying each when the other changes the document. By acting as one of the editors on a document, one can easily insert text into the editor of choice. The next code snippet locates the active editor, gets its document provider, requests the underlying document, and inserts some text into it:

```
IWorkbenchPage page = ...;
IEditorPart part = page.getActiveEditor();
if (!(part instanceof AbstractTextEditor)
    return;
ITextEditor editor = (ITextEditor)part;
IDocumentProvider dp = editor.getDocumentProvider();
IDocument doc = dp.getDocument(editor.getEditorInput());
int offset = doc.getLineOffset(doc.getNumberOfLines()-4);
doc.replace(offset, 0, pasteText+"\n");
```

The provider will notify all other editors to update their presentation as a result.

☞ **FAQ 265** *How do I use the text document model?*

What is the difference between highlight range and selection?

**FAQ
271**

`ITextEditor` has two similar concepts for singling out a portion of the editor contents: *selection* and *highlight range*. The selection is the highlighted segment of text typically set by the user when dragging the mouse or moving the caret around while holding the shift key. The selection can be obtained programmatically via the editor's selection provider:

```
ITextEditor editor = ...;//the text editor instance
ISelectionProvider sp = editor.getSelectionProvider();
ISelection selection = sp.getSelection();
ITextSelection text = (ITextSelection)selection;
```

The selection can also be changed using the selection provider, but `ITextEditor` provides a convenience method, `selectAndReveal`, that will change the selection and also scroll the editor so that the new selection is visible.

Highlight range also defines a subset of the editor contents, but it cannot be directly manipulated by the user. Its most useful feature is that the editor can be toggled to show only the current highlight range. This is used in the Java editor to support the "Show source of selected element only" mode. The default implementation of `ITextEditor` also links the highlight range to the `ISourceViewer` concept of *range indication*. The source viewer in turn creates an annotation in the vertical ruler bar that shades the portion of the editor corresponding to the highlight range. To use the Java editor as an example again, you'll notice this shading indicates the range of the method currently being edited. The following snippet sets the highlight range of a text editor and then instructs the editor to display only the highlighted portion:

```
ITextEditor editor = ...;
editor.setHighlightRange(offset, length, true);
editor.showHighlightRangeOnly(true);
```

FAQ 272

How do I change the selection on a double-click in my editor?

By default, double-clicking in a text editor will cause the complete word under the mouse to be selected. When creating your own text-based editor, you can change this behavior from your `SourceConfiguration` by overriding the method `getDoubleClickStrategy`. The method must return an instance of `ITextDoubleClickStrategy`, a simple interface that gets called whenever the user double-clicks within the editor area.

When double-clicking in a text-based editor, the selection will typically change to incorporate the nearest enclosing syntactic unit. For example, clicking next to a brace in the Java editor will expand the selection to include everything in the matched set of braces. Double-clicking in the sample HTML editor will cause the word under the mouse to be selected or, if no word is under the mouse, the entire HTML element. This involves scanning the document forwards and backwards from the current cursor position and then setting the selection accordingly. The following example is a bit contrived and is English-specific, but it illustrates the usual steps by selecting the text range up to the next vowel. If no vowel is found, nothing is selected:

```
public void doubleClicked(ITextViewer part) {
    final int offset = part.getSelectedRange().x;
    int length = 0;
```

```
IDocument doc = part.getDocument();
while (true) {
   char c = doc.getChar(offset + length);
   if (c=='a'||c=='e'||c=='i'||c=='o'||c=='u')
      break;
   if (offset + ++length >= doc.getLength())
      return;
}
part.setSelectedRange(offset, length);
}
```

Of course, double-clicking doesn't have to change the selection. You can
perform any manipulation you want on the editor or its document from within a
double-click strategy implementation. For example, double-clicking could trigger
Content Assist or present possible refactorings. The only real restriction is that
you can't use double-click to perform a manipulation on an existing text selection
as the first click of the double-click will have eliminated any previous selection.

How do I use a model reconciler?

FAQ
273

Advanced text editors, such as those for programming languages or Web
development, often have an underlying object model that represents the elements
being shown in the editor. Such models are often used for semantic manipulation,
such as refactoring, or for querying by other tools. As the user types in such an
editor, the text can become out of sync with this underlying model. For example,
an HTML editor may have a model that contains information about hyperlinks in
and out of the document. As the user edits the document, adding or removing
links and anchors, this model will invariably become out of date. If another tool
makes a query on this model while it is out of date, invalid results may occur.

When the editor is operating on a file in the workspace, one approach to solving
this problem is to use an incremental project builder to update the model. With
autobuild enabled, the model would be updated every time the user saved the
document. However, if autobuild is turned off, this strategy can result in long
periods of time in which the model is out of date. If the model update is a costly
computation, this might be the only practical trade-off. By turning autobuild off,
the user can control the build frequency.

For a lighter-weight model that can be updated with little overhead, it is
preferable to update the model more frequently. This is where a text editor
reconciler comes into play. When a reconciler is installed on an editor, a queue is

created to record all the changes that occur. Each change is represented as a DirtyRegion object, and the regions are added to a DirtyRegionQueue. The reconciler removes items from the queue and updates the model accordingly. If several edits occur in the document before the reconciler processes them, the DirtyRegion objects in the queue will merge where appropriate. For example, continuously typing in an editor will create one large dirty region rather than individual dirty regions for each character pressed. The reconciler can analyze the DirtyRegion objects to see what portions of the text have been invalidated, allowing it to perform more optimized updates.

A reconciler can be installed by overriding the getReconciler method declared in your subclass of SourceViewerConfiguration. You can choose from a couple of built-in reconcilers, or you can implement the IReconciler interface directly. Most of the time, you can use MonoReconciler, an implementation that does not distinguish between reconciling in different document partitions. This reconciler runs in a low-priority background thread, allowing multiple changes to be added to the queue before processing them. Performing the reconciliation asynchronously allows the user to continue editing the document while it is being reconciled, although this results in a short period in which the document will be out of date.

Note that reconcilers are generally not an adequate replacement for builders but can play a complementary role. For example, in the JDT plug-ins, the reconciler performs a parse of the class as the user makes changes. This parser gathers enough information to update the Java model, allowing accurate content assist, refactoring, and other common operations. When the user saves and builds the file, an incremental builder performs a full compilation, generating class files and recompiling any other files affected by the change. This way, the expensive processing is deferred, but the domain model always stays up to date.

☞ **FAQ 331** *Language integration phase 2: How do I implement a DOM?*

Chapter 16. Help, Search, and Compare

Admittedly, this chapter covers a number of unrelated components in the Eclipse Platform. They have in common the fact that each is designed as an independent plug-in that can be added to any Eclipse-based application. Although they are at home mostly in IDE applications, these plug-ins can also be inserted into RCP applications when help, search, or compare facilities are needed.

How do I add help content to my plug-in?

FAQ
274

Help is added to Eclipse in the form of *help books* that appear in the online help system. Each help book is laid out in table-of-contents files (`toc.xml`) that specify the structure of each help book. These table-of-contents files are then registered with the platform, using the `org.eclipse.help.toc` extension point. The help content must be in the form of standard HTML files. Each major topic should be in a separate file so it can be referenced in the table of contents. Not surprisingly, excellent help content that describes how to integrate help into your plug-in is available, so we don't need to go into further detail here.

☞ Go to **Platform Plug-in Developer Guide > Programmer's Guide > Plugging in help**.

How do I provide F1 help?

FAQ
275

When the user presses F1, context-sensitive help is displayed that briefly describes the action or widget that is currently in focus and provides links to related help topics. You can implement this form of help for your plug-in by associating a *help context ID* with the actions, menus, and controls in your plug-in. Help is designed in such a way that disruption in the code is kept to an absolute minimum. The help text and links are provided via an extension point and don't even need to reside in the same plug-in as the code that the help text refers to. This makes it easy to make help an optional part of your plug-in or to provide help in various languages.

The only code required to associate help with your UI component is to link a help context ID to it. This is accomplished by using the various `setHelp` methods on the `WorkbenchHelp` class. For example, adding help to a view can be done in the view's `createPartControl` method:

```
public void createPartControl(Composite parent) {
    ...
    WorkbenchHelp.setHelp(parent,
        "org.eclipse.faq.examples.books_view");
}
```

The `setHelp` methods can be used to add help contexts to actions, menus, and arbitrary controls. Because context-sensitive help operates on the control that is in focus, it makes sense to associate help contexts only with controls that are able to take focus. See the help documentation for more details.

For actions that are contributed declaratively, help contexts are contributed in the XML action definition. For example, for an action in an `actionSet`, the context is specified using the `helpContextId` attribute:

```
<action
    ...
    helpContextId="org.eclipse.faq.examples.console_action"
</action>
```

Help contexts are specified declaratively for the following extension points in the Eclipse SDK:

- `org.eclipse.ui.actionSets`
- `org.eclipse.ui.editorActions`
- `org.eclipse.ui.popupMenus`
- `org.eclipse.ui.viewActions`
- `org.eclipse.ui.ide.markerHelp`
- `org.eclipse.search.searchPages`
- `org.eclipse.debug.ui.launchShortcuts`
- `org.eclipse.debug.ui.launchConfigurationTabGroups`

☞ **FAQ 35** *Where do I get help?*
FAQ 276 *How do I contribute help contexts?*

How do I contribute help contexts?

Help contexts are added by using the `org.eclipse.help.contexts` extension point. Contexts are usually specified by using a separate help plug-in, making it easier to switch help content for various languages. The context extension specifies the path of a separate XML file where the data is stored:

```
<extension point="org.eclipse.help.contexts">
   <contexts
       file="help_contexts.xml"
       plugin="org.eclipse.faq.examples">
   </contexts>
</extension>
```

The contexts file includes a description for each context and can, optionally, add links to HTML help content files in the plug-in. See the help documentation for more details on the format of help context files.

☞ **FAQ 275** *How do I provide F1 help?*
Go to **Platform Plug-in Developer Guide > Programmer's Guide > Plugging in help**

How can I generate HTML and `toc.xml` files?

You can write the HTML files and the corresponding `toc.xml` file by hand, which is painful. An alternative is to use DocBook for those who swear by XML, style sheets, and XSLT. Perhaps the simplest way is to use the `toc.xml` Explorer and HTML editor included as samples with this book.

☞ DocBook (http://www.docbook.org)

How do I write a Search dialog?

You can add custom search pages to the Eclipse Search dialog by adding an extension to the `org.eclipse.search.searchPages` extension point. This page, which must implement the `ISearchPage` interface, should have input fields for whatever search criteria you want to allow. Figure 16.1 shows an example search page that allows the user to search for files based on their size.

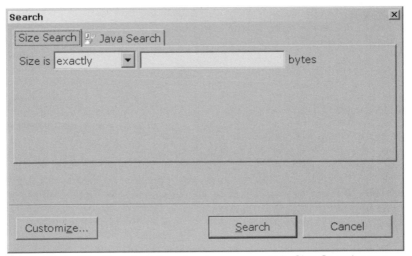

Figure 16.1   The Search dialog showing our example Size Search page

The code for creating the dialog page is much the same as for any other group of SWT widgets. The one caveat is that your `createControl` method must call `setControl` after your widget is created to let the dialog know what your top-level control is. Complete source code for the dialog is included in the FAQ Examples plug-in.

When the **Search** button is clicked, the `performAction` method is called on your search page. This method should perform the search and return `true` if the search was successful. If the user enters invalid search parameters, you should present a dialog explaining the error, and return `false` from the `performAction` method. Returning `false` causes the dialog to remain open so the user can fix the search parameters.

Your query page can, optionally, include a standard area allowing the user to specify a search scope. This scope can be the entire workspace, the selected resources, the selected projects, or a user-defined working set. If you want this scope area to appear in your page, include the attribute `showScopeSection = "true"` in your search page extension declaration. If you do include this, you should consult the chosen scope via the `ISearchPageContainer` instance that is passed to your page and make sure that your search operation honors the value of the scope.

Note that you are not restricted to creating queries based on files. The search dialog has pages for finding plug-ins and help contents as well. Other plug-ins are available on the Web for performing Bugzilla queries, news queries, and more. However, the infrastructure for presenting results in the Search Results view is limited to file-based searches. If your search is not operating on files, you will need to create your own view or dialog for presenting search results.

FAQ 279 *How do I implement a search operation?*
FAQ 280 *How do I display search results?*

How do I implement a search operation?

FAQ
279

A search operation is initiated from the `performAction` method on a search page. The search can run either in a blocking manner, thus preventing the user from doing further work until the search is done, or in the background. To run the search in a blocking manner, use the `IRunnableContext` available from the `ISearchPageContainer` instance:

```
class SearchSizePage extends DialogPage
  implements ISearchPage {
    private ISearchPageContainer container;
    public boolean performAction() {
        // ... validate input ...
        IRunnableWithProgress query = ...;//the query object
        container.getRunnableContext().run(true, true, query);
        return true;
    }
    public void setContainer(ISearchPageContainer spc) {
        this.container = spc;
    }
}
```

To run your query in the background, create and schedule a subclass of `Job`. Regardless of whether the search is run in the foreground or the background, the mechanics of the search operation itself will usually be the same.

If your search is operating on files in the workspace, you should ensure that changes are batched to prevent autobuilds every time a search result is created. Do this by making your operation subclass `WorkspaceModifyOperation` in the blocking case or `WorkspaceJob` in the nonblocking case. For the rest of this FAQ, we'll assume that you're writing a search on the workspace.

The purpose of your search operation is to locate the files that match the search parameters and to generate search result markers for each match. One common method of doing this is to use a resource visitor. Here is the general structure of a simple search operation:

```
class SearchOperation extends WorkspaceModifyOperation
   implements IResourceProxyVisitor {
   public void execute(IProgressMonitor monitor) {
      ResourcesPlugin.getWorkspace().getRoot().accept(
         this, IResource.DEPTH_INFINITE);
   }
   protected boolean isMatch(IFile file) {
      ... test match criteria ...
   }
   public boolean visit(IResourceProxy proxy) {
      if (proxy.getType() == IResource.FILE) {
         IFile file = (IFile) proxy.requestResource();
         if (isMatch(file))
            file.createMarker(SearchUI.SEARCH_MARKER);
      }
      return true;
   }
}
```

If your search is located within a specific portion of the file, you should fill in the appropriate attributes on the search result marker (LINE_NUMBER, CHAR_START, and CHAR_END from IMarker). None of these attributes is required; in some cases, a search can simply identify an entire file.

FAQ 278 *How do I write a Search dialog?*
FAQ 280 *How do I display search results?*
FAQ 290 *How do I prevent builds between multiple changes to the workspace?*
FAQ 304 *Why don't my markers appear in the editor's vertical ruler?*

How do I display search results?

Marker-based search results can be displayed in the Search Results view provided by the `org.eclipse.search` plug-in. To do this, you first need to make sure that the Search Results view is created and then obtain a reference via the `SearchUI` class:

```
SearchUI.activateSearchResultView();
ISearchResultView resultView = SearchUI.getSearchResultView();
```

Before you begin adding search results to the view, you need to call `ISearchResultView.searchStarted`. This method lets the view know that the series of matches about to be added belong to a single search query. This method takes the following:

- `IActionGroupFactory`, a factory object for creating the actions that will appear in the context menu when a search result is selected.

- `String`, the label to use in the view title bar when there is exactly one search result. This label should describe the search thoroughly because it will also appear in the search history list that allows the user to add old searches back to the view.

- `String`, the same label as the preceding, but for multiple search results. The string should contain the pattern `{0}`, which will be replaced with the exact number of occurrences.

- `ImageDescriptor`, the image to use for this group of results. This will also appear in the search history drop-down list. If you don't provide one, a default icon will be used.

- `String`, the ID of the Search dialog page that generated this set of search results. This is the ID attribute from the search page extension declaration.

- `ILabelProvider`, the label provider to use for displaying each search result. If not provided, a reasonable default will be used.

- `IAction`, the action that will cause your search result to be opened in an editor.

- `IGroupByKeyComputer` (described in the next paragraph).

- `IRunnableWithProgress`, a runnable that will execute the search query over again. This can be the exact runnable executed from the Search dialog.

The Search Results view shows results in groups, where each line in the view is a single group. A group typically corresponds to a logical unit, such as a file or a Java method, where the match was found. This serves to reduce clutter in the view so that a large number of results can be aggregated into a smaller space. The `IGroupByKeyComputer` object provided in the `searchStarted` method is used to map from search results to the group that corresponds to each result. If you don't want to group your search results, you don't need to provide this object.

Once the search has been started, each search result is added to the view by using the `addMatch` method. This method takes a description string, a resource handle, the search result marker, and an object that represents the group that the result belongs to. A typical grouping is to use the file as the group identifier. That way, all search results for a given file will be aggregated together in the Search Results view. If you don't want to group search results at all, use the marker itself as the group marker.

Finally, when you have finished adding search results, call the method `searchFinished` on the Search Results view. This method must be called in all circumstances, including failure and cancellation, so it is a good idea to put it in a `finally` block at the end of your search operation.

 FAQ 278 *How do I write a Search dialog?*
FAQ 279 *How do I implement a search operation?*

**FAQ
281**

How can I use and extend the compare infrastructure?

The `org.eclipse.compare` plug-in includes infrastructure for computing the differences between groups of files and the content of individual files. The plug-in also contains UI components that allow a user to browse and manipulate comparisons in editors and dialogs. Eclipse components typically interact with the compare plug-in in two ways. First, they may be compare clients, using the comparison engine to compute differences between various inputs and to display the result of those comparisons. For example, the `Team` plug-ins use the compare support to compute differences between local and remote resources, and to display those comparisons in a comparison editor.

The second way to use the compare plug-in is as a provider. Your plug-in can contribute viewers for displaying the structure of files and for illustrating the differences between two files of a particular type. *Structure merge viewers* are contributed when you have a file with a particular semantic structure that is useful to display to the user. For example, JDT supplies a structure merge viewer that shows the differences between the methods and fields of the files being displayed. Structure viewers are contributed by using the `structureMergeViewers` extension point.

The platform includes compare viewers for text content and for GIF and JPG image files. If you have unique files that need a more specialized compare viewer, you can contribute one via an extension point. All plug-ins that use compare will then be able to make use of those compare viewers for displaying your content type. To contribute a content viewer that does not support merge, use the `contentViewers` extension point. To contribute a viewer that supports the merging of files, use the `contentMergeViewers` extension point.

☞   Go to **Platform Plug-in Developer Guide > Programmer's Guide > Compare support**

How do I create a Compare dialog?

FAQ
282

The Eclipse SDK includes actions for comparing and replacing files in the workspace with one another and with editions in the local history. The same mechanisms can be used for comparing any kind of text content, regardless of its source. `EditionSelectionDialog` is used to ask the user to select from an array of input elements. The inputs must implement several interfaces. First, they must implement `ITypedElement` to provide the name, image, and content type of the object to be compared. Second, they must implement `IModificationDate` to provide a timestamp of the object's creation or modification date. The timestamp is used to sort the input elements chronologically. Finally, they must implement `IStreamContentAccessor` to supply the content to be compared. Here is an example of a class that implements all these interfaces for string-based content:

```
class CompareItem implements IStreamContentAccessor,
        ITypedElement, IModificationDate {
    private String contents, name;
    private long time;
    StringItem(String name, String contents, long time) {
        this.name = name;
        this.contents = contents;
        this.time = time;
    }
    public InputStream getContents() throws CoreException {
        return new ByteArrayInputStream(contents.getBytes());
    }
    public Image getImage() {return null;}
    public long getModificationDate() {return time;}
    public String getName() {return name;}
    public String getString() {return contents;}
    public String getType() {return ITypedElement.TEXT_TYPE;}
}
```

The most interesting method here is the getType method, which should return the file extension of the input element. The file extension is used to determine the viewer for displaying the contents of the object.

The method EditionSelectionDialog.selectEdition accepts an array of objects that implement all the interfaces mentioned earlier. It will open a dialog, allow the user to select one of the available editions, and return the chosen result. The EditionSelectionDialog instance is initialized in a somewhat unorthodox manner by requiring a ResourceBundle object in the constructor. This bundle must supply all the text messages that appear in the dialog, in addition to such parameters as the dialog's default width and height. See the EditionSelectionDialog constructor comment for more details. In the FAQ Examples plug-in, see the CompareStringsAction example for a complete illustration of how this dialog is used.

How do I create a compare editor?

Compare dialogs are typically used in simple contexts that ask the user to select from a list of available editions. For richer comparisons, a compare editor is typically used. The advantage of using an editor is that the user can take as long as needed to browse, modify, and merge the contents.

Compare editors display a tree of DiffNode elements, where each node represents a logical entity, such as a file or programming-language element. These nodes represent either a two-way or a three-way comparison, where the optional third element is the common ancestor of the two elements being compared. Each DiffNode references a left- and right-side element and, possibly, a third element representing the common ancestor. As with compare dialogs, these compare elements should implement ITypedElement and IStreamContentAccessor. You can construct these node trees manually or use the supplied Differencer class to help you construct it.

The DiffNode tree is computed by a CompareEditorInput subclass that is passed as an input to the editor. The subclass must implement the prepareInput method to return the tree represented by the DiffNode. The following example illustrates a compare editor input that uses the CompareItem class described in **FAQ 282**:

```
class CompareInput extends CompareEditorInput {
    public CompareInput() {
        super(new CompareConfiguration());
    }
    protected Object prepareInput(IProgressMonitor pm) {
        CompareItem ancestor =
            new CompareItem("Common", "contents");
        CompareItem left =
            new CompareItem("Left", "new contents");
        CompareItem right =
            new CompareItem("Right", "old contents");
        return new DiffNode(null, Differencer.CONFLICTING,
            ancestor, left, right);
    }
}
```

Once you have a compare editor input, opening a compare editor on that input is trivial. Here is an example action that opens a compare editor, using the preceding input:

```
public class CompareEditorAction implements
  IWorkbenchWindowActionDelegate {
    public void run(IAction action) {
       CompareUI.openCompareEditor(new CompareInput());
    }
}
```

If you want to support merging as well as comparing, two extra steps are involved. First, you need to specify which of the elements is editable. This is done by the CompareConfiguration object that is passed to the CompareEditorInput constructor. Use the setLeftEditable and setRightEditable methods to specify which of the comparison panes should support modification. Second, your editor input class should override the save method to perform the save of the editor contents.

Chapter 17. Workspace and Resources API

A program is never written in isolation but instead depends on other code, icons, data, and configuration files. An extendable IDE should provide access to wherever these artifacts are stored. In Eclipse, the artifacts are referred to as *resources* and are stored in a *workspace*. The FAQs in this chapter show how resources are managed in a workspace and what API is available to control and track their lifecycle.

How are resources created?

FAQ
284

The workspace is manipulated using *resource handles*. Resource handles are lightweight pointers to a particular project, folder, or file in the workspace. You can create a resource handle without creating a resource, and resources can exist regardless of whether any handles exist that point to them. To create a resource, you first have to create a resource handle and then tell it to create the resource. The following snippet uses resource handles to create a project, a folder, and a file.

```
IWorkspace workspace = ResourcesPlugin.getWorkspace();
IWorkspaceRoot root = workspace.getRoot();
IProject project  = root.getProject("MyProject");
IFolder folder = project.getFolder("Folder1");
IFile file = folder.getFile("hello.txt");
//at this point, no resources have been created
if (!project.exists()) project.create(null);
if (!project.isOpen()) project.open(null);
if (!folder.exists())
    folder.create(IResource.NONE, true, null);
if (!file.exists()) {
    byte[] bytes = "File contents".getBytes();
    InputStream source = new ByteArrayInputStream(bytes);
    file.create(source, IResource.NONE, null);
}
```

This example defensively checks that the resource doesn't already exist before trying to create it. This kind of defensive programming is a good idea because an exception is thrown if you try to create a resource that already exists. This way, the example can be run more than once in the same workspace without causing an error. The `null` parameters to the creation methods should be replaced by a progress monitor in a real application.

Can I create resources that don't reside in the file system?

No. Resources are strictly a file system-based model. They cannot be used to represent files on a remote server or in a database. Although this prevents a large amount of the platform's functionality from being used for nonlocal applications, there were strong architectural reasons for taking this approach. A principal design goal of Eclipse from the start was to enable it to interoperate smoothly with other tools. Because most tools operate on resources in the file system, this is an important medium for interaction between applications. If Eclipse were built on an abstract resource model with no necessary connection with the file system, interaction between Eclipse plug-ins and non-Eclipse-aware tools would be very difficult.

Having said that, nothing requires you to use `IResource` as your model layer. Almost none of the base platform is tied to resources, and the text-editing framework can also operate on non-`IResource` models. If you want to build plug-ins that operate on files located remotely, you can define your own model layer to represent them and build views and editors that interact with that remote model rather than with the strictly local `IResource` model. In Eclipse 3.0, the RCP has no relationship at all with the `IResource`-based workspace. Only the Eclipse IDE plug-ins still retain a dependency on this model.

If you use resources, you will be tied to the local file system, but you will have a common layer that allows you to interoperate seamlessly with other tools. If you don't want to be tied to the local file system, you can build your own model at the expense of lost integration with plug-ins that are not aware of it. Seamless integration of disparate tools based on a completely abstract resource model is a lofty idea, but like many lofty ideas, it is one that has yet to take flight.

What is the difference between a path and a location?

In general, the term *location* represents physical file system paths, and *path* represents a resource's logical position within the workspace. Many people are confused by this distinction, as both terms are represented by using the IPath data type.

IPath is in fact an abstract data structure that represents a series of slash-separated strings. Many people assume that paths always correspond to a file-system location, but this is not always the case. In fact, IPath objects are used in a variety of contexts for locating an object within a tree-like hierarchy. For example, a resource path, returned by IResource.getFullPath, represents the position of a resource within the workspace tree. The first segment is the name of the project, the last segment is the name of the file or folder, and the middle segments are the names of the parent folders in order between the project and the file or folder in question. This doesn't always match the path of the resource in the file system!

The file-system location of a resource, on the other hand, is returned by the method IResource.getLocation. Methods on IContainer and IWorkspaceRoot can help you convert from one to the other. The following code converts from a path to a location:

```
IPath path = ...;
IWorkspace workspace = ResourcesPlugin.getWorkspace();
IWorkspaceRoot root = workspace.getRoot();
IResource resource = root.findMember(path);
if (resource != null) {
    location = resource.getLocation();
}
```

Note that in some situations, a resource can have a null location. In particular, resources whose project doesn't exist and linked resources that are relative to a nonexistent path variable will have a null location.

Here is the converse code to convert from a location to the workspace paths that correspond to it:

```
IPath location = ...;
IFile[] files = root.findFilesForLocation(location);
IFolder[] folders = root.findContainersForLocation(location);
if (files.length > 0) {
   for (int i = 0; i < files.length; i++)
      path = files[i].getLocation();
} else {
   for (int i = 0; i < folders.length; i++)
      path = folders[i].getLocation();
}
```

As this snippet shows, a single file-system location can correspond to multiple resources. This is true because linked resources can point to locations inside other projects. Of course, the same file-system location can't correspond to both files and folders at the same time.

When using API from the resources plug-in that involves IPath objects, always read the API javadoc carefully to see whether it deals with paths or locations. These different types of paths must never be mixed or used interchangeably, as they represent completely different things.

**FAQ
287**

When should I use `refreshLocal`?

Resources become out of sync with the workspace if they are changed directly in the file system without using Eclipse workspace API. If your plug-in changes files and folders in this way, you should manually synchronize the workspace with the file system using the method `IResource.refreshLocal`. Some common situations where this is necessary include:

- When files are manipulated using `java.io` or `java.nio`, such as writing to a `FileOutputStream`.

- When your plug-in calls an external editor that is not Eclipse-aware.

- When you do file I/O using your own natives.

- When you launch external builders, tools, or Ant scripts that modify files in the workspace.

Here is an example snippet that sets the contents of a file using a `FileOutputStream`, and then uses `refreshLocal` to synchronize the workspace. This example is a bit contrived, because you could easily use the workspace API in this case. Imagine that the actual file manipulation is buried in some third-party library that you can't change, and this code makes more sense.

```
private void externalModify(IFile iFile) throws ... {
    java.io.File file = iFile.getLocation().toFile();
    FileOutputStream fOut = new FileOutputStream(file);
    fOut.write("Written by FileOutputStream".getBytes());
    iFile.refreshLocal(IResource.DEPTH_ZERO, null);
}
```

You might reasonably ask why the workspace does not refresh out of sync files automatically. The answer in Eclipse 3.0 is that it can, with some caveats. The problem is that there is no way to do this efficiently in a platform-neutral way. Some operating systems have callback mechanisms that send notifications when there are changes to particular sections of the file system, but this support doesn't exist on all operating systems that Eclipse runs on. The only way to perform automatic refresh across all platforms is to have a background thread that periodically polls the file system for changes. This clearly can have a steep performance cost, especially since workspaces might easily contain tens of thousands of files.

The solution in Eclipse 3.0 is to have an auto-refresh capability that is turned off by default. On platforms that have efficient native support for change notification, this can be quite fast. On other platforms, change notification can be very slow. Users who have a need to modify files externally on a regular basis may gladly pay the performance cost to get automatic workspace refresh. Users who do not make external modifications to files, can leave auto-refresh off and avoiding paying a performance penalty for a feature they do not need. This follows the general performance rule of only introducing a performance hit if and when it is actually needed. Auto-refresh can be turned on by checking **Refresh workspace automatically** on the **Workbench** preference page.

The down side of auto-refresh is that programmatic clients of the workspace API still need to check for and defend against out of sync resources. Resources can be out of sync if auto-refresh is turned off, and they can even be out of sync when auto-refresh is turned on. If you are programmatically modifying files in the workspace externally, you should still perform a `refreshLocal` to make sure files come back in sync as quickly as possible.

If you are using Eclipse 2.1, you can install auto-refresh as a separate plug-in. This plug-in is hosted on the Eclipse Platform core team home page, to be found at the Eclipse Web site (http://eclipse.org), by clicking on **Projects > The Eclipse Project > Platform > Core > Development Resources and Planning**.

FAQ 288

How do I create my own tasks, problems, bookmarks, and so on?

Annotations can be added to resources in the workspace by creating `IMarker` objects. These markers are used to represent compile errors, to-do items, bookmarks, search results, and many other types of annotations. You can create your own marker types for storing annotations for use by your own plug-in. Each marker can store an arbitrary set of attributes. Attributes are keyed by a string, and the values can be strings, Booleans, or integers. The `IMarker` interface defines some common attribute types, but you are free to create your own attribute names for your markers. Here is an example snippet that creates a marker, adds some attributes, and then deletes it:

```
final IFile file = null;
IMarker marker = file.createMarker(IMarker.MARKER);
marker.setAttribute(IMarker.MESSAGE, "This is my marker");
marker.setAttribute("Age", 5);
marker.delete();
```

When markers are created, modified, or deleted, a resource change event will be broadcast, telling interested parties about the change. You can search for markers by using the `findMarkers` methods on `IResource`.

The `org.eclipse.core.resources.markers` extension point can be used to declaratively define new marker types. See its documentation for an explanation and examples.

FAQ 289 *How can I be notified of changes to the workspace?*
FAQ 304 *Why don't my markers appear in the editor's vertical ruler?*
FAQ 338 *How do I create problem markers for my compiler?*
eclipse.org article "Mark My Words"

Go to **Platform Plug-in Developer Guide > Programmer's Guide > Resources overview > Resource markers**

FAQ
289

How can I be notified of changes to the workspace?

Resource change listeners are notified of most changes that occur in the workspace, including when any file, folder, or project is created, deleted, or modified. Listeners can also be registered for some special events, such as before projects are deleted or closed and before and after workspace autobuilds. Registering a resource change listener is easy:

```
IWorkspace workspace = ResourcesPlugin.getWorkspace();
IResourceChangeListener rcl = new IResourceChangeListener() {
   public void resourceChanged(IResourceChangeEvent event) {
   }
};
workspace.addResourceChangeListener(rcl);
```

Always make sure that you remove your resource change listener when you no longer need it:

```
workspace.removeResourceChangeListener(rcl);
```

Look at the javadoc for `IWorkspace.addResourceChangeListener` for more information on the various types of resource change events you can listen to and the restrictions that apply. It is important to keep performance in mind when writing a resource change listener. Listeners are notified at the end of every operation that changes the workspace, so any overhead that you add in your listener will degrade the performance of all such operations. If your listener needs to do expensive processing, consider off-loading some of the work into another thread, preferably by using a Job as described in **FAQ 127**.

☞ **FAQ 127** *Does the platform have support for concurrency?*
eclipse.org article "How You've Changed! Responding to resource changes in the Eclipse workspace"
Go to **Platform Plug-in Developer Guide > Programmer's Guide > Resources overview > Tracking resource changes**

How do I prevent builds between multiple changes to the workspace?

Every time resources in the workspace change, a resource change notification is broadcast, and autobuild gets a chance to run. This can become very costly if you are making several changes in succession to the workspace. To avoid these extra builds and notifications, it is very important that you batch all of your workspace changes into a single *workspace operation*. It is easy to accidentally cause extra builds if you aren't very careful about batching your changes. For example, even creating and modifying attributes on `IMarker` objects will cause separate resource change events if they are not batched.

Two different mechanisms are available for batching changes. To run a series of changes in the current thread, use `IWorkspaceRunnable`. Here is an example of a workspace runnable that creates two folders:

```
final IFolder folder1 = ..., folder2 = ...;
workspace.run(new IWorkspaceRunnable() {
    public void run(IProgressMonitor monitor) {
        folder1.create(IResource.NONE, true, null);
        folder2.create(IResource.NONE, true, null);
    }
}, null);
```

The other mechanism for batching resource changes is a `WorkspaceJob`. Introduced in Eclipse 3.0, this mechanism is the asynchronous equivalent of `IWorkspaceRunnable`. When you create and schedule a workspace job, it will perform the changes in a background thread and then cause a single resource change notification and autobuild to occur. Here is sample code using a workspace job:

```
final IFolder folder1 = ..., folder2 = ...;
Job job = new WorkspaceJob("Creating folders") {
    public IStatus runInWorkspace(IProgressMonitor monitor)
        throws CoreException {
        folder1.create(IResource.NONE, true, null);
        folder2.create(IResource.NONE, true, null);
        return Status.OK_STATUS;
    }
};
job.schedule();
```

☞ **FAQ 127** *Does the platform have support for concurrency?*
FAQ 306 *What are* `IWorkspaceRunnable`, `IRunnableWithProgress`, *and*
`WorkspaceModifyOperation`?

Why should I add my own project nature?

FAQ
291

Project natures act as tags on a project to indicate that a certain tool is used to
operate on that project. They can also be used to distinguish projects that your
plug-in is interested in from the rest of the projects in the workspace. For
example, natures can be used to filter declarative extensions that operate only on
projects of a particular type. The `propertyPages` and `popupMenus` extension
points allow you to filter enablement of an extension, based on various properties
of the selected resource. One of the properties that this mechanism understands is
the nature of a project. Here is an example of an `actionSet` declaration that
operates only on files in projects with the PDE nature:

```
<extension point="org.eclipse.ui.popupMenus">
    <objectContribution
        objectClass="org.eclipse.core.resources.IFile"
        id="org.eclipse.pde.ui.featureToolSet">
        <filter
            name="projectNature"
            value="org.eclipse.pde.FeatureNature">
        </filter>
        ...
```

Another reason for using natures is to make use of the nature lifecycle methods
when your plug-in is connected to or disconnected from a project. When a nature
is added to a project for the first time, the nature's `configure` method is called.
When the nature is removed from the project, the `deconfigure` method is called.
This is an opportunity to initialize metadata on the project and to associate
additional attributes, such as builders, with the project.

☞ eclipse.org article "Project Natures and Builders"
Go to **Platform Plug-in Developer Guide > Programmer's Guide >
Resources overview > Project natures**

FAQ
292

Where can I find information about writing builders?

Incremental project builders are used to transform resources in a project to produce some output. As the project changes, the builder is responsible for incrementally updating its output based on the nature of the changes. Some excellent resources are available on how builders work and how to create your own, so we won't get into more detail here.

 FAQ 325 *How do I implement an Eclipse builder?*
eclipse.org article "Project Natures and Builders"
Go to **Platform Plug-in Developer Guide > Programmer's Guide > Resources overview > Incremental project builders**

FAQ
293

How do I store extra properties on a resource?

Several mechanisms are available for attaching metadata to resources. The simplest are session and persistent properties, which affix arbitrary objects (for session properties) or strings (for persistent properties) to a resource keyed by a unique identifier. Session properties are discarded when the platform shuts down, and persistent properties are saved on disk and will be available the next time the platform starts up. Markers are intended to work as annotations to a particular location in a file but in reality can be used to attach arbitrary strings, integers, or Boolean values to a resource. Finally, synchronization information can be attached to a resource (see `ISynchronizer`). Sync info was designed for clients, such as repositories or deployment tools, that need to track differences between local resources and a remote copy. Such clients have some very special features, including the ability to maintain the metadata regardless of whether the resource exists. Although quite specialized, this form of metadata may be appropriate for use in your plug-in.

Table 17.1 provides a high-level view of the various forms of metadata, along with some of their key design features. *Speed* refers to the amount of CPU time required for typical access and storage operations. *Footprint* refers to the memory space required for storing the information during a session. Persistent properties are not stored in memory at all, except for a small cache, which makes them good memory citizens but terrible for performance. *Notify* refers to whether resource change notification includes broadcasting changes to this metadata. Note that this is not always a good thing: Performing a resource change broadcast has a definite performance cost, which will be incurred whether or not you care about the notification. Also, metadata that is included in resource change events cannot be changed by a resource change listener. So if you need a resource change listener to store some state information, you're stuck with either session or persistent properties. *Persistence* describes when the information is written to disk. Full save happens when the platform is being shut down, and snapshot is a quick incremental save that happens every few minutes while the platform is running. *Data types* identify the Java data types that can be stored with that metadata facility.

	Speed	Footprint	Notify	Persistence	Types
Markers	Good	Medium	Yes	Save; snapshot	`String, int, boolean`
Sync info	Good	Medium	Yes	Save; snapshot	`byte[]`
Session Property	Fast	Medium	No	None	`String`
Persistent Property	Slow	None	No	Immediate	`String`

Table 17.1 Forms of resource metadata

Keep in mind that the best solution for your particular situation isn't always as simple as picking one of these four mechanisms. Sometimes a combination of these systems works better. For example, session properties can be used as a high-performance cache during an operation, and the information can then be flushed to a persistent format, such as persistent properties, when your plug-in is not in use. Finally, for large amounts of metadata, it is often better to store the information in a separate file. You can ask the platform to allocate a metadata area for your plug-in, using `IProject.getWorkingLocation`, or you can store metadata directly in the project's content area so that it gets shared with the user's repository.

☞ **FAQ 288** *How do I create my own tasks, problems, bookmarks, and so on?*
FAQ 294 *How can I be notified on property changes on a resource?*

How can I be notified on property changes on a resource?

It depends what you mean by *properties*. For some metadata stored on resources, such as markers and sync info, an `IResourceChangeListener` can be used to be notified when they change. Other metadata, such as session and persistent properties, has no corresponding change notification. This is a design trade-off, as tracking and broadcasting change notifications can be quite expensive. Session and persistent properties are designed to be used only by the plug-in that declared the property, so other plug-ins should never be tracking or changing properties declared by your plug-in.

 FAQ 289 *How can I be notified of changes to the workspace?*
FAQ 293 *How do I store extra properties on a resource?*
FAQ 296 *How can I be notified when the workspace is being saved?*
FAQ 324 *How do I react to changes in source files?*

How and when do I save the workspace?

If you're using the Eclipse IDE workbench, you don't. When it shuts down, the workbench will automatically save the workspace. The workspace will also perform its own periodic workspace saves, called *snapshots*, every once in a while. Note that the most essential information in the workspace—the files and folders that the user is working with—are always stored on disk immediately. Saving the workspace simply involves storing away metadata, such as markers, and its in-memory picture of the projects. The workspace is designed so that if a user pulls the computer power cord from the wall at any moment, the workspace will be able to restart in a consistent state with minimal loss of information.

Nonetheless, it is possible for your plug-in to explicitly request a workspace save or snapshot. If you are writing an RCP application, you are responsible for minimally invoking save before shutdown. The following example saves the workspace:

```
final MultiStatus status = new MultiStatus(...);
IRunnableWithProgress runnable = new IRunnableWithProgress() {
    public void run(IProgressMonitor monitor) {
        try {
```

```
            IWorkspace ws = ResourcesPlugin.getWorkspace();
            status.merge(ws.save(true, monitor));
        } catch (CoreException e) {
            status.merge(e.getStatus());
        }
    }
};
new ProgressMonitorDialog(null).run(false, false, runnable);
if (!status.isOK())
    ErrorDialog.openError(...);
```

Note that the `save` method can indicate minor problems by returning an `IStatus` object, or major problems by throwing an exception. You should check both of these results and react accordingly. To request a workspace snapshot, the code is almost identical: pass `false` as the first parameter to the `save` method.

☞ **FAQ 176** *How do I make the workbench shutdown?*
FAQ 296 *How can I be notified when the workspace is being saved?*

How can I be notified when the workspace is being saved?

FAQ
296

If your plug-in maintains a model based on the workspace, you will want to save your model to disk whenever the workspace is saved. This ensures that your model will be in sync with the workspace every time the platform starts up. Your plug-in can take part in the workspace save process by registering an `ISaveParticipant`. It is a common mistake to try to perform saving directly from your `Plugin.shutdown` method, but at this point it is too late to make changes to the workspace. The workspace is saved before any plug-ins start to shut down, so any changes made to files, markers, and other workspace state from your plug-in's `shutdown` method will be lost.

The three kinds of save events are full workspace saves, snapshots, and project saves. Projects cannot be saved explicitly, but they are saved automatically when they are closed. Snapshots must be fast, saving only essential information. Full saves can take longer, and they must ensure that all information that will be needed in future sessions is persisted.

You must register your save participant at the start of each session. When you register your participant, you receive a resource delta describing all the changes that occurred since the last save you participated in. This allows your model to catch up with any changes that happened before your plug-in started up. This delta is exactly like the resource deltas provided to a resource change listener. After processing this delta, you can be sure that your model is perfectly in sync with the workspace contents.

After the initial registration, your save participant will be notified each time the workspace is saved.

☞ **FAQ 295** *How and when do I save the workspace?*
Go to **Platform Plug-in Developer Guide > Programmer's Guide > Resources overview > Workspace save participation**

FAQ 297

Where is the workspace local history stored?

Every time you modify a file in Eclipse, a copy of the old contents is kept in the local history. At any time, you can compare or replace a file with any older version from the history. Although this is no replacement for a real code repository, it can help you out when you change or delete a file by accident. Local history also has an advantage that it wasn't really designed for: The history can also help you out when your workspace has a catastrophic problem or if you get disk errors that corrupt your workspace files. As a last resort, you can manually browse the local history folder to find copies of the files you lost, which is a bit like using Google's cache to browse Web pages that no longer exist. Each file revision is stored in a separate file with a random file name inside the history folder. The path of the history folder inside your workspace is

```
.metadata/.plugins/org.eclipse.core.resources/.history/
```

You can use your operating system's search tool to locate the files you are looking for. Although not the prettiest backup system, it sure beats starting over from scratch!

How can I repair a workspace that is broken?

In some rare situations, the Eclipse workspace can become corrupt and unreadable. In particular, this can happen when VM errors, such as OutOfMemoryError, occur. The platform core team home page includes a plug-in that can be used to restore a workspace that has become corrupt. This plug-in will be able to restore only basic workspace metadata information, so metadata created by other plug-ins may still be lost. From eclipse.org, select **Projects > Eclipse Project > Platform > Core**, and then look for the workspace restorer plug-in on the development resources page. Be sure to also enter a bug report in the Eclipse Bugzilla with any available log information to help prevent such disasters from happening to others!

What support does the workspace have for team tools?

Repository tools often need special control over how files in the workspace are managed. The workspace API includes special hooks that allow repository tools to reimplement certain methods, validate and veto file changes, and store synchronization state on resources. These facilities are generally well described in the *Platform Plug-in Developer Guide*, but here is a quick tour of special repository integration support in the workspace:

- IFileModificationValidator. This hook is called when a file is about to be edited and immediately prior to a file being saved. This gives repository providers a chance to check out the file being changed or to veto the modification. A repository provider can supply a validator by overriding getFileModificationValidator on RepositoryProvider.

- IMoveDeleteHook. This hook allows repository providers to reimplement the resource move and delete methods. This is used both for validation prior to move and deletion and for transferring version history when a resource is moved. This hook is supplied by overriding getMoveDeleteHook on RepositoryProvider.

- TeamHook. The workspace API developers realized that the existing hook methods could not be extended without breaking API compatibility. To avoid an explosion of specialized hook methods, the developers decided to consolidate future team-integration hooks in a single place. This hook is currently used only for validating linked resource creation, but any future hooks that are added for team plug-ins will appear here.

- `ISynchronizer`. This API associates synchronization information, such as file timestamps, with a resource. The synchronization information is represented as arbitrary bytes, so you can store whatever information you want, using the synchronizer. The workspace will take care of storing and persisting this information across sessions and will broadcast resource change notifications when this information changes.

Note that although these facilities were designed for use by repository tools, sneaky plug-ins have been known to use them for other purposes. If you have very specialized needs in your plug-in, it may be justifiable to use some of these hooks yourself. For example, the plug-in development tools use these hooks for binary plug-in projects to prevent users from deleting content that is linked back into your install directory. Keep in mind that in the case of the hook methods, a project can have only one hook implementation. Using these hooks for your plug-in will prevent other repositories from being able to connect to those projects.

FAQ 310 *What APIs exist for integrating repository clients into Eclipse?*

Chapter 18. Workbench IDE

The remaining plug-ins in the Eclipse Platform are truly oriented toward writing development tools. This chapter covers elements of the Eclipse IDE workbench, found in the `org.eclipse.ui.ide` plug-in. This plug-in includes most of the standard platform views, such as Navigator, Tasks, Problems, Properties, and Bookmark. We also take a quick look at advanced topics, such as writing repository clients and debuggers.

How do I open an editor on a file in the workspace?

FAQ
300

In Eclipse 2.1, use the `openEditor` methods on `IWorkbenchPage` to open files in the workspace. In 3.0, this API was moved to the IDE class in order to remove the dependency between the generic workbench and the workspace. If you use `openEditor(IFile)`, the platform will guess the appropriate editor to use, based on the file extension.

To open an editor to a particular position, you can create a marker in the file and then use `openEditor(IMarker)`. Be sure to get rid of the marker when you're done. You can specify what editor to open by setting the `EDITOR_ID_ATTR` on the marker. If you don't do this, the workbench will guess what kind of editor to open from the file extension. The following code snippet opens the default text editor to line 5, using a marker:

```
IFile file = <choose the file to open>;
IWorkbenchPage page = ;
HashMap map = new HashMap();
map.put(IMarker.LINE_NUMBER, new Integer(5));
map.put(IWorkbenchPage.EDITOR_ID_ATTR,
    "org.eclipse.ui.DefaultTextEditor");
IMarker marker = file.createMarker(IMarker.TEXT);
marker.setAttributes(map);
//page.openEditor(marker); //2.1 API
IDE.openEditor(marker); //3.0 API
marker.delete();
```

FAQ 207 *How do I open an editor programmatically?*
FAQ 301 *How do I open an editor on a file outside the workspace?*
FAQ 302 *How do I open an editor on something that is not a file?*

How do I open an editor on a file outside the workspace?

You can open a read-only editor on a file outside the workspace by creating your own implementation of `IStorage` and `IStorageEditorInput` for the file. Alternatively, you can create a *linked resource* in an existing project, which points to a file elsewhere in the file system. This example snippet creates a project called "External Files," and then prompts the user to select any file in the file system. The code then creates a linked resource in the project to that external file, allowing the platform to open the file in read/write mode in one of the standard editors:

```
IWorkspace ws = ResourcesPlugin.getWorkspace();
IProject project = ws.getRoot().getProject("External Files");
if (!project.exists())
    project.create(null);
if (!project.isOpen())
    project.open(null);
Shell shell = window.getShell();
String name = new FileDialog(shell, SWT.OPEN).open();
if (name == null)
    return;
IPath location = new Path(name);
IFile file = project.getFile(location.lastSegment());
file.createLink(location, IResource.NONE, null);
IWorkbenchPage page = window.getActivePage();
if (page != null)
    page.openEditor(file);
```

 FAQ 36 *How do I accommodate project layouts that don't fit the Eclipse model?*
FAQ 207 *How do I open an editor programmatically?*
FAQ 302 *How do I open an editor on something that is not a file?*

How do I open an editor on something that is not a file?

Most editors will accept as input either an IFileEditorInput or an
IStorageEditorInput. The former can be used only for opening files in the
workspace, but the latter can be used to open a stream of bytes from anywhere. If
you want to open a file on a database object, remote file, or other data source,
IStorage is the way to go. The only downside is that this is a read-only input
type, so you can use it only for viewing a file, not editing it. To use this
approach, implement IStorage so that it returns the bytes for the file you want to
display. Here is an IStorage that returns the contents of a string:

```
class StringStorage extends PlatformObject
  implements IStorage {
    private String string;
    StringStorage(String input) {this.string = input;}
    public InputStream getContents() throws CoreException {
        return new ByteArrayInputStream(string.getBytes());
    }
    public IPath getFullPath() {return null;}
    public String getName() {
        int len = Math.min(5, string.length());
        return string.substring(0, len).concat("...");
    }
    public boolean isReadOnly() {return true;}
}
```

The class extends PlatformObject to inherit the standard implementation of
IAdaptable, which IStorage extends. The getName and getFullPath methods
can return null if they are not needed. In this case, we've implemented getName
to return the first five characters of the string.

The next step is to create an IStorageEditorInput implementation that returns
your IStorage object:

```
class StringInput extends PlatformObject
  implements IStorageEditorInput {
    private IStorage storage;
    StringInput(IStorage storage) {this.storage = storage;}
    public boolean exists() {return true;}
    public ImageDescriptor getImageDescriptor() {return null;}
    public String getName() {
        return storage.getName();
    }
```

```
public IPersistableElement getPersistable() {return null;}
public IStorage getStorage() {
   return storage;
}
public String getToolTipText() {
   return "String-based file: " + storage.getName();
}
}
```

Again, many of the methods here are optional. The `getPersistable` method is used for implementing persistence of your editor input, so the platform can automatically restore your editor on start-up. Here, we've implemented the bare essentials: the editor name, and a tool tip.

The final step is to open an editor with this input. This snippet opens the platform's default text editor on a given string:

```
IWorkbenchWindow window = ...;
String string = "This is the text file contents";
IStorage storage = new StringStorage(string);
IStorageEditorInput input = new StringInput(storage);
IWorkbenchPage page = window.getActivePage();
if (page != null)
   page.openEditor(input, "org.eclipse.ui.DefaultTextEditor");
```

FAQ 303

Why don't my markers show up in the Tasks view?

The Tasks view, also called the task list, shows all markers of type `org.eclipse.core.resources.taskmarker`, as well as any marker type that declares `taskmarker` as a supertype. Prior to Eclipse 3.0, the task list also showed markers of type `problemmarker`. In 3.0, problem markers appear in the Problems view instead. If you define a custom marker with one of these types, it will appear in either the Tasks or Problems view automatically. Note that if you don't see your marker there, it might have been filtered out. Check the filter dialog to ensure that your marker type is selected.

FAQ
304

Why don't my markers appear in the editor's vertical ruler?

Text editors in Eclipse can display markers in a number of ways. Most commonly, they appear as icons in the vertical rule on the left-hand side of the editor pane. Markers can also optionally be displayed as squiggly underlays in the text and in the overview ruler on the right-hand side of the editor. How each type of marker is displayed is chosen by the user on the editor preference pages (**Workbench > Editors > Text Editor > Annotations** and **Java > Editor > Annotations**). The IMarker interface declares a number of frequently used marker types. Any created marker that has either the LINE_NUMBER or CHAR_START and CHAR_END attributes set will be displayed by editors. These attributes must exist when the marker is created for the marker to appear in an editor. The most common mistake is to create the marker and then add the attributes in a separate operation. The text framework provides a utility class called MarkerUtilities to make this easier for you. Here is a sample snippet that adds a marker correctly:

```
int lineNumber = ...;
HashMap map = new HashMap();
MarkerUtilities.setLineNumber(map, lineNumber);
MarkerUtilities.createMarker(resource, map, IMarker.TEXT);
```

☞ **FAQ 288** *How do I create my own tasks, problems, bookmarks, and so on?*

FAQ
305

How do I access the active project?

This question is often asked by newcomers to Eclipse, probably as a result of switching from another IDE with a different interpretation of the term *project*. Similarly, people often ask how to access the "active" file. In Eclipse there is no such thing as an active project or file. Projects can be opened or closed, but many projects may be open at any given time.

Often people are really asking for the currently selected project, folder, or file. The selection can be queried using the UI's ISelectionService.

Once you have the selection, you can extract the selected resource as follows:

```
IResource extractSelection(ISelection sel) {
    if (!(sel instanceof IStructuredSelection))
        return null;
    IStructuredSelection ss = (IStructuredSelection)sel;
    Object element = ss.getFirstElement();
    if (element instanceof IResource)
        return (IResource) element;
    if (!(element instanceof IAdaptable))
        return null;
    IAdaptable adaptable = (IAdaptable)element;
    Object adapter = adaptable.getAdapter(IResource.class);
    return (IResource) adapter;
}
```

If you are looking for the active editor, you can determine that from the
`IPartService`. If an editor is active, you can extract the resource, if available,
like this:

```
IResource extractResource(IEditorPart editor) {
    IEditorInput input = editor.getInput();
    if (!(input instanceof IFileEditorInput))
        return null;
    return ((IFileEditorInput)input).getFile();
}
```

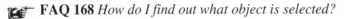 **FAQ 168** *How do I find out what object is selected?*

**FAQ
306**

What are `IWorkspaceRunnable`, `IRunnableWithProgress`, and `WorkspaceModifyOperation`?

`IWorkspaceRunnable` is a mechanism for batching a set of changes to the
workspace so that change notification and autobuild are deferred until the entire
batch completes. `IRunnableWithProgress` is a mechanism for batching a set of
changes to be run outside the UI thread. You often need to do both of these at
once: Make multiple changes to the workspace outside the UI thread. Wrapping
one of these mechanisms inside the other would do the trick, but the resulting
code is cumbersome, and it is awkward to communicate arguments, results, and
exceptions between the caller and the operation to be run.

The solution is to use `WorkspaceModifyOperation`. This class rolls the two mechanisms together by implementing `IRunnableWithProgress` and performing the work within a nested `IWorkspaceRunnable`. To use it, simply create a subclass that implements the abstract method `execute`, and pass an instance of this subclass to `IRunnableContext.run` to perform the work. If you already have an instance of `IRunnableWithProgress` on hand, it can be passed to the constructor of the special subclass `WorkspaceModifyDelegatingOperation` to create a new `IRunnableWithProgress` that performs workspace batching for you.

☞ **FAQ 218** *Actions, commands, operations, jobs: What does it all mean?*
FAQ 290 *How do I prevent builds between multiple changes to the workspace?*

How do I write to the console from a plug-in ?

FAQ
307

Many of the people asking this question are confused by the fact that two Eclipse instances are in use when you are developing plug-ins. One is the *development* platform you are using as your IDE, and the other is the *target* platform—also known as the runtime workbench—consisting of the plug-ins in the development workbench you are testing against. When a plug-in in the target platform writes a message to `System.out` or `System.err`, the message appears in the Console view of the development platform. This view emulates the Java console that appears when Eclipse runs under Windows with `java.exe`. You should be writing to the console only in this manner when in debug mode (see **FAQ 122**).

In some situations however, a plug-in in the development platform has a legitimate reason to write to the development platform Console view. Some tools originally designed for the command line, such as Ant and CVS, traditionally use console output as a way of communicating results to the tool user. When these tools are ported for use with an IDE, this console output is typically replaced with richer forms of feedback, such as views, markers, and decorations. However, users accustomed to the old command-line output may still want to see this raw output as an alternative to other visual forms of feedback. Tools in this category can use the Console view to write this output.

Prior to Eclipse 3.0, each plug-in that wanted console-like output created its own Console view. Eclipse 3.0 provides a single generic Console view that all plug-ins can write to. The view can host several console documents at once and allows the user to switch between different console pages. Each page in the console is represented by an `org.eclipse.ui.console.IConsole` object. To write to the console, you need to create your own `IConsole` instance and connect it to the Console view. For a console containing a simple text document, you can instantiate a `MessageConsole` instance. Here is a method that locates a console with a given name and creates a new one if it cannot be found:

```
private MessageConsole findConsole(String name) {
    ConsolePlugin plugin = ConsolePlugin.getDefault();
    IConsoleManager conMan = plugin.getConsoleManager();
    IConsole[] existing = conMan.getConsoles();
    for (int i = 0; i < existing.length; i++)
        if (name.equals(existing[i].getName()))
            return (MessageConsole) existing[i];
    //no console found, so create a new one
    MessageConsole myConsole = new MessageConsole(name, null);
    conMan.addConsoles(new IConsole[]{myConsole});
    return myConsole;
}
```

Once a console is created, you can write to it either by directly modifying its `IDocument` or by opening an output stream on the console. This snippet opens a stream and writes some text to a console:

```
MessageConsole myConsole = findConsole(CONSOLE_NAME);
MessageConsoleStream out = myConsole.newMessageStream();
out.println("Hello from Generic console sample action");
```

Creating a console and writing to it do not create or reveal the Console view. If you want to make that sure the Console view is visible, you need to reveal it using the usual workbench API. Even once the Console view is revealed, keep in mind that it may contain several pages, each representing a different `IConsole` provided by a plug-in. Additional API asks the Console view to display your console. This snippet reveals the Console view and asks it to display a particular console instance:

```
IConsole myConsole = ...;//your console instance
IWorkbenchPage page = ...;//obtain the active page
String id = IConsoleConstants.ID_CONSOLE_VIEW;
IConsoleView view = (IConsoleView) page.showView(id);
view.display(myConsole);
```

FAQ 122 *How do I use the platform debug tracing facility?*
FAQ 265 *How do I use the text document model?*

How do I prompt the user to select a resource?

Several dialogs are available for prompting the user to select one or more resources in the workspace. Each dialog has its own particular attributes and uses, and supports varying degrees of customization based on your needs. Note that you can change the title of many of these dialogs by using the method `SelectionDialog.setTitle` to suit your particular application. Here is a summary of the available dialogs:

- `ContainerSelectionDialog` prompts the user to select a single project or folder in the workspace. This dialog be configured to allow the user to specify a folder that does not yet exist.
- `ElementListSelectionDialog` is a powerful generic selection dialog that is widely used throughout the workbench. This dialog has a text box at the top that allows the user to enter a pattern. As the user types, the list below narrows down to show only the matching elements. The input elements can be any kind of objects.
- `TwoPaneElementSelector` is much like `ElementListSelectionDialog`, except an extra qualifier list is added at the bottom. When a match is selected in the middle pane, the corresponding qualifiers are shown in the bottom pane. This is used most prominently by the **Open Type** and **Open Resource** actions. In these dialogs, the qualifier is either the package or folder name for the resource that is selected in the middle pane.
- `NewFolderDialog` prompts the user to enter the name of a new folder directly below a supplied parent container. This dialog allows the user to create a linked folder that maps to a directory in the file system outside the project content area.
- `ResourceListSelectionDialog` prompts the user to select a single resource from a flat list of resource names. This dialog can be configured with a resource type mask to narrow the list to only folders, only files, or both. The user can enter a filter pattern to narrow down the list of resources. Filtering and populating the dialog are done in a background thread to ensure responsiveness in large workspaces. This dialog is designed to be subclassed to allow for further customization.
- `ResourceSelectionDialog` prompts the user to select one or more resources below a given root. This dialog displays a table tree of containers on the left-hand side and a list of resources on the right-hand side, just like the panes at the top of the file system export wizard.

- `FileSelectionDialog` is deprecated in Eclipse 3.0. Its intent was to provide a generic dialog to allow the user to make selections from file-system-like structures such as the workspace, zip files, or the actual file system. Most of the functionality of this dialog can be found in other dialogs.
- `SaveAsDialog` has hard-coded title and messages; otherwise, it could be used in any context requiring a file selection. The user can supply the name of a new or existing file. This dialog is the file equivalent of `ContainerSelectionDialog`. The dialog returns an `IPath` result and does not check whether the file or parent folders already exist.

The FAQ Examples plug-in for this book includes an action called `ResourceSelectionAction` that demonstrates the use of all these dialogs.

☞ **FAQ 142** *How do I prompt the user to select a file or a directory?*

FAQ 309

Can I use the actions from the Navigator in my own plug-in?

Yes. All the resource actions in the Navigator view, including **Copy**, **Move**, **Delete**, **Build**, and **Refresh**, are available as API. These actions are found in the `org.eclipse.ui.actions` package of the `org.eclipse.ui.ide` plug-in. These actions expect a selection of either `IResource` objects or `IAdaptable` objects that are able to adapt to `IResource`. You must either install the actions as selection change listeners, such as on a `TreeViewer`, or supply them with the selection before running them:

```
IResource r = ...;//resource to delete
IStructuredSelection ss = new StructuredSelection(r);
DeleteResourceAction delete = new DeleteResourceAction(shell);
delete.selectionChanged(ss);
delete.run();
```

☞ **FAQ 126** *How do I use `IAdaptable` and `IAdapterFactory`?*

What APIs exist for integrating repository clients into Eclipse?

Repositories, or version and configuration management (VCM) tools, are an essential part of software development. A wide variety of code repositories and a larger number of client-side tools for interacting with those repositories are available. These clients range from rudimentary command-line tools to rich graphical clients that are deeply integrated with other development tools. As a tool-integration platform, repository client integration is an important aspect of Eclipse. From the very start, the core architecture of the Eclipse Platform has striven to allow deep integration of these repository client tools.

Early on, Eclipse used the term *VCM* as a label for its repository integration components. Because acronyms in general aren't particularly descriptive and because this particular acronym didn't seem to be widely understood, the Eclipse Platform adopted the term *team tools* as a replacement. This is why the repository APIs are found in the plug-ins `org.eclipse.team.core` and `org.eclipse.team.ui` and why the developers writing this stuff call themselves the *team* team.

As with many Eclipse components, team tooling is divided into a generic, repository-agnostic layer and then separate layers for specific repository clients. The platform includes a reference implementation of the generic team APIs, which implements a powerful graphical client for integrating with *concurrent versions system*, or CVS. The team API centers on the notion of a *repository provider*. Each project in an Eclipse workspace can be associated with a single `RepositoryProvider` subclass that acts as the entry point for repository interaction. The `RepositoryProvider` API and the remainder of the team-integration APIs are extremely well documented, so we don't need to go into more detail here.

The *Platform Plug-in Developer Guide* includes detailed documentation on how to implement your own repository provider. See the section **Programmer's guide > Team support**.

☞ **FAQ 299** *What support does the workspace have for team tools?*

**FAQ
311**

How do I deploy projects to a server and keep the two synchronized?

Some development tools include support for pushing projects to a remote server, using such protocols as FTP and WebDAV. Then an ongoing challenge is to keep the old workspace contents synchronized with the remote content as files in the workspace and on the remote server are added, removed, or changed. The Eclipse team API includes generic infrastructure for deploying workspace contents to a remote location and for keeping the two copies synchronized.

The main entry point for this kind of team integration is the notion of a *team subscriber*. A subclass of `TeamSubscriber` specifies the logic for comparing workspace contents to a remote resource and for performing synchronization. The team API has support for building and maintaining a model of remote resources and the synchronization state between remote and local resources. A subscriber can use the generic Synchronize view to allow users to browse the differences between local and remote copies and for refreshing and synchronizing the two. The `org.eclipse.team.ui.synchronize` package includes API for adding pages to the Synchronize view and for displaying the synchronization model created by a team subscriber.

See the *Platform Plug-in Developer Guide* under **Programmer's Guide > Team support** for complete details on how to implement your own team subscriber and for integrating with the generic Synchronize view.

**FAQ
312**

What is the difference between a repository provider and a team subscriber?

The Eclipse Platform team component supports two categories of tool integration. Of primary interest are *repository providers*, which represent full-fledged versioning and configuration management tools, such as CVS, ClearCase, and Subversion. These tools typically include support for maintaining an arbitrary number of versions of files and file trees, for branching and merging development streams, and for linking versions to bug tracking and other configuration management tools. Clients for interacting with these tools are represented in Eclipse through the `RepositoryProvider` API.

Another class of team tooling is used for deployment of development artifacts to a remote execution target. For example, you may use FTP or WebDAV to deploy code and other resources to a Web server, or a proprietary protocol for deploying code to embedded and hand-held devices. This class of tooling is represented by the *team subscriber* API.

Note the extensive overlap between these two categories of team tooling. In general, team subscribers represent a subset of the functionality provided by a repository client. In other words, if you're writing a client for a repository, you will most likely need both the repository provider and the team subscriber API.

☞ **FAQ 310** *What APIs exist for integrating repository clients into Eclipse?*
FAQ 311 *How do I deploy projects to a server and keep the two synchronized?*

What is a launch configuration?

**FAQ
313**

A launch configuration is a description of how to launch a program. The program itself may be a Java program, another Eclipse instance in the form of a runtime workbench, a C program, or something else. Launch configurations are manifested in the Eclipse UI through **Run > Run...**.

Launching in Eclipse is closely tied to the infrastructure for debugging, enabling you to make the logical progression from support for launching to support for interactive debugging. This is why you will find launch configurations in the `org.eclipse.debug.core` plug-in.

For extensive documentation on how to add your own launch configuration, refer to *Platform Plug-in Developer Guide* under **Programmer's Guide > Program debug and launch support**.

☞ eclipse.org article "We Have Lift-off: The Launching Framework in Eclipse"

FAQ
314

When do I use a launch delegate?

A launch configuration captures all the information required to launch a
particular application, but the launching is performed by a launch delegate. This
separation allows a single launch configuration to be used by several launch
delegates to launch an application in different ways using the same launch
information. For example, there is a single launch-configuration type for
launching Java programs but different launch delegates for launching in run
mode versus debug mode. One could define more delegates for launching Java
programs by associating with the existing Java launch-configuration type. This
example shows a declaration of a launch delegate for launching Java applications
in a special profiling mode:

```
<extension point="org.eclipse.debug.core.launchDelegates">
    <launchDelegate
        id="org.eclipse.faq.example.traceDelegate"
        delegate="org.eclipse.faq.example.TraceLauncher"
        type="org.eclipse.jdt.launching.localJavaApplication"
        modes="trace"/>
</extension>
```

For more information on launch delegates, see the documentation for the
`org.eclipse.debug.core.launchDelegates` extension point and the javadoc
for `ILaunchConfigurationDelegate` in the debug core plug-in.

FAQ
315

What is Ant?

Ant is a Java-based build tool created as part of the Apache open-source project.
You can think of it as a Java version of *make*. Ant scripts have a structure and are
written in XML. Similar to *make*, Ant targets can depend on other targets. For
example, Ant is used in the context of plug-in development in the `build.xml`,
created from a `plugin.xml` file for assembling a deployable version of your
plug-in.

The Ant UI as provided in Eclipse comes with a first-class Ant build-file editor,
including syntax highlighting, Content Assist, templates, and content formatting.
This editor is automatically associated with files named `build.xml` and can be
associated with other file names from the **Workbench > File Associations**
preference page.

The Ant UI also has a wizard for running Ant scripts and a toolbar button for repeating previous builds.

For more details, such as how to run Ant scripts programmatically, refer to *Platform Plug-in Developer Guide* under **Programmer's Guide > Platform Ant support**.

 Apache Ant (http://ant.apache.org)
FAQ 82 *What is the use of the* `build.xml` *file?*

Why can't my Ant build find `javac`?

FAQ
316

Ant tasks that include the `javac` task for compiling Java source will fail if a Java compiler cannot be found. This results in an error message like the following:

```
Unable to find a javac compiler;
com.sun.tools.javac.Main is not on the classpath.
Perhaps JAVA_HOME does not point to the JDK
```

This simply means that Ant could not find a Java compiler. The easiest solution is to make sure that `tools.jar`, which is included with any JDK—as opposed to a JRE—is on Ant's classpath. You can add items to Ant's classpath from the **Ant > Runtime** preference page. If you launch Eclipse by using a full JDK instead of a JRE, `tools.jar` should appear on the Ant classpath automatically.

Alternatively, Ant supports the notion of a *compiler adapter*, allowing you to plug in your own Java compiler, such as the Java compiler that is built into Eclipse. The Eclipse compiler adapter is found in the `org.eclipse.jdt.core` in `jdtCompilerAdapter.jar`. Again, you need to make sure that this JAR is on Ant's classpath from the Ant preference page. Then, simply add the following line to your build file to specify the compiler:

```
<property name="build.compiler"
    value="org.eclipse.jdt.core.JDTCompilerAdapter"/>
```

FAQ 315 *What is Ant?*

**FAQ
317**

How do I add my own external tools?

External tools are applications or scripts that typically act as extensions to your development environment. For example, they may be used to execute scripts to package and deploy your application or to run an external compiler on your source files. External tools allow an end user to achieve a basic level of integration for a non-Eclipse-aware tool without writing a plug-in. External tools are created and configured via **Run > External Tools > External Tools** or from the drop-down menu on the **Run** button with the toolbox overlay.

If you want to write your own category of external tool, such as support for a different scripting language, you need to write a plug-in. The process for defining external tools is almost identical to writing your own launch configuration. Essentially, an external tool is a launch-configuration type that belongs to the special external-tools category:

```
<launchConfigurationType
    name="My Tool"
    delegate="com.xyz.MyLaunchDelegate"
    category="org.eclipse.ui.externaltools"
    modes="run"
    id="com.xyz.MyLaunchType">
</launchConfigurationType>
```

 FAQ 313 *What is a launch configuration?*

**FAQ
318**

How do I create an external tool builder?

An external tool builder is an external tool that runs every time the projects in your workspace are built. End users can add external tool builders by selecting a project in the Navigator, choosing **Properties**, and then going to the **Builders** page. On the **Build Options** tab, you can specify whether the builder should run on autobuild, manual build, or on **Clean**. In most cases, running external tool builders during auto-builds is too disruptive because they are too long running.

As with ordinary external tools, you can define your own type of external tool builder by creating a new launch configuration type. In your launch configuration declaration, you must specify the category for external tool builder launch configurations:

```
<launchConfigurationType
    name="%AntBuild"
    delegate="com.xyz.MyLaunchDelegate"
    category="org.eclipse.ui.externaltools.builder"
    modes="run"
    id="com.xyz.MyLaunchType">
</launchConfigurationType>
```

FAQ 313 *What is a launch configuration?*
FAQ 317 *How do I add my own external tools?*

Chapter 19. Implementing Support for Your Own Language

Through its JDT project, Eclipse has strong support for Java development, such as editing, refactoring, building, launching, and debugging. Likewise, the C development tools (CDT) project aims for similar support for writing C/C++ code. This chapter discusses some of the issues to address when you have your own language and want to host it in Eclipse for writing programs and plug-ins. We look at the various ways of integrating with Eclipse: from no integration to a fully integrated language development environment. To structure our discussion, we take a closer look at eScript, an experimental script language developed especially for this book. As is the case for all examples described in this book, you can find eScript on this book's CD-ROM or Web site (http://eclipsefaq.org). For more details on eScript, see **FAQ 319**.

Many questions have been addressed in other FAQs in this book and may be somewhat repetitive. However, if you are planning to implement support for your own programming language, this chapter might serve well as a comprehensive overview of how to approach this big task.

Any classification of integration of a new programming language with Eclipse is somewhat arbitrary. We have identified the following degrees of integration of a new programming language, such as eScript, with Eclipse:

- *Phase 1—Compiling code and building projects.* To obtain full integration with Eclipse in the area of compilation of programs and build processes for your own language, follow the various steps outlined in **FAQ 320**.

- *Phase 2—Implementing a DOM.* The DOM is an in-memory structural representation of the source code of a program written in your language. Using the structural information contained in the DOM, all kinds of analysis and refactoring tools can be built. For more details, see **FAQ 331**.

- *Phase 3—Editing programs.* After writing a compiler, a builder, and a DOM, you are ready to consider all the individual steps to build the ultimate Eclipse editor for your language. The steps are outlined in **FAQ 334**.

   • *Phase 4—Adding the finishing touches.* To give your language IDE a professional look, follow the steps outlined in **FAQ 342**.

If you carefully observe these four phases, you will find that the visual aspects of your language IDE happen late in the process. You will have to do some legwork before you are able to get to the pretty parts. We recommend patience and restraint. Time spent in phases 1 and 2 will be well spent, and once you get to phase 3 and 4, you will be grateful that you followed all the steps we outlined.

FAQ 319

What is eScript?

We designed and implemented eScript to describe the various steps in adding support for a new programming language to Eclipse. Our eScript is not an official product but simply serves as an experiment for this book.

The idea behind eScript is that someone can implement an Eclipse plug-in by using a simple script language instead of using a sometimes complicated and confusing combination of XML and Java. Figure 19.1 is a sample eScript that declares an update site containing a feature that contains a plug-in that contributes to the `org.eclipse.ui.actionSets` extension point.

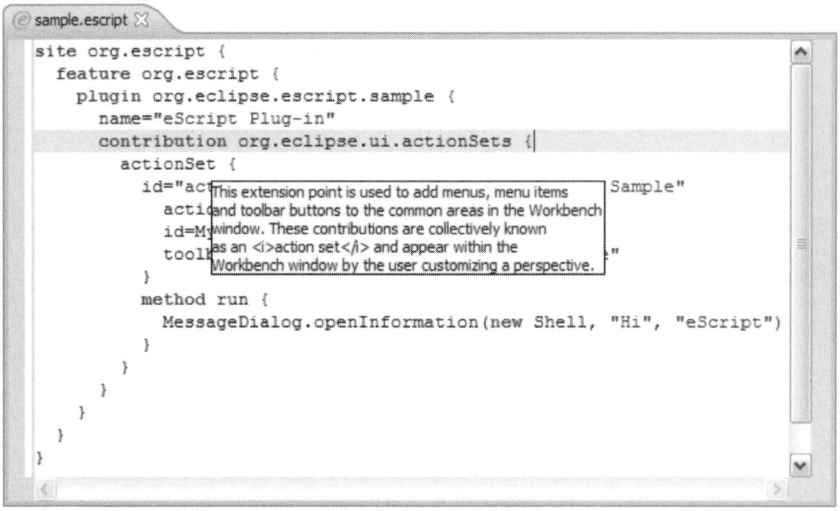

Figure 19.1 An eScript example

The eScript language uses as much inferencing as possible. It does not need import statements, type declarations, or even the declaration of a required interface (the example in Figure 19.1 implements `IActionDelegate`, but nowhere is this specified in the script). Whenever possible, types and identities are inferred from the environment.

Files containing eScript scripts are compiled into Java bytecodes with the eScript compiler. The compiler generates a `plugin.xml` file and a JAR containing autogenerated Java class files.

  See the eScript Web site (http://eclipsefaq.org/escript)

FAQ
320

Language integration phase 1: How do I compile and build programs?

Phase 1 of language integration with Eclipse focuses on compilation of source files and building projects. We can distinguish the following individual steps/approaches to obtain complete integration:

1. *Use no integration.* Edit and compile source code externally and load it into Eclipse. This makes it difficult for the eScript compiler to use such facilities as the PDE plug-in model, which is needed to discover all kinds of attributes about plug-ins to be written. In fact, using an external builder is impractical for any kind of serious integration. For more details, see **FAQ 321**.

2. *Use external builders.* Edit your files with Eclipse, and use an Ant script to compile the source files. A problem is that information exchange between Eclipse and the external builder is severely limited; hence, the name *external builder*, of course. However, using an Ant script allows for some experimentation without the need to write a plug-in. For more details, see **FAQ 322**.

3. *Implement a compiler that runs inside Eclipse.* In other words, write the compiler in Java and run it in the same JVM as Eclipse runs in. One approach could be to add a `PopupMenu` command to eScript files in the Resource Navigator. Running the compiler in this fashion puts Eclipse in control. Files are built when Eclipse wants them and Eclipse does not need to react to changes from outside. For more details, see **FAQ 323**.

4. *React to workspace changes.* Edit files by using Eclipse editors. Whenever the user saves a source file, you can be notified so that the file can be compiled. Integration is definitely improving but still is cumbersome as it does not integrate well with how Eclipse thinks about the way projects are built. For more details, see **FAQ 324**.

5. *Implement an Eclipse builder.* Builders are invoked on a project when any of its resources are changed or when the user manually requests a project to be rebuilt. Multiple builders can be registered on a project, and integration of a compiler into a build process is worth considering owing to its many benefits. For more details, see **FAQ 325**.

After following these steps, you are *almost* ready to focus on writing an editor. First, you have to look at **FAQ 331**.

FAQ 321

How do I load source files edited outside Eclipse?

You can achieve a minimal level of Eclipse integration without writing a single line of Eclipse-specific tooling code. Add resource files to a project in your workspace. Edit and compile the source files outside Eclipse or by using the Eclipse text editor. Make sure that the files get copied into the project's output directory, usually the `bin` directory. Intermittently refresh your Eclipse Navigator so that you can access the generated bytecode files. The only integration is the sharing of class files through the file system. But at least it allows for preliminary and rudimentary experimentation without writing any Eclipse plug-ins.

☞ **FAQ 322** *How do I run an external builder on my source files?*

How do I run an external builder on my source files?

FAQ
322

Use the default Eclipse text editor to edit the eScript source files, and use an Ant script to compile the eScript source into Java bytecodes. Ant scripts are XML-based scripts that can be used to automate certain build processes. You could view them as a much more flexible incarnation of *Make*.

A simple Ant script (`build.xml`) may look like this:

```xml
<?xml version="1.0" encoding="UTF-8"?>
<project name="eScript" default="compile" basedir=".">
    <target name="compile">
        <exec executable="eScriptc.exe" dir="src">
            <arg value="-cp"/>
            <arg value="... long classpath specifier ..."/>
            <arg value="EscriptPlugin/SampleAction.eScript"/>
        </exec>
        <copy file="src/EscriptPlugin/SampleAction.class"
            todir="bin/EscriptPlugin/actions/"/>
        <eclipse.convertPath
                    fileSystemPath="c:\faq\Escript Plugin\"
            property="resourcePath"/>
        <eclipse.refreshLocal resource="${resourcePath}"
            depth="infinite"/>
    </target>
</project>
```

Of course, this script can be made more elegant, but it serves to highlight the main problems with the approach. First, we have to compute the project's classpath, which can be quite complex for a plug-in, and pass it to the eScript compiler. Second, we have to explicitly pass in the name of the source file. Third, we need to replicate the JDT's behavior by copying the resulting class file to the project's `bin` directory. Finally, we have to refresh the workspace so that Eclipse gets notified of the changes in the class files and can rebuild dependant components in the workspace.

It is not easy to discover structure about Eclipse's installed plug-ins from outside Eclipse, so compilation of eScript source files becomes a real challenge when done outside Eclipse. Perhaps most troublesome is that each time the source changes, the user has to manually run Ant on the `build.xml` file. This spins off a new compiler, which has to load the entire classpath to do name and symbol resolution, and the compilation process becomes quite noticeable and annoying after a while.

But even with these limitations, this approach is viable for developers who do not want to write a new plug-in to support their language. Using the Eclipse support for launching external tools and Ant scripts, eScript files can be edited and compiled without having to leave the IDE.

 FAQ 315 *What is Ant?*
FAQ 317 *How do I add my own external tools?*
FAQ 323 *How do I implement a compiler that runs inside Eclipse?*

FAQ
323

How do I implement a compiler that runs inside Eclipse?

First, a compiler like the eScript compiler should, of course, be written as a plug-in. In other words, the compiler will have dependent plug-ins, such as the `core.resources` plug-in to read source files and class files and to write resulting Java class files. The compiler has preferences, so it declares a preference page. Furthermore, to discover all kinds of structural information about the target platform, the compiler leans heavily on PDE to help out.

More important the compiler can itself be a publisher of API and can contribute a set of extension points to which other plug-ins can define extension points.

By making the compiler a plug-in, it automatically runs inside Eclipse, and it can keep information cached for later compilation runs. For instance, it can be quite expensive to compute the full list of classes available for class-name resolution if the compiler sees the word `Shell` and needs to determine that a reference is made to `org.eclipse.swt.widgets.Shell`. Such metainformation has to be recomputed each time the compiler is executed in an external process, such as when run from a command-line compiler. Keeping the metadata in memory allows for *incremental* compilation strategies, greatly improving the user experience and reinforcing the feeling of *integration* with the platform. Later, we discuss how to implement a compiler in Eclipse.

 FAQ 325 *How do I implement an Eclipse builder?*

How do I react to changes in source files?

Register a workspace resource change listener. Inside our eScript plug-in class, we call

```
IResourceChangeListener rcl = new IResourceChangeListener() {
    public void resourceChanged(IResourceChangeEvent event) {
        IResource resource = event.getResource();
        if (resource.getFileExtension().equals("escript")) {
            // run the compiler
        }
    }
};
ResourcesPlugin.getWorkspace().addResourceChangeListener(rcl);
```

We will be notified whenever the file is changed in the workspace under Eclipse's control. Changes made to the files outside Eclipse will not be detected unless the workspace is being explicitly refreshed. Alternatively, a separate worker thread could be used to monitor the file system and inform Eclipse of any files having changed.

If the source files are edited with an Eclipse text editor, this scenario will work, and files can be compiled as soon as saved. We certainly are on the right path for our language integration because all editing and compilation are done inside Eclipse on the same Java VM.

Even though we are more integrated than when running an external builder, reacting to workspace changes remains cumbersome, and a much better approach is to use an integrated builder.

☞ eclipse.org article "How You've Changed! Responding to resource changes in the Eclipse workspace"
Go to **Platform Plug-in Developer Guide > Programmer's Guide > Resources overview > Tracking resource changes**

FAQ
325

How do I implement an Eclipse builder?

To understand how Eclipse builds projects, you need to

- Understand where Eclipse stores its project build specifications (See **FAQ 326**)

- Be able to add a builder to a given project (See **FAQ 327**)

- Implement the builder (See **FAQ 328**)

- Make your compiler incremental (See **FAQ 330**)

If you follow these instructions, but your builder does not seem to be called, consult **FAQ 329**.

☞ **FAQ 326** *Where are project build specifications stored?*
Go to **Platform Plug-in Developer Guide > Programmer's Guide > Resources overview > Incremental project builders**

FAQ
326

Where are project build specifications stored?

A project is built according to the specifications defined in its `.project` file. To see the `.project` file for a given project, click on the **Menu** toggle in the Package Explorer's toolbar, select **Filters...**, and deselect **.* files**. Open the `.project` file. The `.project` file for a plug-in should look similar to this:

```
<?xml version="1.0" encoding="UTF-8"?>
<projectDescription>
    <name>org.eclipse.escript.builder</name>
    <projects>
        ...
    </projects>
    <buildSpec>
        <buildCommand>
            <name>org.eclipse.jdt.core.javabuilder</name>
            <arguments> </arguments>
        </buildCommand>
        <buildCommand>
            <name>org.eclipse.pde.ManifestBuilder</name>
```

```
                <arguments> </arguments>
            </buildCommand>
            <buildCommand>
                <name>org.eclipse.pde.SchemaBuilder</name>
                <arguments> </arguments>
            </buildCommand>
        </buildSpec>
        <natures>
            <nature>org.eclipse.pde.PluginNature</nature>
            <nature>org.eclipse.jdt.core.javanature</nature>
        </natures>
    </projectDescription>
```

☞ **FAQ 327** *How do I add a builder to a given project?*

How do I add a builder to a given project?

To register the eScript builder for a given project, add the builder to the project's build specification as follows:

```
private void addBuilder(IProject project, String id) {
    IProjectDescription desc = project.getDescription();
    ICommand[] commands = desc.getBuildSpec();
    for (int i = 0; i < commands.length; ++i)
        if (commands[i].getBuilderName().equals(id))
            return;
    //add builder to project
    ICommand command = desc.newCommand();
    command.setBuilderName(id);
    ICommand[] nc = new ICommand[commands.length + 1];
    // Add it before other builders.
    System.arraycopy(commands, 0, nc, 1, commands.length);
    nc[0] = command;
    desc.setBuildSpec(nc);
    project.setDescription(desc, null);
}
```

Alternatively, you could edit the project description directly on disk by modifying the .project file:

```
<buildCommand>
    <name>org.eclipse.escript.builder.Builder</name>
    <arguments> </arguments>
</buildCommand>
```

A builder is normally added to a project in the project creation wizard but can be added later on.

 FAQ 328 *How do I implement an incremental project builder?*

How do I implement an incremental project builder?

To implement an incremental project builder, you first have to create an extension for `org.eclipse.core.resources.builders`:

```
<extension
      id="Builder"
      name="eScript Builder"
      point="org.eclipse.core.resources.builders">
   <builder>
      <run class="org.eclipse.escript.builder.Builder">
         <parameter name="optimize" value="true"/>
         <parameter name="comment" value="escript Builder"/>
      </run>
   </builder>
</extension>
```

The second step is to create a builder class that must extend the abstract `IncrementalProjectBuilder` superclass:

```
public class Builder extends IncrementalProjectBuilder {
   protected IProject[] build(int kind, Map args,
    IProgressMonitor monitor) {
      if (kind == IncrementalProjectBuilder.FULL_BUILD) {
         fullBuild(monitor);
      } else {
         IResourceDelta delta = getDelta(getProject());
         if (delta == null) {
            fullBuild(monitor);
         } else {
            incrementalBuild(delta, monitor);
         }
      }
      return null;
   }
    private void incrementalBuild(IResourceDelta delta,
     IProgressMonitor monitor) {
       System.out.println("incremental build on "+delta);
```

```
        try {
           delta.accept(new IResourceDeltaVisitor() {
              public boolean visit(IResourceDelta delta) {
                 System.out.println("changed: "+
                    delta.getResource().getRawLocation());
                 return true; // visit children too
              }
           });
        } catch (CoreException e) {
           e.printStackTrace();
        }
     }
     private void fullBuild(IProgressMonitor monitor) {
        System.out.println("full build");
     }
  }
```

It is important to return `true` in the `visit` method for those folders that contain the resources of interest. If you return `false`, the children of the resource delta are not visited.

FAQ 329 *How do I handle setup problems for a given builder?*

How do I handle setup problems for a given builder?

FAQ
329

When running a build in a runtime workbench, you might get the following message:

```
!MESSAGE Skipping builder com.xyz.builder for project P.
Either the builder is missing from the install, or it
belongs to a project nature that is missing or disabled.
```

This message means that something is wrong with the builder plug-in or with the attribution of the builder specification in the `.project` file. The builder plug-in might load fine but still be broken, perhaps because it is missing an ID in the extension point declaration.

If everything else seems right to you, double-check the ID specified in the builder extension point. The ID should not be the plug-in ID of your builder, but rather the concatenation of the *plug-in ID* and the *builder ID*. In other words, if the plug-ins ID is `org.eclipse.escript.builder`, and the ID of the builder is

Builder, the builder ID reference in the .project file should be
org.eclipse.escript.builder.Builder.

 FAQ 330 *How do I make my compiler incremental?*

How do I make my compiler incremental?

The Eclipse Platform distinguishes between *full* and *incremental* builds.
Incremental builds are much faster than a complete rebuild of a project because
only the resources that have changed since the last build need to be considered
for compilation.

Incremental builders are invoked each time a file is saved. To prevent a bad user
experience, take special care to make the incremental builder as fast as possible.
To make a compiler fast, it helps to understand that in most compilers little time
is spent in compilation at all. Most time is spent resolving the context of the
program, such as the build classpath.

In the case of eScript, two kinds of information need to be discovered from the
target environment:

1. Starting with the Java classpath and the list of plug-ins referenced by a
   given script, the eScript compiler needs to find all possible external class
   types, as well as their methods and fields. This information is needed to
   determine whether a given input string refers to a class, an interface, a
   method, a field, or a local variable.

2. To facilitate the easy creation of the underlying Java class files for a
   given script, the eScript compiler, when it reads the contribution to a
   certain extension point, needs to interrogate the PDE to find out the class
   to extend or interface to implement.

The overhead of building the context is surprisingly constant for eScript and
dwarfs the memory consumption needed for compiling a script. The scripts tend
to be small, but the universe of plug-ins is large. The eScript compiler easily
loads about 14,000 classes, simply to bind strings to type names. Rebuilding this
contexts adds about three to four seconds to a compilation. The compilation of
the script itself is less than a second, and is hardly noticeable.

By not discarding the context information after a compilation, performance of the next compilation run is greatly improved. The first compilation will be slow, but the next ones will be non-interruptive. However, note that optimization is always a time/space trade-off. The price we pay for faster compilation is about 15 MB of state that needs to be cached. JDT suffers from the same dilemma. Load a big Java project and close all perspectives, including the Java perspective, and the entire Java model with its thousands of classes is being held onto by the JDT.

Incremental builders that are run sporadically may be wise to run a timer and clean up their cache after a certain expiration time to free up heap memory used by the platform.

☞ **FAQ 331** *Language integration phase 2: How do I implement a DOM?*

Language integration phase 2: How do I implement a DOM?

FAQ
331

In phase 1 of our language integration, we focused on the compilation of source code and the build process of programs written in our new language. Our experience is that it is smart to follow this bottom-up approach. It may be tempting to start with the visual components, such as the editor, but developing an IDE is like building a home. Excavation and foundation pouring is a useful step and should not be skipped too hastily.

Therefore, before we can implement an editor, we need to follow phase 2. Even though phase 2 has only one step, it is a very important one and should be given plenty of attention. Namely, by carefully designing a Document Object Model (DOM) first, many of the following steps will be a lot easier to implement. After doing phase 1—implementing a compiler and a builder—and finishing phase 2—implementing a DOM—you are ready to move to **FAQ 334**.

FAQ 332

How do I implement a DOM for my language?

A DOM represents the structure of your programming language. Its design and implementation are dependent of the target language and follow a few simple guidelines:

- The DOM is hierarchical in nature and directly represents concrete elements in the program it represents (such as the program itself and its functions, declarations, and statements).

- A DOM is used for defining context for Content Assist (see **FAQ 336**).

- A DOM is useful for generating text hovers (see **FAQ 337**).

- Creating outline views without a DOM is difficult (see **FAQ 341**).

- A DOM is essential in architecting and implementing support for refactoring (see **FAQ 340**).

- A program may be represented with various DOMs. In the case of eScript we have a DOM for describing the program structure and a second DOM for the method bodies.

- A DOM is implemented as a data structure with access API. In the case of eScript, we move Content Assist and text-hover support into the DOM nodes. This makes handling those in the editor very easy.

- A DOM can be generated in two modes:

  1. The same compiler that also compiles source code can save its abstract syntax tree (AST) and expose it for use by the editor. Using an AST is a pretty standard way to implement a computer language, and piggybacking on that infrastructure makes life a lot easier when writing your editor. This is the way the eScript editor works.

  2. If the underlying AST is not accessible or is to too fine-grained for use in an editor, you may decide to implement a lightweight parser and generate a DOM more efficiently. This is the way the JDT implements its Java model.

Figure 19.2 shows the inheritance hierarchy for the DOM that was develloped for the eScript's language. As you can see, each node in the DOM extends `Element`. It defines the following fields:

```
int startOffset, endOffset; // source positions
Hashtable attributes;       // things like ID, label, ...
ArrayList children;         // children of this element
Element parent;             // the owner of this element
String hoverHelp;           // cached value of hover help
...more fields....
```

The subclasses of `Element` implement useful methods:

```
public String getAttributeValue(String name)
public String getHoverHelp()
public void getContentProposals(...., ArrayList result)
```

For instance, the `getHoverHelp` method easily allows us to use the DOM to find the element at a given offset and then ask it for what hover help is appropriate.

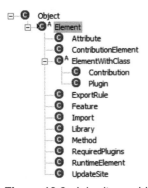

Figure 19.2   Inheritance hierarchy for eScript's DOM

☞ **FAQ 333** *How can I ensure that my model is scalable?*

FAQ
333

How can I ensure that my model is scalable?

Because eScript programs are assumed to be small, we did not put too much care into the optimization of the memory usage of our DOM. However, for languages in which programs tend to get much larger, such as C, Pascal, or C#, the definition of each individual field has to be carefully weighed. To represent `<windows.h>`, the number of DOM elements easily runs into hundreds of thousands or even millions.

When writing a model that needs to scale to large systems, you must pay careful attention to the memory your model uses. Traditional performance optimization techniques apply here, but *lazy loading* and *most recently used (MRU) caching* are particularly effective. The JDT's Java model, for example, is populated lazily as the elements are accessed. Java element handles do not exist in memory at any one time for every Java project in your workspace. Most Java elements implement the `Openable` interface, indicating that they are lazily populated when you invoke methods on them that require access to underlying structures. Although all `Openable` elements can be explicitly closed when no longer needed, the model automatically closes the MRU elements by storing references to all open elements in a least recently used (LRU) cache. The abstraction layer of thin Java element handles allows expensive data structures to be flushed even if clients maintain references to those Java elements indefinitely. Abstract syntax trees are also generated lazily as they are needed and are quickly discarded when no longer referenced.

Although some of these performance enhancements can be added retroactively to your model implementation, it is important to think about scalability right from the start. Performance aspects of your model and of the tools built on top of it, need to be considered early in architectural planning. In particular, an architecture that does not let clients of your API maintain references to large internal data structures is essential to the scalability of your model.

FAQ 334 *Language integration phase 3: How do I edit programs?*
FAQ 350 *How do I create Java elements?*

Language integration phase 3: How do I edit programs?

After creating a compiler, a builder, and a DOM, writing an editor is a snap. To write an editor for a particular programming language, a few steps can be distinguished, all relying heavily on the existence of a DOM.

1. *Implement an language-specific editor.* The JDT places the bar high for any subsequent language implementers. No matter how fast the compiler is and how well the build process is integrated, if your language has to be edited in the default text editor, you fail to even get close to being worthy of comparison to JDT. Writing an editor is not difficult. Many examples exist. The platform wizard has one for an XML editor. The examples shipped with Eclipse show a simplified Java editor. This book has a sample that shows how to write an HTML editor. For more details, see **FAQ 335**

2. *Add Content Assist.* (see **FAQ 336**). The DOM, developed in phase 2, allows us to navigate the source code, analyze it, present it in multiple modes, and manipulate its structure, a process also known as *refactoring.* Content Assist uses the DOM to figure out all the possible context-sensitive continuations for a given input. Quick Fixes know how to solve a given compilation error. Refactoring relies on the DOM to find all call sites for a given method before we can change its name. An Outline view uses the DOM to show the structure of the code in a hierarchical summary format.

3. *Add Quick Fixes* (see **FAQ 339**). After compilation errors have been detected, suggest how to fix the problem. How would you reason about code without an underlying model?

4. *Add refactoring* (see **FAQ 340**). Implement operations on source code to restructure program constructs, following the semantics of your language. Again, without a model of the underlying language, this is a daunting, error-prone task.

5. *Add an Outline view* (see **FAQ 341**). The Outline view presents a summary of the structure of a particular program. Using the same compiler and/or DOM saves a lot of time developing your language IDE.

After completing your editor, you are ready to enter the Holy Grail of language IDEs; see **FAQ 342**.

How do I write an editor for my own language?

An editor contributes to the `org.eclipse.ui.editors` extension point, and, in practice, the class implementing the editor is typically a subclass of `org.eclipse.ui.editors.text.TextEditor`. The simplest way to familiarize yourself with the Eclipse editor framework is by creating a new plug-in with a sample XML editor (use **New > Plug-in Development > Plug-in Project > ... > ... > Plug-in with an editor**). This will provide you with an editor supporting syntax color highlighting, Content Assist, hover help, and more. Also be sure to check out Chapter 11 of this book, which describes an HTML editor framework. Both the XML and HTML editors show how to design and arrange your code in manageable packages.

If you want to see what the minimalist editor looks like, we did the experiment of reducing our eScript editor to a single source file with the bare minimum code required to make the smallest possible Eclipse editor ever (see Figure 19.3). We don't suggest that you organize your code this way, but it will show you the basic information you will have to provide to give your editor have a professional look and feel with syntax highlighting and hover help.

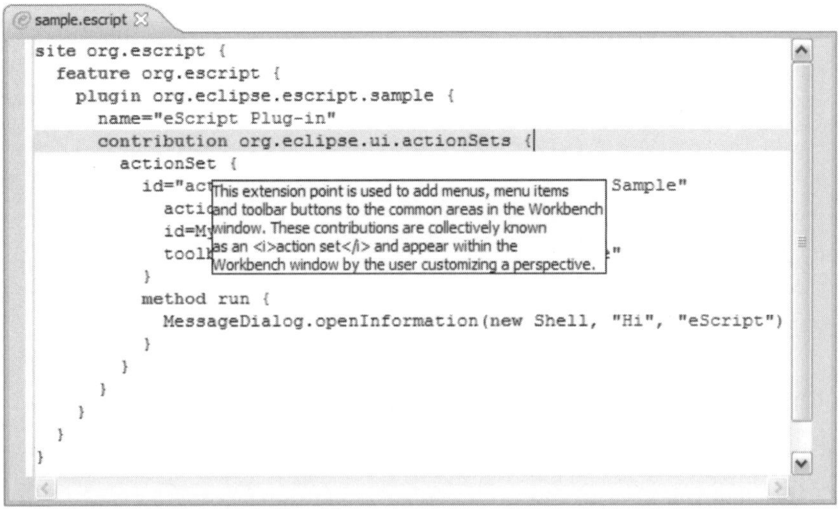

Figure 19.3 The eScript editor

Here is the structure of our minimalist eScript editor:

```
public class Editor extends TextEditor {
    ...
    public Editor() {
        super();
        setSourceViewerConfiguration(new Configuration());
    }
    protected void createActions() {
        ...
    }
    ...
}
```

In the constructor, we set up a source viewer configuration, handling such issues as Content Assist, hover help, and instructing the editor what to do while the user types text. In the inherited `createActions` method the editor creates its Content Assist action, used when Ctrl+Space is pressed in the editor.

Our configuration looks like this:

```
class Configuration extends SourceViewerConfiguration {
    public IPresentationReconciler getPresentationReconciler(
        ISourceViewer sourceViewer) {
        PresentationReconciler pr =
            new PresentationReconciler();
        DefaultDamagerRepairer ddr =
            new DefaultDamagerRepairer(new Scanner());
        pr.setRepairer(ddr, IDocument.DEFAULT_CONTENT_TYPE);
        pr.setDamager(ddr, IDocument.DEFAULT_CONTENT_TYPE);
        return pr;
    }
    IContentAssistant getContentAssistant(ISourceViewer sv) {
        ContentAssistant ca = new ContentAssistant();
        IContentAssistProcessor cap = new CompletionProcessor();
        ca.setContentAssistProcessor(cap,
            IDocument.DEFAULT_CONTENT_TYPE);
        ca.setInformationControlCreator(
            getInformationControlCreator(sv));
        return ca;
    }
    public ITextHover getTextHover(ISourceViewer sv,
        String contentType) {
        return new TextHover();
    }
}
```

We use the default presentation reconciler, and we do not distinguish between sections in our documents. In other words, reconciliation of layout will be the same all over the document, whether we are inside a feature, a plug-in, or a method. We declare a scanner, implemented by us, and rely on the text editor framework to parse the document using our parser when it suits it.

Next, we enable Content Assist by creating a default Content Assistant and defining our own Content Assist processor. When Content Assist is activated, our processor will map the current cursor position to a node in the abstract syntax tree for the underlying document and present relevant continuations based on the currently entered string. See **FAQ 336** for the implementation of our completion processor.

Finally, we create a text-hover that will return a relevant string to be shown in a hover window when we move over a given node in our abstract syntax tree. See **FAQ 337** for the implementation of our `ITextHover` implementation.

For scanning the underlying document to draw it using different colors and fonts, we deploy `RuleBasedScanner`, one of the simplest scanners offered by the editor framework:

```
class Scanner extends RuleBasedScanner {
    public Scanner() {
        WordRule rule = new WordRule(new IWordDetector() {
            public boolean isWordStart(char c) {
                return Character.isJavaIdentifierStart(c);
            }
            public boolean isWordPart(char c) {
                return Character.isJavaIdentifierPart(c);
            }
        });
        Token keyword = new Token(new TextAttribute(
            Editor.KEYWORD, null, SWT.BOLD));
        Token comment = new Token(
            new TextAttribute(Editor.COMMENT));
        Token string = new Token(
            new TextAttribute(Editor.STRING));
        //add tokens for each reserved word
        for (int n = 0; n < Parser.KEYWORDS.length; n++)
            rule.addWord(Parser.KEYWORDS[n], keyword);
        setRules(new IRule[] {
            rule,
            new SingleLineRule("#", null, comment),
            new SingleLineRule("\"", "\"", string, '\\'),
            new SingleLineRule("'", "'", string, '\\'),
            new WhitespaceRule(new IWhitespaceDetector() {
```

```
                    public boolean isWhitespace(char c) {
                        return Character.isWhitespace(c);
                    }
                }),
            });
        }
    }
```

For each of the keywords in our little language, we define a word entry in our
WordRule. We pass our keyword detector, together with rules for recognizing
comments, strings, and white spaces to the scanner. With this simple set of rules,
the scanner can segment a stream of bytes into sections and then use the
underlying rules to color the sections.

FAQ 211 *How do I create my own editor?*
FAQ 264 *How do I get started with creating a custom text editor?*
FAQ 336 *How do I add Content Assist to my language editor?*

How do I add Content Assist to my language editor?

In **FAQ 335** we describe how Content Assist is installed through our
configuration class, as follows:

```
class Configuration extends SourceViewerConfiguration {
    ...
    public IContentAssistant getContentAssistant(ISourceViewer
      sourceViewer) {
        ContentAssistant ca = new ContentAssistant();
        IContentAssistProcessor cap =
                        new CompletionProcessor();
        ca.setContentAssistProcessor(cap,
            IDocument.DEFAULT_CONTENT_TYPE);
        ca.setInformationControlCreator(
            getInformationControlCreator(sourceViewer));
        return ca;
    }
    ...
}
```

A completion processor takes the current insertion point in the editor and figures out a list of continuation proposals for the user to choose from. Our completion processor looks something like this:

```
class CompletionProcessor implements
                                IContentAssistProcessor {
    private final IContextInformation[] NO_CONTEXTS =
        new IContextInformation[0];
    private final char[] PROPOSAL_ACTIVATION_CHARS =
        new char[] { 's','f','p','n','m', };
    private ICompletionProposal[] NO_COMPLETIONS =
        new ICompletionProposal[0];

    public ICompletionProposal[] computeCompletionProposals(
        ITextViewer viewer, int offset) {
        try {
            IDocument document = viewer.getDocument();
            ArrayList result = new ArrayList();
            String prefix = lastWord(document, offset);
            String indent = lastIndent(document, offset);
            EscriptModel model =
                        EscriptModel.getModel(document, null);
            model.getContentProposals(prefix, indent,
                                        offset, result);
            return (ICompletionProposal[]) result.toArray(
                new ICompletionProposal[result.size()]);
        } catch (Exception e) {
            // ... log the exception ...
            return NO_COMPLETIONS;
        }
    }
    private String lastWord(IDocument doc, int offset) {
        try {
            for (int n = offset-1; n >= 0; n--) {
                char c = doc.getChar(n);
                if (!Character.isJavaIdentifierPart(c))
                    return doc.get(n + 1, offset-n-1);
            }
        } catch (BadLocationException e) {
            // ... log the exception ...
        }
        return "";
    }
    private String lastIndent(IDocument doc, int offset) {
        try {
            int start = offset-1;
            while (start >= 0 &&
                doc.getChar(start)!= '\n') start--;
            int end = start;
```

```
            while (end < offset &&
                Character.isSpaceChar(doc.getChar(end))) end++;
            return doc.get(start+1, end-start-1);
        } catch (BadLocationException e) {
            e.printStackTrace();
        }
        return "";
    }
    public IContextInformation[] computeContextInformation(
        ITextViewer viewer, int offset) {
        return NO_CONTEXTS;
    }
    char[] getCompletionProposalAutoActivationCharacters() {
        return PROPOSAL_ACTIVATION_CHARS;
    }
    // ... remaining methods are optional ...
}
```

Basically, Content Assist completion has three steps. First, we have to figure out what string has already been started by the user (see `lastWord`). Second, we have to find appropriate completions. Third, we have to return strings so that when they are inserted, they lay out acceptably (see the use of `lastIndent`).

FAQ 267 *How do I add Content Assist to my editor?*
FAQ 337 *How do I add hover support to my text editor?*

How do I add hover support to my text editor?

In **FAQ 335** we describe how text hover is enabled for our editor through our configuration class:

```
class Configuration extends SourceViewerConfiguration {
    ...
    public ITextHover getTextHover(ISourceViewer sv,
      String contentType) {
        return new TextHover();
    }
    ...
}
```

When the user moves the mouse over an area that corresponds to a given node in our AST, it is easy for us to provide a symbolic description of the node. Namely, the editor framework helps out by registering for the mouse events, setting timers, calling us at the right time, and drawing the box that will show the text hover. All that we need to do is match a certain location in the editor to a symbolic string. We do this by providing our own implementation of `org.eclipse.jface.text.ITextHover` as follows:

```
public class TextHover implements ITextHover {
    public IRegion getHoverRegion(ITextViewer tv, int off) {
        return new Region(off, 0);
    }
    public String getHoverInfo(ITextViewer tv, IRegion r) {
        try {
            IDocument doc = tv.getDocument();
            EscriptModel em = EscriptModel.getModel(doc, null);
            return em.getElementAt(r.getOffset()).
                getHoverHelp();
        }
        catch (Exception e) {
            return "";
        }
    }
}
```

The first method we implement is meant for optimizing the drawing of the text hover. We answer the question, If I am going to show a hover for character x in the text viewer, for what region should the hover be the same? We don't try to be too smart here. We simply return an empty region.

The next method implements the real logic of the text hover. We convert the current cursor location to an AST element in the document and ask it to return a string relevant to the current context. Note that we assume that the `EscriptModel` implements a cache and that the `getModel` method is inexpensive as we will call it many times during editing.

☞ **FAQ 338** *How do I create problem markers for my compiler?*

How do I create problem markers for my compiler?

Adding problem markers for eScript compilation happens in two simple steps.

1. Right before we compile the resource, we remove all problem markers from the resource:

```
void compileResource(IResource resource) {
    resource.deleteMarkers(IMarker.PROBLEM,
        true, IResource.DEPTH_INFINITE);
    doCompileResource(resource);
}
```

2. During compilation, errors are attached to the resource as follows:

```
void reportError(IResource res, int line, String msg) {
    IMarker m = res.createMarker(IMarker.PROBLEM);
    m.setAttribute(IMarker.LINE_NUMBER, line);
    m.setAttribute(IMarker.MESSAGE, msg);
    m.setAttribute(IMarker.PRIORITY, IMarker.PRIORITY_HIGH);
    m.setAttribute(IMarker.SEVERITY, IMarker.SEVERITY_ERROR);
}
```

To simplify matters, we use the existing problem-marker type. See the online Eclipse article "Mark My Words" for an explanation on how to declare your own marker types.

Simply by attaching a marker to a resource, the IDE will take care of placing visual indicators at the two indicator bars in the editor. The IDE will also add entries to the Problems view. If we indicated additional information in the marker for IMarker.CHAR_START and IMarker.CHAR_END, the editor will also draw a red squiggly line under the offending problem. Figure 19.4 shows the result of a compilation of a problematic eScript file.

☞ **FAQ 339** *How do I implement Quick Fixes for my own language?*

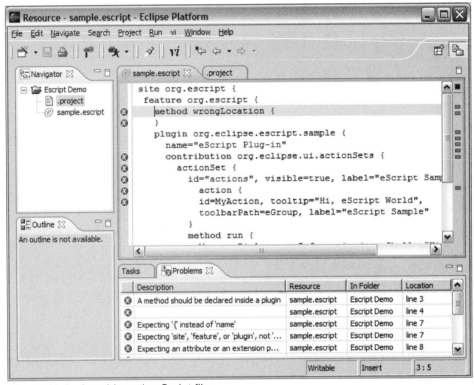

Figure 19.4 A problematic eScript file

FAQ
339

How do I implement Quick Fixes for my own language?

The JDT has support for so-called Quick Fixes. Whenever a marker is generated, a set of resolutions is associated with it for users to click on and choose an automatic fix of the problem as shown in Figure 19.5. Quick Fixes are implemented through the `org.eclipse.ui.ide.markerResolution` extension point:

```
<extension point="org.eclipse.ui.ide.markerResolution">
   <markerResolutionGenerator
      markerType="org.eclipse.core.resources.problemmarker"
      class="org.eclipse.escript.quickfix.QuickFixer"/>
</extension>
```

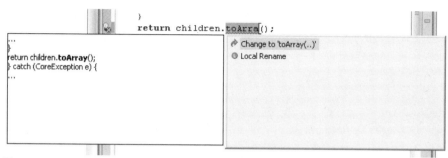

Figure 19.5 Quick Fixes in the Eclipse Java editor

The implementation class implements the `IMarkerResolutionGenerator` interface. Use the `IMarkerResolutionGenerator2` when resolutions are expensive to implement. See the javadoc for the interface for an explanation. Here is what the implementation class may look like:

```
class QuickFixer implements IMarkerResolutionGenerator {
    public IMarkerResolution[] getResolutions(IMarker mk) {
        try {
            Object problem = mk.getAttribute("WhatsUp");
            return new IMarkerResolution[] {
                new QuickFix("Fix #1 for "+problem),
                new QuickFix("Fix #2 for "+problem),
            };
        }
        catch (CoreException e) {
            return new IMarkerResolution[0];
        }
    }
}
```

An array of Quick Fixes has to be returned for the problem associated with the current marker.

Each marker resolution, or Quick Fix, implements `IMarkerResolution` or, when a description and an image are available, `IMarkerResolution2`. Here is what the implementation may look like:

```
public class QuickFix implements IMarkerResolution {
    String label;
    QuickFix(String label) {
        this.label = label;
    }
    public String getLabel() {
        return label;
    }
```

```
public void run(IMarker marker) {
    MessageDialog.openInformation(null, "QuickFix Demo",
        "This quick-fix is not yet implemented");
    }
}
```

The problem indicator—in our sample, the WhatsUp attribute— is associated with the marker by the parser. Typically, the Quick Fix handler that resolves the problem, as shown in this example, lives somewhere in the UI. Following this paradigm is advisable as it separates the problem detection in the compiler/parser from how it is presented to the user.

Quick Fixes can be inspected and executed by using the context menu on a given problem in the Problems view. Note how the JDT uses a context menu and the double-click action on a marker to active Quick Fix.

 FAQ 340 *How do I support refactoring for my own language?*

**FAQ
340**

How do I support refactoring for my own language?

Refactoring is the process of restructuring code for the purpose of readability, performance improvements, reuse, or simply for the regular evolutionary quest for elegance. The kind of refactoring your language will support is heavily dependent on the nature of your language. Almost all languages provide support for expressing *abstraction*. Therefore, it makes most sense to focus on the processes of encapsulating certain expressions into a more abstract form, such as *extracting a method*, and the reverse, such as *in-lining a method*.

To implement refactorings, you need the UI mechanisms for implementing them. Implement a new menu with your refactoring options; use the JDT for inspiration. See the org.eclipse.jdt.ui plug-in's manifest file and open the **Refactor** menu. Note how all possible refactorings are exhaustively listed here. Each refactoring can be fired by the user, and Java code will have to determine whether the refactoring is appropriate for the given selection and context. Figure 19.6 shows the refactoring menu for the Java perspective.

Figure 19.6   Refactor menu for the Java perspective

In addition to having a menu in the global menu bar, you will want to add a pop-up menu to your editor to activate a given refactoring from the current selection. Here you can be more creative and restrict the choices given to the user to relate directly to a given selection. Figure 19.7 shows the context menu for the JDT showing the refactoring options for a few selected statements.

Now that we have decided what UI support to provide, how do we actually implement the refactorings? As we said earlier, refactorings can be expressed as a restructuring of code. Let us think. What do we have that describes the structure of our program? Right, the DOM. In the case of JDT, all refactoring is directly expressed as operations on the Java model. The fact that an editor is open and will redraw the changes as a result is just a side-effect. Many refactorings go beyond the current text file. Imagine renaming a given method name. You will have to visit all the places where the original method is called and rename each instance accordingly. Without a model, this is very difficult to implement.

In Eclipse 3.0, the generic portions of the JDT refactoring infrastructure were pushed down into a generic IDE layer called the Eclipse Language Toolkit (LTK). The LTK projects provide a model for refactoring operations, a mechanism to allow third parties to participate in your refactorings, and some basic UI components for refactoring wizards. This infrastructure is a logical starting point for writing refactoring support for your own language.

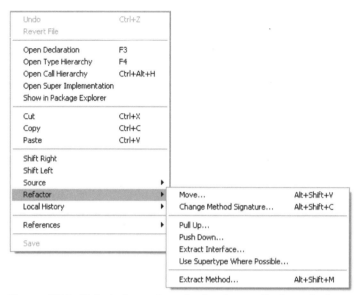

Figure 19.7 Refactoring options for the Java editor's context menu

The price of success is adoption. When you release your language plug-ins, you have to assume the worst: that people may like them. You may end up with many programmers who use them. However, these programmers are very much like you and will probably want to enhance your tools.

One of the first things people will want to do is obtain access to your DOM to do code generation, extraction, and analysis. The second thing they will want to do is provide their own refactorings and easily tie them to your existing refactorings. Prepare for this to happen and define your own extension point schema before starting to implement any refactorings. If you define all your refactorings using your own extension point schema, you will iron out the bugs, and people will be grateful once they start using your language IDE.

FAQ 341 *How do I create an Outline view for my own language editor?*
FAQ 361 *What is LTK?*

How do I create an Outline view for my own language editor?

The Outline view is not generated by the editor framework. In fact, this view is offered by the `org.eclipse.ui.views` plug-in. When the user changes editors, your editor will be asked to provide an `IContentOutlinePage` adapter for an Outline view. This is how you could implement your outline viewer:

```
public Object getAdapter(Class required) {
    if (IContentOutlinePage.class.equals(required)) {
        if (myOutlinePage == null) {
            myOutlinePage = new CoolLanguageContentOutlinePage(
                            getDocumentProvider(), this);
            myOutlinePage.setInput(getEditorInput());
        }
        return myOutlinePage;
    }
    return super.getAdapter(required);
}
```

Most programming languages are inherently hierarchical. Therefore, to show the content outline of a certain program file, most editors deploy a tree. If you think that a tree is the most appropriate way to show the outline of your programs, you should consider subclassing from class `ContentOutlinePage` in the `org.eclipse.ui.views.contentoutline` package. This class already sets you up with a `TreeViewer`, and all you need to provide are a content provider, a label provider, and the input:

```
public void createControl(Composite parent) {
    super.createControl(parent);
    TreeViewer viewer= getTreeViewer();
    viewer.setContentProvider(new MyContentProvider());
    viewer.setLabelProvider(new MyLabelProvider());
    viewer.addSelectionChangedListener(this);
    viewer.setInput(myInput);
}
```

You will want to update the selection in your Outline view when the cursor is moved in the editor. Similarly, if the structure of the program changed—code added or removed—the outline has to be updated. This is typically performed with a JFace text model reconciler.

When the user selects a node in the Outline view, the editor should change selection to the selected element and make it visible.

 FAQ 273 *How do I use a model reconciler?*
FAQ 342 *Language integration phase 4: What are the finishing touches?*

Language integration phase 4: What are the finishing touches?

After following the steps in phases 1 to 3, you have successfully written a compiler, a builder, a DOM, and an integrated editor. What remains are a few finishing touches:

1. *Add a project wizard.* Your language may benefit from similar wizards as provided by JDT to create projects, classes, and interfaces. See **FAQ 343**.

2. *Declare a project nature.* Natures can be used to facilitate the enablement of builders on certain projects. See **FAQ 344**.

3. *Declare a perspective.* Perspectives can be used to organize views and editors into a cohesive, collaborative set of tools. See **FAQ 345**.

4. *Add documentation.* Traditionally this is done as one of the last steps in any agile software project. Eclipse has support for adding documentation to a set of plug-ins through its help system, accessed with **Help > Help Contents...**. Context-sensitive help can be activated by using F1. For more information about how to add documentation and help for your language, see **FAQ 346**.

5. *Add source-level debugging support.* Implementing support for source-level debugging is arguably the most difficult to implement, even in the highly configurable Eclipse. See **FAQ 347** for a discussion.

Congratulations. You followed all steps outlined in the four phases of language integration and are to be commended for getting this far. Writing an IDE in Eclipse is the most elaborate and wide-ranging exercise to perform on top of Eclipse.

What wizards do I define for my own language?

This depends on your language. For instance, the PDE offers wizards for creating plug-ins, features, plug-in fragments, and update sites. In addition, the PDE provides support for converting something existing into a form it can work with, such as converting a regular project to a plug-in project.

In the case of Java, the JDT offers wizards for the obvious things—Java projects, packages, classes, and interfaces—as well as for less obvious ones such as a wizard for creating a scrapbook page and a source folder. The CDT offers wizards for generating a C++ class and for creating either a standard make file project or a managed make project for C or C++. Furthermore, the CDT has a wizard for converting a normal project to a C/C++ project.

If we look at eScript, the only appropriate wizard type seems to be the creation of an eScript file, where the user would choose whether the generated code should include the definition of a feature and an update site. An extra wizard page could be added to generate code to implement plug-ins that contribute a view, editor, and so on.

When certain wizards are used frequently, consider showing them in the toolbar by contributing an action set.

For instructions on writing wizards, look at **Help > Platform Plug-in Developer Guide > Programmer's Guide > Dialogs and Wizards > Wizards**.

 FAQ 155 *What is a wizard?*
FAQ 344 *When does my language need its own nature?*
eclipse.org article "Creating JFace Wizards"

When does my language need its own nature?

This topic is explained in **FAQ 291**.

 FAQ 345 *When does my language need its own perspective?*

When does my language need its own perspective?

Your language needs its own perspective only when you have a certain collection of views and editors that work together and would be cumbersome to open individually. Adding a new perspective should be done with reservation, though. If you add a new perspective and bring users there to do programming in your language, you have made many hidden assumptions about how programs are developed and in what sequence. Ask yourself, What if people want to develop programs written in my language and at the same time in Java and/or C? Will my perspective be a help or hindrance?

Think of perspectives as one of the windows in a virtual desktop manager. When you start using a virtual desktop, you like the separation of function. You use one of the windows for editing, one for reading mail, one for browsing, one for programming. This is great. You can switch between tasks with a clever keyboard shortcut or a simple mouse click. Inevitably though, you get sloppy, separation rules are broken, and all applications end up in one window. The virtual desktop ends up as a useful tool for demos, but that's about it. The same issues apply to perspectives. People like them for their separation of context and their memory of what views are chosen with their layout. However, people can manage only a limited number of perspectives and are particularly annoyed when an application rudely jumps to another perspective. Be sure to ask permission from the user, as the Debug perspective does.

Perspectives are created by using the `org.eclipse.ui.perspectives` extension point:

```
<extension
      point="org.eclipse.ui.perspectives">
   <perspective
         name="Cool Perspective"
         icon="icons/cool.gif"
         class="org.eclipse.faq.sample.CoolPerspective"
         id="org.eclipse.faq.sample.coolPerspective">
   </perspective>
</extension>
```

☞ **FAQ 346** *How do I add documentation and help for my own language?*

How do I add documentation and help for my own language?

Documentation for plug-ins, including those that implement a programming language is done by contributing to the extension point. Open the plug-in Manifest Editor on your plug-in and switch to the Extensions page. Click on **Add...** and choose **Extension Templates > Help Contents** (see Figure 19.8).

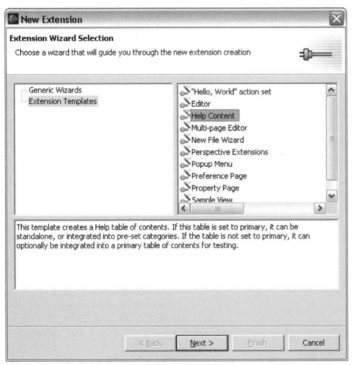

Figure 19.8   Using the Manifest Editor

Click **Next** and provide details. Click **OK**. Voila, your plug-in now has documentation exported in the standard Eclipse Help format, provided through **Help > Help Contents...**.

FAQ 277 *How can I generate HTML and* `toc.xml` *files?*
FAQ 347 *How do I support source-level debugging for my own language?*

How do I support source-level debugging for my own language?

Writing an integrated source debugger for a language is a highly specialized topic requiring major study and a lot of work, and many subtleties are involved. To do the topic justice, we can only refer you to the platform documentation and to JDT debugging as a reference implementation. Start by looking in the *Platform Plug-in Developer Guide* under **Programmer's Guide > Program debug and launch support**.

FAQ 313 *What is a launch configuration?*
FAQ 314 *When do I use a launch delegate?*

Chapter 20. Java Development Tool API

From the outset, Eclipse has been used to develop Eclipse itself. The plug-ins that make up Eclipse are written in Java, and the concept of self-hosting has propelled the JDT to their current maturity level. When you are writing your plug-ins, you will also spend considerable time inside the JDT. A full coverage of JDT's functionality is way beyond the scope of the list of FAQs in this chapter; however, we do focus on topics that are directly related to writing plug-ins and discuss aspects of JDT that warrant a discussion about how they are implemented rather than used.

It is important to realize that JDT itself has been written as a set of plug-ins and receives no special support from the platform. JDT represents a wealth of knowledge and is by far the most elaborate and advanced set of plug-ins in Eclipse. It is definitely worth spending some time to observe how JDT extends the platform and how its own extension points and API have been designed. It is likely that your plug-ins will deploy very similar patterns of extensions, extendibility, and reuse.

Finally, the JDT is a useful set of plug-ins in its own right, but it has also been carefully designed for extension by other plug-ins. By having a published API, it is easy to create new Java projects, generate Java source code, manage Java builds, inspect and analyze Java projects, and implement special refactorings. Refer to **Help > Help Contents > JDT Plug-in Developer Guide** for extensive documentation and tutorials describing the extension points and API published by JDT. For a comprehensive guide to Java development using Eclipse, see Shavor et al. (2003).

 Sherry Shavor, et al., Chapter 27, "Extending the Java Development Tools," in *The Java Developers Guide to Eclipse* (Addison-Wesley, 2003)

How do I extend the JDT?

FAQ 348

The first step is to read **Help > Help Contents... > JDT Plug-in Developer Guide**. This guide provides an excellent description of how the Java development tools maintain a model of a Java program and what can be done with it.

The `org.eclipse.jdt.core` plug-in provides API for querying and manipulating Java programs. Its major capabilities include

- Parsing and compiling Java source code

- Manipulating Java source files, using various object models

- Evaluating (running) code snippets

- Searching, formatting, and invoking Content Assist on source files

The `org.eclipse.jdt.ui` plug-in is responsible for all UI elements of the Java development tools, including all the Java browsing views and the Java editor. The plug-in also provides API in a number of areas to allow other plug-ins to customize or extend the Java development tools:

- Action classes for adding JDT actions to views in other plug-ins

- Export code into JARs

- Participation in refactorings

- Java text editors and text hovers

- Wizard components for creating Java projects and files

In addition to these two principal JDT plug-ins, a number of other plug-ins also provide APIs relating to Java development. The `org.eclipse.jdt.debug` plug-in provides support for launching and debugging Java programs. The `org.eclipse.jdt.launching` plug-in provides API for installing and configuring Java VMs and for looking up the source code corresponding to a Java library. Finally, the `org.eclipse.jdt.unit` plug-in has support for running JUnit tests and for programmatically monitoring the execution of JUnit tests.

☞ Extend Eclipse's Java development tools (http://www.ibm.com/developerworks) JUnit (http://www.junit.org)

What is the Java model?

The Java model is a hierarchical representation of the Java projects in your workspace. Figure 20.1 is a sample Spider graph of the Java model, showing the `java.lang.VerifyError` class and its two constructors.

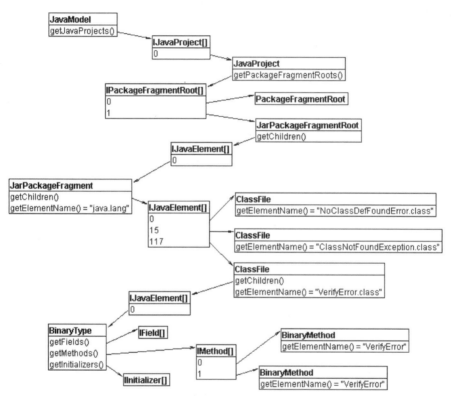

Figure 20.1 Spider diagram of the Java model

Using a utility method provided by `JavaCore`, a Java model is obtained for the workspace. Using the `IJavaModel`, the Java projects can be inspected. Each project contains a classpath, consisting of multiple package fragment roots, such as source directories in the project or referenced JARs from required plug-ins. Each fragment contains a number of class files. An example of its use is given in the following piece of code:

```
IWorkspace workspace = ResourcesPlugin.getWorkspace();
IJavaModel javaModel = JavaCore.create(workspace.getRoot());
IJavaProject projects[] = javaModel.getJavaProjects();
for (int n = 0; n < projects.length; n++) {
```

```
IJavaProject project = projects[n];
IPackageFragmentRoot[] roots =
   project.getAllPackageFragmentRoots();
int nClasses = 0;
for (int k = 0; k < roots.length; k++) {
    IPackageFragmentRoot root = roots[k];
    IJavaElement[] elements = root.getChildren();
    for (int i = 0; i < elements.length; i++) {
        IJavaElement element = elements[i];
        PackageFragment fragment = (PackageFragment)
           element.getAdapter(PackageFragment.class);
        if (fragment == null) continue;
        IJavaElement fes[] = fragment.getChildren();
        for (int j = 0; j < fes.length; j++) {
            String className = fes[j].getElementName();
            nClasses++;
        }
    }
}
String projectName = projects[n].getElementName();
System.out.println("Classpath for project "+
   projectName +" contains "+nClasses+" classes.");
}
```

The output of this code for a workspace with a single empty Java project is

```
Classpath for project P contains 12187 classes.
```

In other words, before you start adding your own classes or start referring to any other Eclipse plug-ins, you already have access to more than 12,000 classes in the Java 2, Standard Edition (J2SE) libraries.

The Java model is declared in package org.eclipse.jdt.core, which consists of 55 types providing access to anything you would ever need to analyze and manipulate your Java programs.

FAQ 350

How do I create Java elements?

The Java model is made up of IJavaElement objects. Java elements represent all levels of a Java project, from the project itself all the way down to the types, methods, and fields. The Java model can be seen as a logical view of the underlying IWorkspace resource model.

An important characteristic of IJavaElements is that they are *handle objects*. This means that simply obtaining a Java element instance does not imply that the Java element exists. You can create IJavaElement handles for Java projects, packages, and compilation units that do not exist in your workspace. Conversely, IJavaElement instances do not always exist for all portions of the Java projects that do exist. IJavaElement handles are created lazily as they are requested by various clients. If multiple clients request handles on the same Java element, they will get equal, but not necessarily identical, handle objects.

The implication here is that creating a Java element has two meanings. You can create IJavaElement handles by asking the parent element for one. For example, IType.getMethod will return an IMethod handle but will not create that method in the file on disk. The JavaCore class also provides factory methods for creating Java elements for a given file, folder, or project in the workspace. For example, the following will create an ICompilationUnit handle for a given file handle:

```
IFile file = ...;//a file handle
ICompilationUnit unit =
   JavaCore.createCompilationUnitFrom(file);
```

To create the contents on disk, you need to use the various create methods on the handle objects. For example, IType.createMethod will create a Java method on disk. Because creation will fail if such a method already exists, you should first use a method handle to find out whether the method already exists:

```
IType type = ...;
String body = "public String toString() {"+
   "return super.toString();}";
IMethod method = type.getMethod("toString", new String[0]);
if (!method.exists())
   method = type.createMethod(body, null, false, null);
```

FAQ 284 *How are resources created?*
FAQ 349 *What is the Java model?*

FAQ
351

How do I create a Java project?

Several steps are required to create and properly initialize a Java project. Start by creating and opening an `IProject`:

```
String name = "MyProject";
IWorkspace workspace = ResourcesPlugin.getWorkspace();
IWorkspaceRoot root= workspace.getRoot();
IProject project= root.getProject(name);
project.create(null);
project.open(null);
```

Next, you need to add the Java nature to the project. This in turn will cause the Java builder to be added to the project:

```
IProjectDescription desc = project.getDescription();
desc.setNatureIds(new String[] {
    JavaCore.NATURE_ID});
project.setDescription(desc);
```

Next, you must set the Java builder's output folder, typically called `bin`. This is where the Java builder will place all compiled `*.class` files:

```
IJavaProject javaProj = JavaCore.create(project);
IFolder binDir = project.getFolder("bin");
IPath binPath = binDir.getFullPath();
javaProj.setOutputLocation(binPath, null);
```

Finally, you need to set the project's classpath, also known as the build path. You will need to minimally create a classpath entry that points to the Java runtime library, `rt.jar`, and additional entries for any other libraries and projects that the project requires:

```
String path = "c:\\jre\\lib\\rt.jar";
IClasspathEntry cpe= JavaCore.newLibraryEntry(
    path, null, null);
javaProj.setRawClasspath(new IClasspathEntry[] {cpe});
```

FAQ 77 *When does PDE change a plug-in's Java build path?*
FAQ 284 *How are resources created?*
FAQ 291 *Why should I add my own project nature?*

How do I manipulate Java code?

JDT offers a number of mechanisms for manipulating Java programs. It can be a daunting task to figure out which of these options best suits your needs. Each mechanism has different capabilities and trade-offs, depending on exactly what you want to do. Here is a quick rundown of what's available.

The first option is to use the *Java model* API. This API is intended primarily for browsing and manipulating Java projects on a macro scale. For example, if you want to create or browse Java projects, packages, or libraries, the Java model is the way to go. The finest granularity the Java model supports is the *principal structure* of Java types. You can browse the method and field signatures of a type, but you cannot manipulate the bodies of methods or any source file comments. The Java model is typically not used for modifying individual Java files.

The Java document object model (JDOM), is used for manipulating an individual Java file, also known as a *compilation unit*. JDOM also supports only manipulation of the principal structure of Java files but has more power than the Java model for modifying files. In particular, JDOM lets you modify the source characters for each method and field in a file. For performing manipulation of the principal structure only, such as adding methods and changing parameter or return types, JDOM is the way to go.

Last but not least is the *abstract syntax tree (AST)* API. By creating an AST on a Java file, you have ultimate control over browsing and modifying a Java program, including modification of method bodies and source comments. For complex analysis or modification of Java files, the AST is the best choice. Support for modifying and writing ASTs was introduced in Eclipse 3.0. Prior to 3.0, you could use the AST for analyzing Java types but had to use the JDOM for source modification.

Of course, you can modify Java files without using any of these facilities. You can obtain a raw character buffer on the file contents and perform arbitrary transformations yourself. Regardless of what mechanism you use to modify Java files, you should always use a *working copy* to do so.

FAQ 353 *What is a working copy?*
FAQ 354 *What is a JDOM?*
FAQ 355 *What is an AST?*

What is a working copy?

The Java model supports the creation of so-called working copies of compilation units. A working copy is an in-memory representation of the compilation unit on disk. Any changes made to the working copy will have no effect on the file on disk until the copy is explicitly reconciled with the original. Using a working copy to manipulate a Java program has a number of powerful advantages over using your own private memory buffer. Most importantly, working copies can be shared between multiple clients. For example, you can programmatically modify the working copy being used by a Java editor, and your changes will appear immediately in the editor. JDT can also detect and report compilation problems on working copies, thus allowing you to preview or warn the user about possible adverse side effects of a change before the copy on disk is modified.

Working copies should generally be used whenever you modify a compilation unit. This ensures that you are modifying the most up-to-date contents of that file, even if they have not yet been written to disk. If you do not use working copies, and a dirty Java editor is open on that file already, the user will be forced to reconcile your changes manually. The following example of using a working copy to replace a compilation unit's contents is from the implementation of ChangeReturnTypeAction included in this book's FAQ Examples plug-in:

```
ICompilationUnit unit = ...;//get compilation unit handle
unit.becomeWorkingCopy(null, null);
try {
   IBuffer buffer = unit.getBuffer();
   String oldContents = buffer.getContents();
   String newContents = ...;//make some change
   buffer.setContents(newContents);
   unit.reconcile(false, null);
} finally {
   unit.discardWorkingCopy();
}
```

You should always put discardWorkingCopy in a finally block to ensure that the working copy opened by becomeWorkingCopy is discarded even in the case of an exception. Although in this example, we simply replaced the old file contents with new contents, the IBuffer API can be used to perform modifications on smaller parts of the buffer, to replace a region, or to append contents to the end of the file.

FAQ 352 *How do I manipulate Java code?*
FAQ 354 *What is a JDOM?*

What is a JDOM?

A JDOM is a Java document object model. DOM is a commonly used term for an object-oriented representation of the structure of a file. A Google definition search turned up this Web definition:

Document Object Model: DOM is a platform- and language-neutral interface, that provides a standard model of how the objects in an XML object are put together, and a standard interface for accessing and manipulating these objects and their interrelationships.
—http://www.google.com/search?q=define:Document+Object+Model

In the context of JDT, the JDOM represents a hierarchical, in-memory representation of a single Java file (compilation unit). The DOM can be traversed to view the elements that make up that compilation unit, including types, methods, package declarations, import statements, and so on. The main purpose of the JDOM API is manipulating Java code, allowing you to add and delete methods and fields, for example. All this manipulation occurs on the in-memory object model, so it does not affect the Java file on disk until the DOM is saved. However, the DOM allows you to access only the *principal structure* of the compilation unit, so you cannot easily modify document elements, such as javadoc comments and method bodies.

The class `ChangeReturnTypeAction` in the FAQ Examples plug-in uses the JDOM to change the return type of a selected method. Here is the portion of the action that creates and manipulates the JDOM:

```
String oldContents = ...;//original file contents
IMethod method = ...;//the method to change
String returnType = ...;//the new return type
ICompilationUnit cu = method.getCompilationUnit();
String unitName = cu.getElementName();
String typeName = method.getParent().getElementName();
String mName = method.getElementName();
DOMFactory fac = new DOMFactory();
IDOMCompilationUnit unit =
    fac.createCompilationUnit(oldContents, unitName);
IDOMType type = (IDOMType) unit.getChild(typeName);
```

```
IDOMMethod domMethod = (IDOMMethod) type.getChild(mName);
domMethod.setReturnType(returnType);
```

Note that modifications to the DOM occur on a copy of the file contents in memory. If the DOM is modified and then discarded, any changes will also be discarded. The current string representation of the in-memory DOM can be obtained by calling `IDOMCompilationUnit.getContents()`. To save modifications to disk, you should use a working copy.

 FAQ 332 *How do I implement a DOM for my language?*
FAQ 352 *How do I manipulate Java code?*
FAQ 353 *What is a working copy?*

What is an AST?

In traditional compiler design, a lexical scanner first converts an input stream into a list of tokens. The tokens are then parsed according to syntax rules for the language, resulting in an abstract syntax tree or AST. Aho, Sethi, and Ullman (1986) distinguish between an *abstract syntax tree* and a *parse tree*. The AST is used for semantic analysis such as type resolution, and is traditionally converted to an intermediate representation (IR) for optimization and code generation. The Eclipse Java compiler uses a single AST structure from the initial parse all the way through to code generation. This approach allows for heavy optimization of the compiler, avoiding the garbage collection required when using different structures for different phases of the compilation process.

Because it powerfully captures the semantic structure of a Java program, an AST is a very useful data structure for any tools that want to perform complex queries or manipulation of a program. The AST was initially not exposed as API, but many tools were making use of it anyway to perform such manipulation as code refactoring. However, because the compiler's AST is used for parsing, type resolution, flow analysis, and code generation, the code is very complex and difficult to expose as API. The Java core team decided not to expose its internal AST but instead to expose a clean, new AST. This AST is available in the `org.eclipse.jdt.core.dom` package. Although this isn't the same AST used by the compiler, it nonetheless provides a rich semantic representation of a Java program, right down to every expression and statement in methods and initializers. This AST optionally supports resolution of all type references but does not provide advanced capabilities such as flow analysis and code generation. Clients can build and manipulate ASTs for any Java source code, whether or not it's in the workspace.

FAQ 349 *What is the Java model?*
Alfred Aho, Ravi Sathi, and Jeffrey Ullman, *Compilers, Principles, Techniques, and Tools* (Addison-Wesley, 1986).

How do I create and examine an AST?

FAQ
356

An AST is created by using an instance of `ASTParser`, created using the `newParser` factory method. You will typically create an AST for a compilation unit in the workspace, but you can also create ASTs for class files or source code from other locations. A powerful feature introduced in Eclipse 3.0 is the ability to produce a partial AST. For example, you can create a skeletal AST representing only the principal structure of the file or with only a single method body fully resolved. This offers a considerable performance gain over a full-blown AST if you need to extract information from only a small portion of a file. See the javadoc of `ASTParser` for more details.

Once an AST is created, the most common way to traverse or manipulate it is through a visitor. As with the traditional visitor pattern, each variety of AST node has a different `visit` method, so you can implement a visitor that analyzes only certain kinds of expressions or statements. Outside of visitors, each AST node offers accessor methods for each child type that is appropriate for that node. For example, a `MethodDeclaration` node has `getBody` and `setBody` methods for accessing or replacing the block statement representing the body of the method. There are no methods for generically accessing the children of a node, although there is a generic `getParent` method for accessing the parent of a node.

The `PrintASTAction` class in the FAQ Examples plug-in shows a simple example of constructing and traversing an AST for the currently selected compilation unit. A visitor prints out the name of each AST node in the file with braces surrounding the children of each node:

```
class ASTPrinter extends ASTVisitor {
    StringBuffer buffer = new StringBuffer();
    public void preVisit(ASTNode node) {
        //write the name of the node being visited
        printDepth(node);
        String name = node.getClass().getName();
```

```
        name = name.substring(name.lastIndexOf('.')+1);
        buffer.append(name);
        buffer.append(" {\r\n");
    }
    public void postVisit(ASTNode node) {
        //write a closing brace to indicate end of the node
        printDepth(node);
        buffer.append("}\r\n");
    }
    void printDepth(ASTNode node) {
        //indent the current line to an appropriate depth
        while (node != null) {
            node = node.getParent();
            buffer.append("  ");
        }
    }
}
...
//java model handle for selected file
ICompilationUnit unit = ...;
ASTParser parser = ASTParser.newParser(AST.JLS2);
parser.setKind(ASTParser.K_COMPILATION_UNIT);
CompilationUnit ast =
             (CompilationUnit)parser.createAST(null);
ASTPrinter printer = new ASTPrinter();
ast.accept(printer);
MessageDialog.openInformation(shell, "AST for: " +
    unit.getElementName(), printer.buffer.toString());
```

☞ **FAQ 352** *How do I manipulate Java code?*
FAQ 355 *What is an AST?*

FAQ
357

How do I distinguish between internal and external JARs on the build path?

The Java build path differentiates between internal JARs and external JARs. To find the file-system location for an internal JAR, the workspace path needs to be converted into a file-system location, as follows:

```
IClasspathEntry entry = ...
IPath path = entry.getPath();
IWorkspace workspace = ResourcesPlugin.getWorkspace();
IResource jarFile= workspace.getRoot().findMember(path);
if (jarFile != null) {
```

```
      return jarFile.getLocation();
   } else {
      // must be an external JAR (or invalid classpath entry)
   }
```

☞ **FAQ 286** *What is the difference between a path and a location?*

How do I launch a Java program?

FAQ
358

JDT has support for launching Java programs. First, add the following plug-ins to your dependent list:

- `org.eclipse.debug.core`
- `org.eclipse.jdt.core`
- `org.eclipse.jdt.launching`

With those plug-ins added to your dependent plug-in list, your Java program can be launched using the JDT in two ways. In the first approach, an IVMRunner uses the currently installed VM, sets up its classpath, and asks the VM runner to run the program:

```
void launch(IJavaProject proj, String main) {
   IVMInstall vm = JavaRuntime.getVMInstall(proj);
   if (vm == null) vm = JavaRuntime.getDefaultVMInstall();
   IVMRunner vmr = vm.getVMRunner(ILaunchManager.RUN_MODE);
   String[] cp = JavaRuntime.
      computeDefaultRuntimeClassPath(proj);
   VMRunnerConfiguration config =
      new VMRunnerConfiguration(main, cp);
   ILaunch launch = new Launch(null,
      ILaunchManager.RUN_MODE, null);
   vmr.run(config, launch, null);
}
```

The second approach is to create a new launch configuration, save it, and run it. The cfg parameter to this method is the name of the launch configuration to use:

```
void launch(IJavaProject proj, String cfg, String main) {
   DebugPlugin plugin = DebugPlugin.getDefault();
   ILaunchManager lm = plugin.getLaunchManager();
   ILaunchConfigurationType t = lm.getLaunchConfigurationType(
      IJavaLaunchConfigurationConstants.ID_JAVA_APPLICATION);
   ILaunchConfigurationWorkingCopy wc = t.newInstance(
```

```
        null, cfg);
    wc.setAttribute(
      IJavaLaunchConfigurationConstants.ATTR_PROJECT_NAME,
      proj.getElementName());
    wc.setAttribute(
      IJavaLaunchConfigurationConstants.ATTR_MAIN_TYPE_NAME,
      main);
    ILaunchConfiguration config = wc.doSave();
    config.launch(ILaunchManager.RUN_MODE, null);
  }
```

More information is available at **Help > Help Contents > JDT Plug-in Developer Guide > JDT Debug > Running Java code**.

 FAQ 313 *What is a launch configuration?*

FAQ 359

What is JUnit?

JUnit is a simple testing framework shipped with Eclipse. JUnit can be used to write tests for Java programs developed with the JDT and is also used heavily by the platform to test plug-ins.

When inspecting the Eclipse plug-ins in CVS, you will notice quite a few projects like `org.eclipse.core.tests.resource`. All these projects contain PDE JUnit tests to perform regression tests on plug-ins.

 FAQ 78 *What is a PDE JUnit test?*
FAQ 79 *Where can I find the Eclipse plug-ins?*
The JUnit Web site (http://junit.org)

FAQ 360

How do I participate in a refactoring?

In Eclipse 3.0, the JDT introduced new API to allow other plug-ins to participate in simple refactorings. For example, if a user renames a method, JDT can fix up method references only in other standard Java files. If references to that method exist in Java-like files, such as JSPs, UML diagrams, or elsewhere, the plug-ins responsible for those files will want to update their references as well.

New extension points are defined by `org.eclipse.jdt.ui` for participation in renaming, creating, deleting, copying, and moving Java elements. The refactoring participant API is based on the new language-independent refactoring infrastructure in the LTK plug-ins. You can find more details by browsing through the extension point documentation for the new refactoring participant extension points.

☞ **FAQ 361** *What is LTK?*

What is LTK?

At the EclipseCon conference in 2004, a great deal of interest sparked the idea of adding more generic language IDE infrastructure to Eclipse. Many people have been impressed by the powerful functionality in the Eclipse Java tooling and would like to be able to leverage that support in other languages. This is often currently done by cloning JDT and then hacking out the Java-specific parts and replacing them with a different language. Clearly, this is not very efficient and results in an ongoing effort to catch up to JDT as it continues to add new features.

Eclipse 3.0 includes a first attempt at "bubbling up" some of the JDT functionality into a generic layer. This generic programming-language tooling layer is called the Eclipse Language Toolkit, or LTK. To start, this generic layer has infrastructure for language-independent refactorings in two new projects:

- `org.eclipse.ltk.core.refactoring`
- `org.eclipse.ltk.ui.refactoring`

The `Refactoring` class represents the entire refactoring lifecycle, including precondition checks, generating the set of changes, and post-condition checks. The `Change` class itself performs more expensive validation on the input to determine whether the refactoring is appropriate and performs the workspace modifications induced by the refactoring. A `Change` instance can also encapsulate an undo for another change, allowing the user to back out of a refactoring after it has completed. Look for this to be a growing area of innovation in future releases of Eclipse.

☞ **FAQ 360** *How do I participate in a refactoring?*

Index

informIT

CD-ROM Warranty

Addison-Wesley warrants the enclosed CD-ROM to be free of defects in materials and faulty workmanship under normal use for a period of ninety days after purchase (when purchased new). If a defect is discovered in the CD-ROM during this warranty period, a replacement CD-ROM can be obtained at no charge by sending the defective CD-ROM, postage prepaid, with proof of purchase to:

Disc Exchange
Addison-Wesley Professional
Pearson Technology Group
75 Arlington Street, Suite 300
Boston, MA 02116
Email: AWPro@aw.com

Addison-Wesley makes no warranty or representation, either expressed or implied, with respect to this software, its quality, performance, merchantability, or fitness for a particular purpose. In no event will Addison-Wesley, its distributors, or dealers be liable for direct, indirect, special, incidental, or consequential damages arising out of the use or inability to use the software. The exclusion of implied warranties is not permitted in some states. Therefore, the above exclusion may not apply to you. This warranty provides you with specific legal rights. There may be other rights that you may have that vary from state to state. The contents of this CD-ROM are intended for personal use only.

More information and updates are available at:
http://www.awprofessional.com/